PHILOSOPHICAL MEDITATIONS
ON ZEN BUDDHISM

This book addresses significant philosophical issues that arise in the Zen tradition of East Asian Buddhism as it has come to be transmitted to the West in the twentieth century. It focuses on the figure of the ninth-century Chinese Buddhist master, Huang Po, whose recorded sayings exemplify the spirit of the "golden age" of Zen in medieval China, and on the historic transmission of these writings to the West in the work of the well-known English Asianist, John Blofeld. Outlining ways in which Blofeld's understanding of Huang Po stands within the romantic tradition of western thought, these philosophical meditations make a bold attempt to articulate a post-romantic understanding of Zen applicable to contemporary world culture. The book asks: how should we understand the roles of language and history in the Buddhist "enlightenment" of Huang Po? What do contemporary ways of thinking entitle us to think Zen enlightenment is, and how does this differ from the romantic account of "awakening" given by John Blofeld? If the Zen master, Huang Po, is described as living in ecstatic freedom, how should we understand the form that this freedom would take in realistic terms? If Huang Po's enlightenment is described as a state of transcendence, what is it that we can now imagine the Zen master transcending?

Dale S. Wright is Professor of Religious Studies and Chair of the Program in Asian Studies at Occidental College in Los Angeles. His area of academic speciality is the philosophy and religion of East Asia. His publications focus on Buddhist philosophy, with particular attention to Chinese and Japanese traditions of Buddhist thought. He is co-editor, with Steven Heine, of *The Kōan: Text and Context in Zen Buddhism* (forthcoming 1999).

CAMBRIDGE STUDIES IN RELIGIOUS TRADITIONS

Edited by
John Clayton, *Boston University* (General editor)
Steven Collins, *University of Chicago*
Nicholas de Lange, *University of Cambridge*
William Graham, *Harvard University*

PHILOSOPHICAL MEDITATIONS ON ZEN BUDDHISM

DALE S. WRIGHT

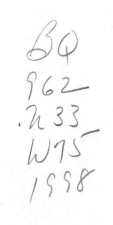

CAMBRIDGE
UNIVERSITY PRESS

PUBLISHED BY THE PRESS SYNDICATE OF THE UNIVERSITY OF CAMBRIDGE
The Pitt Building, Trumpington Street, Cambridge CB2 1RP, United Kingdom

CAMBRIDGE UNIVERSITY PRESS
The Edinburgh Building, Cambridge CB2 2RU, United Kingdom
40 West 20th Street, New York, NY 10011–4211, USA
10 Stamford Road, Oakleigh, Melbourne 3166, Australia

First published 1998

Printed in the United Kingdom at the University Press, Cambridge

Typeset in 11/12½ pt Monotype Baskerville   [SE]

A catalogue record for this book is available from the British Library

Library of Congress Cataloguing in Publication data
Wright, Dale S.
Philosophical meditations on Zen Buddhism / Dale S. Wright.
p.   cm.
Includes bibliographical references and index.
ISBN 0 521 59010 8 (hardback)
1. Huang Po, d. 850.   2. Zen Buddhism – Doctrines.   I. Title.
BQ962.U33W75   1998
294.3′927–dc21   97–38793   CIP

ISBN 0 521 59010 8 hardback

Contents

Introduction

In 1934, under the influence of *The Light of Asia*, Sir Edwin Arnold's romantic representation of the Buddha, the young English adventurer, John Blofeld, boarded a Japanese trading ship bound for China. Having just graduated the week before from Cambridge University where he had eagerly studied the available literature on "the Orient," Blofeld was as much prepared for this adventure as he could have been. "Of course," Blofeld wrote years later, "everything in China differed enormously from what I had imagined."[1] This difference, however, would never disrupt Blofeld's lifelong commitment to the idea that present within the Buddhist tradition were insights making possible "the Ultimate Transformation" of the human mind. Blofeld had converted to Buddhism during his years at Cambridge, and would, by the end of his life, become one of the most influential twentieth-century transmitters of Buddhism to the west. His first transmission would be *The Zen Teaching of Huang Po on the Transmission of Mind (Huang Po Ch'uan Hsin Fa Yao)*. Taking the name P'u Lotao, Blofeld immersed himself in Chinese culture in order to make himself a fit vehicle for the transmission of Huang Po to the west.

Why Huang Po? This text came highly recommended by the Buddhist monks whom Blofeld had encountered while in China. Huang Po was well known throughout East Asia as one of the most powerful figures of the "golden age of Zen." Placed at the center of the sacred genealogy of Zen Buddhism, Huang Po was the student of the great Pai-chang Huai-hai, the reputed organizer of the Zen monastic system, and the teacher of the renowned Lin-chi I-hsuan, the founder of Rinzai Zen. Stories about the powerful and unnerving Huang Po had circulated in China for over a millennium by the time Blofeld was in position to receive them. Blofeld was so impressed with the Huang Po transmission

[1] Blofeld, *The Wheel of Life*, p. 33.

vii

that he would claim in his introduction that this text was one of "the most brilliant expositions of the highest Wisdom which have so far appeared in our language,"[2] and the one "best suited to the needs of Western readers."[3] Although these claims might later seem somewhat inflated, his choice was indeed a good one. Besides being a formative text from the "golden age of Zen," the *Huang Po Ch'uan Hsin Fa Yao* was also an innovative philosophical text, one that took provocative and insightful positions on key issues. Several years of work went into the translation, including time spent in Zen monasteries. Although he wrote humbly about the text, Blofeld's *Huang Po* was no small achievement. By 1958 the text was complete and ready for copyright; in 1959 Grove Press distributed the first of several printings. Although not a big sales item at first, its day would soon come.

In 1968, under the influence of the spirit of the age, I received Blofeld's transmission. Purchasing a paperback copy of *Huang Po* from the "Oriental Wisdom" section of my local bookstore, I too began reading Zen. The activity of reading Zen at that time placed one within a specific cultural tradition, and entailed a particular style of reading. It meant reading "romantically," and thus receiving the transmission of Huang Po through the mediation of a prominent lineage of modern romantics – Blake and Wordsworth, Emerson and Thoreau, all the way up through Kerouac, Watts, . . . and John Blofeld. Romantics in Blofeld's era could be characterized by their openness to cultural and historical ideals quite other than their own. They assumed that through speculative, imaginative excursions beyond the conventions of their own time and place, fundamental forms of wisdom and transformation were possible.

In this minimal sense, the *Philosophical Meditations* before you still stand within the modern tradition of romanticism. But, as we approach the turn of the century, it is easy to see that many changes have occurred since Blofeld first introduced the Zen teachings of Huang Po to the English literary world. For some intellectuals, these changes are so far-reaching and so dramatic that it has become tempting to claim that the opening of a new historical era has occurred, an era that for lack of its own name has come to be called simply "post-modern," and "post-romantic," and "post-". . . .many things. The "post" in each of these cases marks the recognition, hope, or presumption that, in some respects at least, we live in a world fundamentally different from the cultural

---

[2] Blofeld, *Huang Po*, p. 8.   [3] Blofeld, *Huang Po*, p. 8.

world that sent the young Blofeld off to China in the thirties and that was inscribed in his Huang Po translation in the fifties. These meditations will seek to explore how these differences have recast the context for a philosophical meditation on Zen Buddhism, and how a contemporary reading of Huang Po might differ from its predecessors in both outcome and style.

English-language books on Buddhism have increased in number almost exponentially since they began to appear in the nineteenth century. Until very recently, virtually all of them have taken one of two distinct modern forms: either they position themselves within the modern scientific tradition in order to analyze the history and sociology of Buddhism, or, romantically, they attempt to transmit the truth and transformative power of this tradition to the west. Representatives of each of these forms have tended to criticize each other severely. From a scientific point of view, romantic transmissions of Buddhism are simply inaccurate. They project forms of Buddhism more in line with contemporary ideals than with anything that has ever existed in Asia. And from a romantic point of view, scientific studies miss the point of Buddhism altogether. They inadvertently transmit the mentality of modern science, and do nothing to enlighten or alleviate suffering. This duel is well known to us. It constitutes one of the most basic oppositions of the modern era. Scientific rationalism and romantic spiritualism are the twin siblings of modern culture, and the two poles within which the modern personality has been constructed. The bond between them is so close that it was inevitable that both would be implicated in the transmission of Buddhism to the west. The scientific motive for the study of Buddhism was accurate knowledge – enlightenment defined as a thorough understanding of world culture and history. The romantic motive for the study of Buddhism was a breakthrough to a new kind of understanding – enlightenment defined as a fundamental transformation of the human mind. Until recently, these two formative motives have seemed to be irreconcilable.

One factor that lends credence to contemporary claims that we are now moving beyond the modern era is the realization that this conflict may be illusory, and that, in many ways, the opposition between these two essential forms of modernity has hidden their more fundamental similarity. It is now possible to see that both share a set of presuppositions that have made the debate between them possible. If scientific rationalism and modern romanticism can now be seen to share a worldview, the perspective from which this can be seen is no longer completely within either one of them and therefore in some sense "post" both of them. This historical development sets the stage for the claim that reading Zen today is a significantly different matter than it was in Blofeld's time: it will follow different methods and styles, and arrive at quite different conclusions. Many of these methods, styles, and conclusions will show the various marks of contemporary culture and thought. Our Huang Po will not look like Blofeld's. Why not? Isn't this fluctuation with "the times" a symptom of our being somewhat too impressionable? Blofeld reads Huang Po through the lens of romanticism and we read Huang Po through "post-romantic" specters – why not just read Huang Po on his own and set aside the influences of the current intellectual context?

The persuasive force of these questions shows the hold that romantic and scientific doctrine still have on our minds, as well as the need to press beyond them. The romantic quest to behold "spirit" directly without mediation through any particular culture is analogous to the scientific demand to set aside all prejudices and just examine the data, or read the text, in and of itself. In both cases, the mind of the one who understands is thought to exist independent of its own context which leaves no traces on the understanding developed within it. When, however, from our contemporary point of view, we reflect on the assumptions hidden in these questions, we discover that the questions presuppose an understanding of the human mind that is no longer tenable. Just like the objects of our experiments and the texts we read, our minds are context-dependent; they come to the particular form of understanding that they do within particular cultural, historical settings. Once this is seen, the questions above begin to dissolve, and lose their point. We cannot "just read" anything, without demonstrating the shaping power that tradition in its current form has upon us. These powers may take scientific form, or romantic form, or some form beyond those two, but one possibility that we can no longer maintain is that the imprint of tradition will take no form at all, thus allowing us to see Huang Po's Zen on its own. Contemporary Zen readers will thus be able to see what Blofeld could not have seen: that every understanding of Zen will be mediated through some particular development of historical culture. Moreover, this realization is not simply an unfortunate concession that must now be made. It is instead an insight providing the best point of departure for contemporary reflection on Zen because, like Zen, this insight demands an examination of the background factors currently shaping our experience. In the language of Zen, it calls forth "the one who is right now reading," and refuses to allow the reader to cling to his or her own invisibility. Because of its centrality to both contemporary reflection and Zen, this point of departure will be a recurring theme throughout these meditations.

Taking this point of departure in these meditations on Zen will direct us to the possible significance of one of Huang Po's themes: transmission. Transmission is the process through which all forms of culture, including Zen "enlightenment," make their way from one generation to the next, one form leading to a transformed other and to another, without end. How should we understand this process? What is the process through which the minds and experiences of a generation are shaped by the past to become what they are? How should we understand the process through which we, turn-of-the-century English-language readers, have received a transmission from Huang Po, a ninth-century Chinese Buddhist monk? What is revealed, about the principles of transmission, and about us, in our own activity of reading Zen? And what will the effect be, over time, of the fact that, given Blofeld's transmission and thousands of others like it, our education in reading and understanding now includes the great texts of many cultures and historical eras quite other than our own?

The philosophical meditations that follow work in and around these questions by entering into a sustained dialogue with themes that appear to be crucial to a contemporary effort to understand Huang Po's Zen. Blofeld's essential role in this process is to provide an initial understanding in relation to which our own thoughts can be developed and honed. The meditations will, accordingly, move back and forth in dialogue between Blofeld's understanding of a theme and another understanding that will have become possible since Blofeld's time.

In what sense are these meditations philosophical? In the same sense, perhaps, that Descartes' classic "meditations" are that they pose a series of questions intended to yield something important about the very bases of human experience. One difference is crucial, however, and shows an interesting distinction between contemporary thought and the modern mentality shown in the Cartesian meditations. Descartes' philosophical meditations strive to set aside all previous thinking on these matters in order to delve directly into the mind itself. By contrast, our meditations are first and foremost "readings." They regard mediation through language, culture, and prior texts to be as direct as philosophical meditations can be. Therefore, instead of taking the autonomy of "critical doubt" as their first principle, these meditations

feature a prior interest in the underlying activities of reading and interpretation. Although critical reflection is crucial to any mature practice
of reading, it is neither sufficient nor comprehensive. From a contemporary point of view, larger processes and influences render Descartes'
efforts at self-purification unattainable. This becomes clear when we
realize that hidden beneath our activity and intentions in reading,
numerous processes are in effect. What we intend to do in reading is but
one element in determining what in fact happens. Beyond our work on
the text in reading it is the work that the text performs upon us. And
beyond both of these is the work performed upon both thinker and
object of thought by larger cultural and historical forces which set the
stage for the interaction between them. Neither these meditations nor
Descartes' can step out of their own genealogy of transmission to see
how things are on their own. In fact, the universal fate of immersion in
a lineage of understanding is anything but regrettable.

As points of departure, however, intentions are crucial. By calling the
practices of reading demonstrated here "meditations," I intend three
basic points.

First, a meditative reading practice will be thoughtful. Although
receptivity is essential, reading is not primarily a mode of passivity; it is
active and engaged. In order to receive transmission, the reader must do
what the author has done – think. For this reason, at the end of a "*dharma
talk*," the great meditation master, Dogen, would beseech his readers to
"ponder this day and night." Meditative reading is a philosophical,
reflective activity. It is never content with the obvious; it will refuse to
hold onto customary forms of understanding in order to push beyond
what is already within grasp. The initial act of reading serves to lure the
mind out of complacency and inertia by challenging it to consider something new, or to experience more deeply what has already been thought.
A critical reader seeks freedom through the practice of reading, freedom
from immature forms of grasping, self-deception and confinement.
Because these goals are primary, this book is not just about Huang Po; it
is about issues that emerge in the process of engaging Huang Po's Zen
in philosophical meditation. Huang Po is therefore not so much its object
of knowledge as he is its medium, the figure of Zen through which both
writer and readers will seek cultivation of mind.

Second, meditative reading will be reflexive, that is, it will use the text
as a mirror upon which the reader's own mind can be reflected and
observed. Self-awareness is essential to a meditative practice of reading.
In this sense, reading is a form of dialogue, a back-and-forth movement

between the reader and the text. Reading critically, we question what is said in the text; reading reflexively, we allow what is said in the text to question us. For every statement made in the text, an implicit question probes the reflexive reader: what do you think? A unilateral reading, which seeks only to absorb what the author has said, casts no light back upon the reader. It fails to bring the reader's own mind to awareness. Meditative reading is a practice requiring the full presence of the practitioner; it is a practice taking that very presence as one of its goals. Be aware that this book – and every other – displays before the reader a specific practice of reading. When you are reading critically and thoughtfully, you will see the reading practice of the author. You will see not just what the author has read, but how, why, and to what effect. Even this first step is not enough, however. The value of the exercise is to develop awareness of your own reading practice, and, beyond that, to change it. Reading at its best is an engagement of the mind that alters the mind.

Therefore, third, the goal of meditative reading is self-transformation. Through the practice of reading, some change of mind and character is sought. Change, however, requires openness to change, which is never easy. This transformation can only be accomplished in an open process of questioning. Whether questioning Huang Po's Zen, or using that Zen to question ourselves, we open our mind to something that is other than its current identity. In reading, the open mind is attentive to real possibility. Its meditations are explorations, experiments with forms of experience that are taken to be its own possibilities or potential. In this sense, John Blofeld provides an excellent model for us in our reading. Blofeld made of his own life an experiment in Buddhist ideas. His writings show clearly that he sought always to experience the meaning of the Buddhist ideas that he encountered in his own life. The extent of his sincerity in this enterprise, and the openness of his mind in experimenting with alien ideas, made him both an excellent disciple and a ground-breaking navigator across cultural lines. Experiments of this kind require that our own ideas and states of mind be placed at risk, open to transformation by being tested against those of the other. When these practices are operative, philosophical meditation becomes a practical, ethical activity, one through which our own forms of enlightenment will be shaped.

These meditations will follow a series of topics that adhere to their own logical sequence. No doubt, both Huang Po and Blofeld would have chosen a different set of topics and arranged them in an alternative order that made better sense in their intellectual contexts. Nevertheless, the logical progression of these meditations is as follows. Because our access to Huang Po's Zen Buddhism is through texts, we take up a variety of questions about what that means. They ask what a "text" was in Huang Po's time and how reading in that context would have differed from Blofeld's account and ours. The first two chapters encourage us to ask ourselves: what is a Buddhist text and how should we read it? Because we read in language with the goal of understanding, the next few chapters address these philosophical topics. What would it mean to understand Huang Po's Zen and how does the medium of language through which we understand it affect the kind of understanding that emerges? Raising the issue of language takes us deeply into the philosophical domain of Buddhism where sophisticated reflections on language as such, and upon the specifics of Zen rhetoric, were widely discussed. What is the role of language in the enlightened mind of the Zen master? Questions about the immersion of our minds in language lead to other basic questions about human history and the extent to which Zen Buddhism encourages some form of historical awareness. While acknowledging that cultural forces like language and history determine the shape of life, Zen Buddhists nevertheless strive for forms of freedom that transcend a whole range of constraints. Chapters 7 and 8 probe the character of freedom attained in Huang Po's Zen and ask what forms of transcendence are humanly possible. The final two topics are suggested by Huang Po and guide us toward addressing the fundamental point of his Zen. They are "mind," which Huang Po's texts project as the "great matter" of Zen, and enlightenment, the ultimate goal of Zen Buddhism. Our goal in meditating on these topics is to ask ourselves as clearly as possible – how can we, in our time and place, best understand the enlightened mind of Huang Po? In this context, our task is not so much to describe Huang Po's ancient thought as it is to develop our own contemporary thought. Based upon the question, "how did they think?" – ours is "how should we?"

Because these meditations take up ideas that reflect on our own lives, East Asian words are given, when appropriate, in their most common English form. Hence this book engages in meditation on "Zen" even though the proper Chinese transliteration in the case of Huang Po would have been "Ch'an" or "Chan." The word "Zen," in other words, is now our own, for various historical reasons. The traditional Wade-Giles system of "romanizing" Chinese characters has been used in order to retain connections to John Blofeld's use of that system.

Making something one's own is never simply an individual matter. As

Huang Po knew, transmission always entails the convergence of innumerable forces. Among those responsible for making up my mind on these matters are my teachers, especially Alan Anderson, Wang Pachow, and Robert Scharlemann. Close friends, through their conversation and critical reading of these ideas, have helped hone the specific character of these meditations: Elmer Griffin, Steven Heine, David James, Karen King, David Klemm, Donna Maeda, Keith Naylor, Martha Ronk, and Diana Wright. And all of these influences converge upon the basic quest for understanding instilled in me by my parents. Therefore, it is to the precious memory of my father – Harold D. Wright – and in ongoing love of my mother – Marion M. Wright – that this book is gratefully dedicated.[4]

I would like to express my gratitude to Glenda Epps, Mary Pullen, Linda Whitney and the editors and staff at Cambridge University Press for their invaluable assistance in the preparation of this volume.

---

[4] Segments of chapters 5, 6, and 7 have appeared in earlier publications and are reprinted here with the generous permission of publishers: "The Discourse of Awakening: Rhetorical Practice in Classical Ch'an Buddhism" (*Journal of the American Academy of Religion* 61/1, 1993); "Historical Understanding: The Ch'an Buddhist Transmission Narratives and Modern Historiography" (*History and Theory* 31/1, 1992); "Emancipation from What? The Concept of Freedom in Classical Ch'an Buddhism" (*Asian Philosophy* 3/3, 1993).

CHAPTER 1

TEXTUALITY:
the "dependent origination" of Huang Po

> If things could be expressed like this with ink and paper, what would be the purpose of Zen?
>
> Huang Po[1]

> It is clear from Huang Po's own words that he realized the necessity of books and teachings of various kinds for people less advanced.
>
> John Blofeld[2]

When the early Buddhists proclaimed that impermanence is the fundamental condition of all things, they were certainly onto something. Almost nothing remains today of the ninth-century Zen Buddhist world of Huang Po. Nothing, that is, but texts. In the absence of everything else, it is the presence of texts that transmits this distant world of Zen to us. Although they don't supply us with much from which to reconstruct the historical details of Huang Po's life,[3] John Blofeld is certainly right when he says that these texts present us with a vivid picture of the Zen master. Huang Po was a powerful Zen master, the abbot of one of the largest and most important monasteries in South-central China where Zen came to prominence. He is placed in the genealogical charts of Zen ancestry as the student of the famous Zen master, Pai-chang Huai-hai, and as the teacher of the great Lin-chi I-hsuan (Rinzai). Huang Po is described as large in physical stature and overpowering in his presence and voice. He is presented as having evoked in his followers both fear and the experience of ecstatic freedom.

---

[1] Blofeld, *Huang Po*, p. 22 [2] Blofeld, *Huang Po*, p. 102
[3] We sample our ignorance at the outset when we discover that neither Huang Po's birth nor his death can be accurately dated. Variant dates for his death are given in different texts as 849 and 857, but neither is verifiable in any sense. Several texts mention that he was born and raised in the Fukien area, but neither his family name nor given name, nor the name of his native village, are recorded. His official biography (*Sung Kao seng ch'uan*) tells us only that he entered monastic life at an early age in the monastery on Mount Huang Po in Fukien and was given the Buddhist name Hsi-yun.

Huang Po's ways of teaching seem surprisingly diverse. On the one hand, he lectured on abstruse philosophical topics like the nature of "mind," while on the other hand, he intimidated disciples with his strange behavior and uproarious laughter. Some sections of text show his impressive knowledge of the vast and complicated literature of Buddhist philosophy, while others present him speaking in riddles and scoffing at philosophical seriousness. Although the tension between variant images of the master was perplexing, John Blofeld could proceed with his translation fully confident that, because Huang Po was speaking "from some deep inner experience,"[4] whatever contradictions seemed to appear on the surface were either reconcilable at some deep level or simply unimportant.

Later in his life, however, Blofeld expressed some doubts about the purity of the Huang Po texts. What worried him was that these texts didn't come directly from the hand, and therefore, the mind, of Huang Po. Instead, they came to be through a mediator, P'ei-hsiu, who wrote what he thought Huang Po thought. So the next time Blofeld chose a Zen text to translate, he picked one that seemed to be authored directly and without mediation, "whereas what remains to us of the teachings of Huang Po and others consists only of what their disciples chose to record."[5] Blofeld's concern here is quintessentially modern; it expresses the scientific concern for accuracy and the parallel romantic concern for authenticity and originality. If Huang Po's Zen is our interest, we want it direct from the source – no intermediaries. This is not what we get, however. In order to attain some clarity about what these texts are and, therefore, what we are doing when we are reading Zen, we will need to consider the origins and history of the Huang Po literature.

Had John Blofeld any idea what scientific historiography would soon discover about the Huang Po texts, he would never have entertained the idea of translating them. His worst fears have come true. Not only are these texts not directly from the mind of Huang Po, but they have passed through more mediations than anyone can count. Blofeld's own mediation ("My rendering is, to a small extent, interpretive"[6]) was just the latest of thousands that occurred before the text came to him.

---

[4] Blofeld, *Huang Po*, p. 8.
[5] Blofeld, *The Zen Teaching of Hui Hai*, p. 33. Blofeld obviously didn't consider this too serious a problem, however, since he could say in the same Preface that his Huang Po translation "was even then affording some people insight into the marvelous workings of an enlightened mind" (pp. 14–15).   [6] Blofeld, *The Zen Teaching of Hui Hai*, p. 17.

One fruitful way to understand the status of these texts entails calling upon the seminal Buddhist concept of "dependent origination." As Buddhists in many eras have known, this idea is useful to explain *how* it is that things are impermanent, and how they come to be the particular things that they are. According to this traditional Buddhist theory, all things, including texts, are always changing because they depend, at the moment of their origin and at all times, on other things which are themselves changing. All things come to be exactly what they are at any given moment not because it is their own inherent nature to do so, but because other things influence them, shape them, and make them what they are. To understand what the Huang Po texts are – their very essence – we need to trace in some detail just some of the factors that have brought them to be what they are today. Blofeld's doubt about the purity of these texts turns out to be more appropriate than he could have imagined. If we work hard however, to understand the "lack of true self" that we discover in these texts through the Buddhist concept of "dependent origination," we will be able to get over our disappointment about the status of these texts and discover something extremely important about the processes of transmission.

Through what mediation do we receive the Zen teachings of Huang Po? One place to begin would be to imagine just some of the ways in which the words and thoughts spoken by Huang Po – the supposed origin of these texts – would themselves have "originated dependent" upon a whole network of prior factors. Although we can concede, with Blofeld, that "Huang Po spoke from some deep inner experience,"[7] we can also acknowledge the multiple ways in which that experience has been shaped by other factors: his teachers, the ideas and texts of Buddhism, his parents, his historical setting, and so on. Huang Po was not just an independent and isolated entity; he stood within a particular lineage, within the Buddhist tradition, within the resources available to him through the Chinese language and culture of his time.

In the extensive footnotes to Iriya Yoshitaka's modern Japanese translation of Huang Po,[8] we get a sense of just how widespread the "intertextuality" of Huang Po's text and mind was. His language is rarely just *his* language. So familiar with the corpus of Chinese Buddhist texts is Iriya that no paragraph goes by without his noticing familiar language, language taken, either consciously or unconsciously, from other texts and other speakers and added to Huang Po's. Sometimes the Huang Po texts simply quote sutras and other texts to substantiate a point. At other

[7] Blofeld, *Huang Po*, p. 8.   [8] Iriya, *Denshin Hoyo.*

times, however, they just borrow language and ideas without citation and acknowledgment. Were Huang Po a modern author, we would be concerned about plagiarism charges. Medieval Chinese Buddhists, however, were not modern individualists; they assumed that borrowing certified ideas and phrases, and being influenced by them, was exactly what one ought to do. The use of prior texts is so prevalent in the Huang Po literature that it seems to be composed essentially of other writing, now grafted together and rewoven into a new form and directed at new purposes. For the modern historical philologist, these texts are a nightmare – or a dream come true – hinting at a never-ending task of tracing antecedent sources. And if dependent origination is, as the early Buddhists claimed, a truth about all things, then this task will indeed be endless, even for the computers that are now being trained for the job.

All of this is just to say that, wherever we begin our process of tracing the origins and history of the Huang Po texts, it will not be a true origin; there will always be more "dependencies," more background, to uncover. If even the enlightened mind of Huang Po, where it all may have seemed to begin, is itself a product of innumerable coalescing factors, then our starting there in the lecture hall of Huang Po monastery is just an arbitrary point of selection. Nevertheless, this is where we begin.

So, once again, through whose mediation do we receive *The Zen Teaching of Huang Po*? Blofeld knew that the answer to this was through P'ei-hsiu, the lay Buddhist devotee of Huang Po, who explains in his Preface to the literature how it came to be that he is the real author. Knowing who P'ei-hsiu was will help us understand what he wrote and why.[9] In 842, P'ei-hsiu, the newly appointed Governor of the Hung-chou area,[10] met Huang Po, who at that time had a strong local reputation as one of the leading

---

[9] P'ei-hsiu (797–860) was born into a well-known and politically important family in Hunan. He, like his brothers, passed the Imperial civil service exam at the highest level (*chin-shih*) and served in a series of official posts until being elevated to the position of Prime Minister of China in 853. He had the finest education available, and was in consultation throughout his life with China's most famous philosophers. Although a master of the Confucian classics for political purposes, P'ei seems to have turned more and more toward Buddhist thought as he grew older. In the middle of his career he became a student of the Hua-yen and Zen scholar/master Tsung-mi. He was also associated with the Hua-yen scholar Cheng-kuan and, later in his life, with Wei-shan Ling-yu, a well-known Zen master in Hunan and contemporary of Huang Po. His biographies tell of his immersion in the world of Buddhist texts, sometimes enclosing and isolating himself for extended periods of study. His calligraphy is regarded as among the finest of his era. P'ei-hsiu's official biographies are found in *Chiu T'ang-shu* (177) and *Hsin T'ang-shu* (182). See Broughton, *Kuei-Feng Tsung-mi*, and Gregory, *Tsung-mi*, for details about his association with Tsung-mi.

[10] This was the area in South-central China settled two generations earlier by the famous Zen master Ma-tsu, and, by the mid ninth century, was spotted with numerous newly opened temples and monasteries of the new, avant-garde Zen tradition.

figures in the newly emerging – avant-garde – form of Buddhism, Zen. Very shortly thereafter, P'ei-hsiu became a lay disciple of Huang Po, and, as a wealthy and powerful figure, ordered a monastery built for Huang Po off in the rural mountains, several days' walk west of the capital of Hung-chou.[11] It was named Mount Huang Po after the mountain temple in Fukien where the Zen master first entered the Buddhist order, and it is after this mountain that our protagonist came to be named Huang Po.[12] In 845 a massive government suppression of Buddhism was ordered by Emperor Wu-tsung, deposing and sending into exile the thousands of monks resident in numerous monasteries like Huang Po. None of the accounts of Huang Po's life discuss his whereabouts during this period. A biographical note on one of his students, however, mentions that, at the end of the suppression, P'ei-hsiu invited Huang Po to come out of the mountains and to serve as his teacher where he was then posted, in the district of Wan-ling.[13] In his Preface to the Huang Po texts, P'ei describes how "day and night" he received the teachings from Huang Po with eagerness and exactitude: "After leaving him [Huang Po], I recorded what I had learnt and, though able to set down only about a fifth of it, I esteem it as a direct transmission of the Doctrine."[14] Then, sometime either shortly before or after Huang Po's death,[15] P'ei was called to the capital to become Prime Minister. After a few years of service in that prestigious office, he retired, turning his attention entirely to Buddhist practice.

One practice that he initiated right away was the textual practice of reconstructing the teachings of Huang Po. From voluminous notes that

[11] Recently, Japanese Buddhist scholars, searching this area for traces of the early Zen tradition, located the monastery site of Mount Huang Po. Shortly after this "rediscovery," I made my way to this rural area in search of Huang Po. According to locals, the monastery had functioned, although at significantly reduced levels, all the way into the mid twentieth century. It was used by Maoist revolutionaries as a base camp during and following the "long march." The monastery itself was destroyed during the chaos of the Cultural Revolution, so that nothing remains of the original edifice but the monastery well. The building materials from the monastery were used to build new structures, including the commune store that now sits on the ancient temple site. Having undergone a "revolutionary" name change sometime in the fifties, local residents have now renamed the community the "Huang Po commune." They now seek "foreign investment money" to rebuild the edifice into a functioning Buddhist monastery and, not insignificantly, into a tourist attraction for wealthy Japanese travelers on pilgrimage to the ancient "holy land" of Zen. Impermanence indeed!

[12] This Fukien temple, rather than the Kiangsi temple featured in our story, is the place of origin for the Obaku or Huang Po sect of Zen Buddhism in Japan, which traces its lineage to the Fukien area in the Ming Dynasty.　　[13] *Sung kao-seng ch'uan*, T. 50, p. 817c.

[14] T. 48, p. 379c; Blofeld, *Huang Po*, p. 28.

[15] An event which is not precisely datable. The revival of interest in the ancient site of Mount Huang Po has made it possible to locate a grave marker for Huang Po Hsi-yun in the hills near the old monastery site, along with grave markers for hundreds of other important monks and subsequent abbots of the monastery over the last millennium.

he claimed to have written following two intensive sessions with Huang Po, he did his best to reproduce the "essential teachings on the transmission of mind."[16] Now, let's consider some possible effects of the fact that the Huang Po texts "originated dependent" upon the mind and notes of P'ei-hsiu.[17] First, without P'ei as medium, there may never have been a text of Huang Po's teaching. Or, even if there was, P'ei is clearly a condition without which *this* text would have never existed. Second, let us consider that one form that P'ei's mediation may have taken was the systematization and rationalization of what may have been less systematic and rational in the spoken original. Why should we postulate this? Several reasons. Written versions of oral discourse are frequently and naturally brought into sharper focus when they appear as text. We don't notice our rambling when we speak; but when we see a written transcription we are often appalled at our own rhetorical incoherence. P'ei was offering Huang Po to the world; most importantly, to his world of highly educated Chinese scholars. No doubt Huang Po's best and most sophisticated foot was placed forward. Another reason might be that P'ei himself was trained to be a systematic Buddhist philosopher by his earlier and equally famous teacher, Tsung-mi. By the time P'ei would have met Huang Po, he was already himself a Buddhist philosopher in his own right. What he learned from Huang Po would have been added to the system already organized in his mind. Given their prior training, P'ei-hsiu's ears would have heard Huang Po "systematically." This would be true even though one of the most important things P'ei-hsiu would have learned from Huang Po would have been how to dislodge and disrupt mental systems, how to free the mind from rational structure by seeing its inadequacy and emptiness. We can see P'ei-hsiu's eagerness to teach in his Preface. There, before we even get to Huang Po, P'ei can be found offering his own teachings on the nature of mind. He had something he needed to teach, regardless of where he had gotten it.

A third effect of P'ei Hsiu's transmission surfaces when we consider the character of the language through which Huang Po comes to the reader of Zen. Whose is it? P'ei-hsiu was a highly educated, highly polished member of the wealthy *literati* class. Huang Po was a rising star in

---

[16] One of the titles later given to the text.

[17] A lot has been thought and written recently about what occurs to spoken discourse when it makes its way into textual form, and about the differences between speech and writing. In *Chan Insights and Oversights*, Bernard Faure reflects on the bearing this recent literature might have on the medieval Zen tradition. The sources he draws upon in doing so – Derrida, LaCapra, Ong, and Ricoeur – are the best places to look for ways to understand the orality/textuality relation.

a newly emerging rural Buddhist movement that mocked cultural polish and that purposefully employed the most shocking slang of the day. In whose rhetoric is Huang Po's "transmission of mind" made? "Both" would be a good guess. P'ei-hsiu would not have become Huang Po's disciple unless he was attracted to the form and content of his teachings. He must have liked the way Huang Po spoke, however shocking it may have been to his urbane disposition. On the other hand, it is hard to imagine the Prime Minister writing that way himself, particularly when he knew that his highly educated friends might end up reading it. Indeed, an analysis of the form of writing does show both tendencies. Much of the text is written in a polished, literate style. But even these sections occasionally burst into colloquialisms. Other sections (to which we will return later) show no *literati* polish, featuring their slang in both form and content.[18]

Fourth, and finally, let us consider how the fate of the text – what ended up happening to it – would have "originated dependent" upon the enormous prestige of P'ei-hsiu. P'ei was no ordinary lay disciple. In fact, a better advocate of Huang Po's Zen could not have been found. It was P'ei-hsiu's fame and legitimacy, when placed in the service of Huang Po, that would have brought the Zen master to national attention. P'ei's advocacy would have deeply affected who would have sought this text and in what numbers. In the long run, of course, Huang Po's fame would outrun P'ei-hsiu's. Blofeld had no interest in transmitting P'ei-hsiu to the west; he wanted the great Huang Po. The question still remains, however: who did he get?

It is only because Blofeld thought that the story of the text's origins ended here that he was, initially at least, satisfied. The truth is, however, that this is just one of many beginnings. What happened to the text after P'ei-hsiu wrote it? "I gave the manuscript to the monks T'ai Chou and

---

[18] To get a glimpse of how significant these last two factors might have been, compare the images of Huang Po that we receive from two distinct sources, P'ei-hsiu and Lin-chi. Huang Po would have taken the young monk, Lin-chi I-hsuan, into his "Great Peace Temple" (*Ta-an ssu*) in the capital city of Hung-chou province several years before meeting P'ei-hsiu, but the *Lin-chi lu*, or *Record of Rinzai*, is a text that comes to us from a later period than P'ei-hsiu's. P'ei-hsiu, the wealthy, influential scholar–official, projects a Huang Po well-versed in Buddhist doctrine and texts, articulate and convincing in his sermons before throngs of respectful listeners. Lin-chi, famed for his unconventional style of Zen, projects Huang Po as overpowering in his ridicule of unenlightened speech and action, and unconcerned with the intricacies of traditional doctrine. Perhaps these accounts differ because Zen monks (like Lin-chi) differ from scholar–officials (like P'ei-hsiu) or because Sung dynasty images of greatness differ from those of the T'ang. Or perhaps they can be reconciled, as Yanagida suggests (in Iriya, *Denshin Hoyo*), in one complex individual. The point here, however, is that perspective shapes who and what is seen, and that this is a vital dimension of the fate of these texts.

Fa Chien, requesting them to return to the Kuang T'ang Monastery on the old mountain and to ask the elder monks there how far it agrees with what they themselves used frequently to hear in the past."[19] How far might it have agreed? No sane monk would have risked saying that it was just plain wrong, no matter what he thought. After all, this was the manuscript of the former Prime Minister! In such circles, caution is wisdom. Furthermore, P'ei-hsiu's continued attention to their master would have been considered a great opportunity. On the other hand, P'ei-hsiu did ask to be corrected, at least implicitly. He didn't want to misrepresent his revered teacher; therefore, he called for editorial assistance from those who had heard Huang Po many more times than he had. No one now knows what corrections or deletions were made.

There is strong evidence, however, that substantial additions were made. This can be seen from a "form-critical" analysis of the text. Some passages are written in a different style and presuppose an entirely different point of view. That point of view is clearly monastic, coming from the monks at Mount Huang Po to whom the manuscript was given. What did they add? Yanagida Seizan thinks that many of the elder monks would have had in their possession "private notes" compiled over many years of encounter with the abbot Huang Po, and that the arrival of P'ei-hsiu's manuscript would have enticed them to bring these forth so that they could be used to check P'ei's version of the teachings.[20] This makes sense. It also fits nicely with our understanding of the overall genre of Zen literature within which the Huang Po texts have been placed.[21]

The "recorded sayings" genre of Zen literature is at the very center of the emergence of this sect of Buddhism. The sheer fact that such literature was ever written tells us a lot about Zen. As we will see in the next chapter, Zen masters were frequently, almost stereotypically, critical of texts and textual practices. They didn't want their students focusing on sutra study, and they didn't want them writing down or even memorizing Zen phrases.[22] For example, the *Lin-chi lu* harshly criticizes students who "revere the words of some decrepit old man as being the profound truth writing them down in a big notebook, which they then wrap up in

---

[19] T. 48, p. 379c; Blofeld, *Huang Po*, p. 28.   [20] Yanagida in Iriya, *Denshin Hoyo*, p. 172.

[21] See Yanagida, "The Recorded Sayings Texts."

[22] P'ei-hsiu was certainly aware of the ambiguity of his writing practice. One story in the texts shows Huang Po mocking P'ei for trying to express "Zen" in poetry. Also, P'ei says in his Preface, as any pious Zen Buddhist would do before publishing: "At first I was diffident about publishing what I had written. But now fearing that these vital and penetrating teachings will be lost to future generations, I have done so" (T. 48, p. 379c; Blofeld, *Huang Po*, p. 28).

numerous covers and not let anyone else see."[23] Without seeming to notice the irony, the Ma-tsu "recorded saying" text says that the "sayings of Ma-tsu written down by people who cherished facts" do not really capture the spirit of the real Ma-tsu.[24] This, in any case, was the widespread attitude toward texts. In view of this harsh criticism, we can understand why this tended to be done secretly. But why was it done at all? Yanagida explains the process like this:

The greater the number of disciples that surrounded a great teacher became, the smaller each student's opportunities for individual instruction. Hence moments of direct contact with the teacher became prized experiences for the disciples involved, some of whom soon began making secret notes of the events. Eventually certain monks prone to such activity started making anthologies of the teacher's words and actions based on what they heard from other students in addition to their own experience. This was a perfectly natural development.[25]

Why should we think that this was a "perfectly natural development?" Primarily because, in spite of Zen rhetoric on the matter, and in spite of our own modern romantic and utilitarian views of language, the link between what the Zen master said and his enlightened mind was assumed to be very close.[26] When Huang Po spoke, everyone in the monastery listened. Nor was listening enough. Huang Po's utterances literally evoked memorization, mental repetition, and reflection. These were enlightened words, words which bear repeating over and over in one's own mind. In order to do that, and to get it right, what better way than to write them down, secretly perhaps, so that the mind is relieved of the burden of continual memorization, and so that accuracy and authenticity are guaranteed? Freed from the work of just keeping the saying straight in one's mind, one could focus on the saying itself in contemplation and meditation.

Very likely such secret collections of sayings existed on Mount Huang Po and very likely they emerged, perhaps with a smirk of embarrassment and pride, when P'ei-hsiu's manuscript arrived for verification.[27] When someone's saying collection contained something important which was missing from P'ei-hsiu's version, an addition might have been made. The manuscript must have grown; how much, no one knows.

---

[23] See Yanagida, "The Recorded Sayings Texts," p. 188.
[24] Pas, *The Recorded Sayings of Ma-tsu*, p. 39.
[25] Yanagida, "The Recorded Sayings Texts," p. 187.
[26] This is one of my topics in chapters 4 and 5.
[27] One early text, the *Chodang Chip*, refers to "notes" about Huang Po which were in circulation at the time of its writing in the mid to late tenth century. See Iriya, *Denshin Hoyo*, p. 172.

Which sayings would have been jotted down over the years, waiting there in reserve to be included in the "recorded sayings" texts? Certainly not everything Huang Po said would have been recorded. Some things must have seemed too pedestrian, too ordinary to qualify – things already known or not worth remembering. Sayings which met with awe and enthusiasm would have stuck in the mind most forcefully – whatever really seemed to strike home.[28] Most worth recording might have been sayings that stood at the very edge of understanding, those that, with just a little reflection, might open great reserves of insight. Those that pushed too far beyond the graspable might have been too hard to remember, unless, of course, they were so strange, so Zen-like, as to capture the imagination. Sayings noted for their extravagance, for their irregular and unusual qualities, are commonly found in these collections. Some sayings were just so far out of context and out of the ordinary that they became focal points of meditation. A few of these made it all the way into later *koan* collections, puzzles for subsequent generations of minds.

Consider the following enigmatic event on Mount Huang Po: "One day the master entered the hall. When the monks were all assembled, he lifted his staff as if to hit and drive them away. As they were leaving he called to them and when they turned, he said: 'The crescent is like a bent bow, very little rain but only strong winds.'"[29] Perhaps, like us, no one had the slightest idea what Huang Po was talking about. Or perhaps there were clues, present only in that immediate context or decipherable only to an exclusive few. Either way, this was a memorable event, one well worth writing down to see what it might yield upon more thorough meditation.

Here we see two kinds of editorial gatekeeping. Not only did sayings have to make it past the editors who formed and reformed the collections. First, they had to survive the mechanisms of censorship inherent in human interpretation – someone had to notice, remember, write, and preserve the saying in the first place. Transmission, both oral and written, presupposes more forgetting than it does remembering. But we can imagine the excitement generated by the arrival of P'ei-hsiu's manuscript version of their master's teaching on Mount Huang Po. If the secret wasn't out already, this would have been the occasion for confession –

---

[28] Consider Ma-tsu's now famous saying: "Do not remember my words!" (Pas, *The Recorded Sayings of Ma-tsu*, p. 39) It is hard to imagine a more memorable saying, nor one more difficult to put into practice. In attempting to carry it out, you would be violating it.

[29] *Ku-tsun yu-lu*, Lu K'uan Yu, *Ch'an and Zen Teachings*, p. 125.

"okay, I did jot down a few notes now and then!" Who wouldn't have been thankful for their "inauthentic" lapses? Who wouldn't have wished at that point that *they* had taken notes?[30]

The origin of these teachings and the image of Huang Po preserved in them is thus "dependent" upon numerous minds, some no doubt more influential than others. Someone, perhaps a committee, had to serve as editor, the organizer of the text as a whole. Since the Huang Po texts, like many others in this genre, are not in full narrative order from beginning to end,[31] someone had to decide where to place each of the entries. Which aphorisms, sermons, or stories would be featured up front, which later, and which just eliminated altogether? The character of the Huang Po text depends on these decisions. Or, perhaps no single orthodox version of the teachings of Huang Po was formed at all. Since getting a copy of the text probably meant copying your own, it may be that different monks selected different parts of the manuscript to copy, leaving others out or rearranging the order.

Although printing – the process of stabilizing the impermanence of texts through the widespread dissemination of an official version – had been invented in China sometime before this,[32] China was still by and large a "manuscript culture."[33] What this meant in the monastic context of ninth-century China was that texts were hand-copied by individuals for specific purposes, and thus occasionally modified to fit those purposes. Texts were not regarded as fixed and unalterable entities. They could be added to, subtracted from, corrected, and improved. Texts could also take others into themselves. Whereas the Huang Po texts draw upon isolated fragments of many other texts, later texts, even more voracious, often took the entire Huang Po corpus into themselves – and then added some more! Relations between texts, as between spoken discourses, were fluid, always open to some new twist or turn. Although this fluidity was especially prevalent before the widespread use of printing, it continued long after printing came to be common. Printing just made the wholesale incorporation of one text by a later predator all that much easier.

---

[30] We sense a modern, romantic version of this same tension in the account of Thomas Hoover, who writes: "Huang-po is known to us today primarily through the accident of having a follower obsessed by the written word" (*The Zen Experience*, p. 123). In other words, "we can be thankful, but he shouldn't have done it!"

[31] As Tsung-mi has his questioner say: "There is no order to it. I see no beginning and no end" (Broughton, *Kuei-feng Tsung-mi*, p. 104).

[32] For a brief history of print in China, see Liu Guojun, *The Story of Chinese Books*.

[33] Following Gerald Bruns, I distinguish here between "the closed text of a print culture and the open text of a manuscript culture" (*Inventions: Writing, Textuality, and Understanding in Literary History*, p. 44).

Prior to printing, however, Zen texts circulated in handwritten form and, therefore, as manuscripts, remained open to further acts of writing. In this Zen culture, readers were enjoined to their texts in ways that encouraged emendation and extension of the text. Since the text was for their own spiritual use, they felt free to amplify, highlight, and fill in the gaps. Rewriting is thus a method of keeping a text up-to-date, of bringing out whatever in the text really does speak to the present situation.

One cultural practice in medieval Zen which accentuated the pace at which textual, linguistic, and ideological change took place was the institution of travel. When Zen monks traveled from one monastic complex to another they would invariably encounter new ideas, new phrases, and new texts. Many Hung-chou Zen texts allude to the practice of sending "messengers" to another monastery to observe their discourse and practice, and to engage in dialogical exchange about the "great matter" of Zen. These were certainly note-taking occasions. Upon return, monks were expected to report back on what they had observed. Monasteries were so readily interlinked that communication was constant. When Huang Po's biography says that his sayings were in "circulation throughout the world," the world they imagine is this circuit of interdependent monasteries.[34] As they circulated, many of Huang Po's sayings made their way into the minds and texts of other Zen masters. As new ideas and expressions arrived at Huang Po monastery, some of them would eventually find their way into the Huang Po literature.

Naturally it is difficult for us to conceive of this editorial license in anything but negative light. To us it constitutes defacement of an original – the real Huang Po – and distortion of a historic form. In a "manuscript" mode of textuality, however, rewriting is a positive necessity, without which the transmission of mind and text would not be possible. The impermanence of text and tradition are best understood as the actualization of previously unseen possibilities. From the perspective of modern historicism, however, this impermanence is a significant problem. If, following this modern practice, we regard a text as representing its own unique culture and historical epoch, then any later alteration obstructs that representation. Medieval Zen practitioners were clearly not historicists. They took their texts to represent not another era, but the "great matter" of Zen as a possibility for actualization in their own era. So if the text's language or ideas needed updating to fulfill that task, editors were always available for the task of rewriting.

---

[34] T. 50, p. 842bc.

Later editors of Huang Po, for example, felt free, indeed compelled, to alter some of the vernacular language, especially slang expressions. Because language changes – slang expressions perhaps most quickly – old formulations lose their power, not to mention their sense. For Huang Po to be effective in a later era, some accommodation in its language was required. Paradoxically, therefore, amending a manuscript by editing its language served textual preservation, rather than being a sign of its demise. The text is preserved in its alteration precisely because its form must be brought to address the present if it is to continue to have any-thing like the power it had in the time of its origin.

What Tsung-mi, P'ei-hsiu's earlier teacher, says in critique of Huang Po's Zen is right to the point here: "Essentially speaking, these [Zen sayings] are merely things in accordance with the present time. They are in response to the abilities of present-day people."[35] What Tsung-mi didn't fully realize was that this was true of all successful texts – even his own – and that the few "classic" texts which manage to speak meaning-fully to other eras or places, in addition to their own, become "classics" out of sheer contingency – a network of "dependent origins" so complex as to be neither predictable in advance nor fully traceable in retrospect.

The alterations required to fit a new group of readers in a new time and place occur invisibly and with relative ease when the transformation required is translation from one language to another. When John Blofeld wrote in English what the Huang Po texts meant to him when he read them in Chinese, a fundamental alteration of the texts' form occurred in an entirely natural way. Since romanticism was the preferred language of spir-itual quest in the modern, English-speaking world, as well as Blofeld's own orientation in the world, Blofeld could just put Huang Po into the idioms of romanticism and be assured that the text would be able to communi-cate in its new location. This transformation of the Huang Po texts is more radical, to be sure, but not unlike the series of transformations that had already occurred in China in the movement of the text from one context or time to another. A successful text must be just as impermanent over time and place as its readers. To regret this impermanence and the "dependent origination" of Huang Po over time is to miss the Buddhist point.[36] Indeed,

---

[35] Broughton, *Kuei-feng Tsung-mi*, p. 105. Yanagida calls this focus in Zen literature of the Hung-chou area a "transition from substance to function" or from essence to act (*Mu no Tankyu*, p. 177).

[36] A few medieval Chinese, lamenting the impermanence of great texts, tried to overcome or at least to forestall the flux by carving them in stone. It is ironic, however, that the Chinese prac-tices of copying texts for repeated transmission proved to be much more enduring. Ancient stone texts have wasted away while the texts themselves continue to circulate in ever-new forms.

the entire Buddhist tradition councils explicitly against this regret. Since all grounds are fluid and all priorities already dependent, grasping for secure foundations and stable originals can only be misguided – and painful. Better to see the continued transformation of the texts as a sign of health, each new version "originating dependent" upon, and impermanent in accordance with, the complexities of a new situation.

In view of these highly "dependent origins" of the Huang Po texts, let us reflect on their history in rough outline. Because the history of this literature is far too complex ever to write, we focus on occasional and, from our vantage point, interesting stops along the path just to bring them to mind as dimensions of the transmission process.

P'ei-hsiu's Preface to his text, written sometime after having sent the manuscript to Mount Huang Po, is dated October 8, 857, and written in the capital city of Ch'ang-an.

The *Wan-ling lu*, the second of the two texts translated by Blofeld and attributed to P'ei-hsiu, is, because of its language and the nature of its stories, more likely the product of monks on Mount Huang Po.[37] It circulates separate from the P'ei-hsiu text until at least the early eleventh century, after which the two are joined together as a set.

The early Huang Po texts had no title although they may have been known orally as the Huang Po Discourse Collection (Huang-po yu-pen). Later on, when titles are appended, they differ, but the most significant and enduring of these titles is *Zen Master Huang Po Hsi Yun's Essential Teachings on the Transmission of Mind* (*Huang-po Hsi-yun Ch'an-shih Ch'uan-hsin fa yao*).

The earliest extant version of Huang Po's recorded sayings comes from the *Ancestral Hall Anthology* (*Tsu-t'ang chi*), written in 952 and only recently rediscovered in Korea. Along with biographical materials on numerous other Zen masters, this anthology gathers an extensive and purportedly chronological set of stories about the career of Huang Po.

A half-century later, the *Ching-te Records of the Transmission of the Lamp* (*Ching-te ch'uan-teng lu*) collects a slightly more extensive and somewhat different set of texts about Huang Po, and includes, in a subsequently added appendix, an early version of his recorded sermons that would later come to be known in different forms as the *Essentials of the Transmission of Mind*. We don't have the original of this text, only a 1283 edition.

---

[37] This is the view of Yanagida in Iriya, *Denshin Hoyo*.

The canonization and sanctification of Huang Po was established during the Sung dynasty when officially sanctioned versions of the Buddhist classics were published with the Emperor's "imprimatur," and printed in numerous high-profile editions of the canon. The Huang Po texts came to have a status virtually equivalent to that of the sutras.

Printing, which was used for sutras and other classic texts in the T'ang dynasty, came to be used for other Buddhist texts in the Sung. This slowed the impermanence of texts like the Huang Po, which were no longer handwritten manuscripts. Variant texts now had standards against which they could be judged. Printing also meant easier access to texts, wider dissemination, and ease of reading.

The *Record of Lin-chi* becomes a widely circulated text because of the status of the Lin-chi school of Zen. Many stories in this text add to the Huang Po legends as they describe exchanges between the master, Huang Po, and his wild disciple, Lin-chi. This radical image of Huang Po becomes much more popular in the Sung and post-Sung eras than the rational and ideological Huang Po of the *Transmission of Mind*.

The *Transmission of Mind* was first published in Japan in 1283, the first Zen discourse record to appear there. When it arrived in Japan is not clear, but the Zen scholar Ui Hakuju suspects that it came to Japan in the hands of Eisai, the founder of Rinzai Zen. In any case, the *Fu-chou Tripitaka* arrived in Japan at about that time and Huang Po was in it. The Huang Po texts were favorites of the samurai swordsmen who brought Zen to prominence in the Kamakura era.

By the late Sung, *koan* practice appears to have been well established in Zen monasteries. As the classic *koan* collections took shape, Huang Po's name and stories of his acts held a prominent place, no doubt due to his status as the teacher of Lin-chi. This interest in *koans*, however, affected which texts of Huang Po would continue in popularity. From this point on, the sermons on "mind" recede to the background, while the anecdotes and stories take prominence – "strangeness" rather than doctrinal insight becomes the criterion of selection.

Numerous other editions of the Buddhist classics are published and continue the dissemination of Huang Po texts. Of these many texts, each bringing us a slightly different Huang Po, the most important may be *The Four House Discourse Record (Ssu-chia yu-lu)*, first compiled in the early Sung as a product of another Zen lineage in the Hung-chou area. Its importance is the certified link it makes between four masters in the Hung-chou lineage: Ma-tsu, Pai-chang, Huang-po, and Lin-chi. By the time of its printing, these four masters had come to represent the "golden age" of Zen, a time when Zen masters were "really" enlightened. This image of the golden age of Zen served as a counter-image to the present, against which the corruption of current times could be measured and to which contemporaries could look for pure ideals and practices.

By the mid fourteenth century, Neo-Confucianism had begun to displace Buddhism as the avant- garde tradition of the educated elite. This occurred, however, only after their deep appropriation of Buddhist thought and practice as contained in texts like the Huang Po literature. The particular status of the Huang Po texts during the long reign of Neo-Confucianism is that they tended not to be objects of criticism due to their logical and ideological form. More vulnerable to critique were the radical texts of Zen which had given up altogether on logical proposition. As Yanagida points out, these texts may have been exempt from critique because they had been composed by the *literati* figure, P'ei-hsiu. Criticized or not, however, they ceased being read and fell into centuries of relative disuse.[38]

At just the time when D. T. Suzuki began to write about Huang Po and other Zen masters in English, the Huang Po texts and other Zen texts were banned in China as counter-revolutionary even though almost no one knew what they said since they hadn't been read in centuries. By the time I purchased *The Zen Teaching of Huang Po* in Blofeld's version, Buddhist texts were being burned in China during the Cultural Revolution.

In light of this complex story about the origins and history of the Huang Po texts, what can we now say about the question of authorship? Who should be regarded as the writer of these texts and whose mind do they represent? Before our attempt to answer this, we would do well to recognize, reflexively, the status of this question. The question of authorship is a peculiarly modern question. Medieval Zen monks would have been puzzled that we would insist that the project of reading Zen begin here. The heritage of romanticism entices us to seek out Huang

---

[38] Other kinds of change affected textuality from the Sung dynasty onward. Books became popular items for private collections, and public libraries began to be built. A new form of text called "leaf binding" or "sutra binding" began to replace scrolls (although both were called "scrolls," which simply meant "text"). This change is significant because it allows the reader to leap into the text at any point without having first to unroll the lengthy paper or silk. Also, texts began to be stored in boxes called "book clothes" which served to preserve them for longer periods of time.

Po's texts only to the extent that we can legitimately consider them an accurate disclosure of the enlightened mind of the individual Huang Po. For us it almost goes without saying that a text of this kind is successful if it genuinely reveals to us the creative personality behind it. Therefore we seek to look through the text to the authorial voice expressed in it. This orientation to texts became so "natural" to us in the twentieth century that only very recently has it been noticed in literary studies that there might be other options.

Fully ensconced within this romantic tradition of textuality, John Blofeld would insist that neither P'ei-hsiu's mediation nor his own have obstructed the pure expressivity of the Zen master himself. What we get is still the real Huang Po behind the text.[39] In order to sustain this conception of the text, Blofeld accepts at face value P'ei-hsiu's humble deference to the authority of Huang Po: P'ei-hsiu claims to be a neutral medium through which the enlightened mind of Huang Po has been transmitted.[40] Only romantic piety will encourage our efforts to believe this, however. We now understand too much about history, writing, and interpretation not to see the significance of P'ei-hsiu's role in the authorship of the texts. P'ei-hsiu was not just recording; he was composing a text in a newly emerging genre. He was writing what Huang Po never wrote and, if the stories are true, never wanted written.[41]

Beyond these originating circumstances we have seen that numerous other authors have entered the scene of creation. First, the monks on Mount Huang Po who were asked to verify and to edit the text joined Huang Po and P'ei-hsiu in the act of origination. Ironically, the text's initial audience was in fact its author. Second, we know that this process continued for centuries. The text was amplified, extended, and revised to produce what would have been taken to be a better text in subsequent eras. The authorial process seems to have broadened as time went on.

---

[39] This emphasis surfaces most directly in Blofeld's translation of Hui Hai, where he writes that the text "brings us closer to him, because he seems to be addressing us straight from his heart as though we were actually face to face with him" (*The Zen Teaching of Hui Hai*, p. 33). The text succeeds if it manages to get the reader back into the "heart" of its author.

[40] We can easily resist P'ei-hsiu's claims here by pointing out the fact that one of his official government positions was in the "censorship bureau" (*Chiu T'ang Shu*, clxxvii, p. 7b)!

[41] It is clear enough that Huang Po Hsi-yun's area of greatness was Zen oratory. Texts tell us that the quality of his spoken discourse was extraordinary, and that it carried a presence and intensity that compelled attentive listening. Like other Zen masters of his time, he was perhaps first and foremost a skilled speaker, both on the lecture dais and in personal encounter. Buddhist priests of this time either gained fame, or failed to do so, primarily based upon their mastery in these domains. The master spoke from the position in the Dharma Hall traditionally given to the image of the Buddha and, therefore, spoke as an instantiation of enlightenment. See Collcutt, *Five Mountains*, p. 195, for a description of this monastic context.

From Huang Po the teachings were transmitted to P'ei-hsiu; from P'ei they were written and transmitted to Huang Po's monastic community; from there the text was transmitted on from generation to generation, "circulating" outward into the larger world of Zen monasteries where other editors and writers made their contributions.

Our question about authorship is best answered, therefore, by saying that the Huang Po texts available for our reading should be attributed, not to any one creative individual or mind, but rather to the Zen tradition in China as it took shape over many centuries. Communal composition, the collection into a composite form of the community's most influential sayings, stories, and wisdom, problematizes our romantic expectations about individual authorship by inserting in its place an anonymous, selfless collectivity. In the gradual alteration of the manuscript we find the unfolding and transformation of the community's highest ideals. The texts *do* hold out an image of the person Huang Po as a paradigm for practice and emulation. But this image is best conceived as the monastic community's most significant projection, the projection of what Huang Po was, and, therefore, what each of them aspired to become. Moreover, this image of Huang Po changes over time.[42]

The Buddhist image of "no self" at the authorial helm of these texts can be made clear if we recall the origins of the name "Huang Po." The words "Huang Po" were selected by the Zen master to name his new mountain monastery. Therefore, they name, first of all, a place and an institution, an alpine monastic community. It is by virtue of the fact that he was the long-time abbot of this mountain monastery that the monk, Hsi-yun, comes to be named "Hsi-yun of Huang Po monastery." Following his death a succession of abbots were also named "Huang Po"; they too propagated the "Zen Teachings of Huang Po." Although the original master, Huang Po Hsi-yun, does come to be paradigmatic, the actual sources of this impressive paradigm can be more truly located in the innumerable Zen authors who wrote under the overall sign of the monastery. In China, "Huang Po" never did refer just to an individual person and, given what we have discovered to be true of the Huang Po texts, we would be well advised to follow that practice now.

It would be difficult to find a concept more suited to understanding this manner of textuality than the early Buddhist concept "dependent

---

[42] Bernard Faure makes a similar point about the fruitlessness of historicist efforts "to reconstitute an original text," suggesting that we read the texts in light of their constitution through ongoing "supplementarity" (*The Rhetoric of Immediacy*, p. 55).

origination." Dependent origination makes clear to Buddhists how things lack independent and autonomous status. All things come into being and change over time through their interactions with other things which also share this same "selfless" status. Our discovery is that, not only does the person Huang Po come to us in complex interdependence, but so does his text. The extent to which this continues to disappoint us is the extent to which reading Zen is just what we need.

"Reading," however, is no more exempt from this "dependent" status than are texts. The character of your reading "originates dependent" upon a whole host of factors that you may never have noticed.

CHAPTER 2

READING: *the practice of insight*

I am convinced that, if one were to read the Hua Yen Sutra – especially if it were by candlelight in some lonely place – and ponder its
awe-inspiring imagery, a profound mystical experience might burst
upon one unawares!

John Blofeld[1]

You are too fond of reading all manner of books.
The Venerable Neng Hai to John Blofeld[2]

In the massive corpus of Zen reading material, few stories are more fer-
vently read than the account of how Hui-neng, the renowned Sixth
Patriarch of Zen, could not read. As the Zen school gradually took shape
and began to formulate the point of its heritage, great pride was taken
in the thought that Zen arose as a powerful critique of the prevalent
scholastic tradition. Although the historical accuracy of the traditional
account of the origins of Zen is now questionable in a number of ways,
it is nevertheless true that, in Sung dynasty textual images of the Zen
tradition in Huang Po's time, a certain kind of anti-scholasticism was
indeed a rallying point for Zen monastic communities. The practices of
reading and textual study, which had been central to Chinese Buddhism
up through the mid-T'ang, were exposed to a forceful critique. What,
after all, did reading have to do with the enlightened comportment of
the Buddha and other great sages? Textual images of Huang Po, along
with his most famous teachers and disciples, reveal a condescending attitude toward the practice of reading:

The fruit of the path is not attained through textual study, which was cut off by
the ancient sages.[3]

---

[1] Blofeld, *Beyond the Gods*, p. 98. [2] Blofeld, *The Wheel of Life*, p. 151.
[3] T. 48, p. 382c; Blofeld, *Huang Po*, p. 55.

The Buddhas, on manifesting themselves in the world, seized dung-shovels to rid themselves of all such rubbish as books containing metaphysics and sophistry.[4]

Following Huang Po's metaphor, his disciple, Lin-chi, calls texts "dung clods"[5] and "worthless dust"[6], and the genealogy of rejection goes on for generations. These anti-reading passages in Zen literature are so prominent that one might even interpret their point to be that the value of texts lies primarily in their rejection, not in their reading, and that more insight may derive from one irreverent act of anti-textuality than from years of reverent study. So much for reading and the scholastic interests of the orthodox line of Chinese Buddhism!

Yet a strange irony persists in this admonition against reading – like many generations of Zen monks, we inherit it for contemplation primarily in the act of reading. Bending these anti-reading passages back upon the texts in which they can be read lands us in reflexive paradox – self-contradiction. Yet this point never seemed to cause much perplexity in Zen. In writing their anti-reading rule, Zen authors seem to have intended at least one exception; they wanted their best anti-reading texts to be read. This should give us grounds for reflection. The critique of reading is intended to valorize its opposite – immediate experience. If we look closely, however, we will see that the very opposition between the literary world and the world of immediate experience is itself a literary construct, one which functions to bolster the reality of immediate experience by tilting the antithesis against its own textual form. In this sense, Zen texts work on their readers to make the "real world" more real than it was before the act of reading. This way of describing the matter, however, will lead us to think that the anti-reading admonitions in Zen literature may have important limits and qualifications, and that we should therefore be on guard against too literal a reading of them. Indications that reading could not have been eliminated as a primary practice in Zen are not at all difficult to find in Zen literature and in the Huang Po texts. Let us read some.

First, from P'ei-hsiu's narration, we have a story which, even in making its anti-textual point, repeatedly revives the status of reading to at least a position of inevitability. P'ei-hsiu writes: "Once I gave a poem I had written to Huang Po. He took it in his hands, and then set it aside. 'Do you understand?' he asked me. 'No,' I replied. 'Think a little. If things could

[4] Blofeld, *Huang Po*, p. 130.   [5] T. 47, p. 500b; Sasaki, *The Recorded Sayings of Lin-chi*, p. 25.
[6] T. 47, p. 499a; Sasaki, *The Recorded Sayings of Lin-chi*, p. 16.

be expressed like this with ink and paper, what would be the purpose of a sect like ours?'" P'ei-hsiu's story doesn't go on to tell us how he responded to this criticism, or even to elaborate on Huang Po's point – the point is apparently clear. The text does go on, however; it recites the poem for us anyway, even though its pointlessness had just been asserted. Either P'ei-hsiu didn't get Huang Po's message, or he didn't believe it. Or perhaps he was so fond of this poem that he just couldn't leave it out, irrelevant to Zen or not. Moreover, numerous Zen editors of subsequent editions of the text left it there for our reflection. Then, following P'ei-hsiu's poem, the story takes another surprising turn, almost to the point of embarrassing the reader. Having just lashed P'ei-hsiu for writing a poem, Huang Po composes another one in response. Although his poem strives to make its anti-textual point, the master must enter into the textual world to do so, thus abandoning the position of "no dependence on texts" (*pu-li wen-tzu*) and conceding the inescapability of reading.

Second, one cannot help but notice that the recorded sayings of many of the Hung-chou masters, especially Huang Po, are strewn with quotations from other texts. Since these are "recorded sayings" texts, we are encouraged to assume that Huang Po was quoting from memory this vast repertoire of literature. Apparently, Huang Po had not just read these texts, he had read them frequently and carefully, appropriating them to memory. Huang Po is represented as citing an extensive body of literature; his own reading was obviously wide-ranging and influential. Therefore, among other attributes, Huang Po is presented to us as having been a voracious and astute reader. How could this be?

The fact of Huang Po's reading does not go unnoticed in Blofeld's interpretation. Nor does Blofeld lack an explanation for it. On his account, reading is a worthy practice at preliminary stages in the practice of Zen, but can be eliminated once less mediated forms of experience begin to take hold. He writes:

It is clear from his own words that he [Huang Po] realized the necessity of books and teachings of various kinds for people less advanced . . . Hence the Doctrine of Words must inevitably precede the Wordless Doctrine, except in certain rare cases.[7]

Ch'an masters do not just dispense with books from the beginning, as some people in the West seem inclined to think. They dispense with books when they have acquired sufficient preliminary knowledge to be able to transcend writings by direct experience.[8]

---

[7] Blofeld, *Huang Po*, p. 22.   [8] Blofeld, *The Zen Teaching of Hui Hai*, p. 139.

How the highly mediated practice of reading would lead to immediate, "direct experience," is not explained, nor is the tension between them noted. Nevertheless, one can easily find Zen texts which support this succession from reading to non-reading. Huang Po's student, Lin-chi, gives some account of it. The *Lin-chi lu* reports how, after he had "made a wide study of the sutras and sastras," he "threw them all away," having "realized that they were only medicines for salvation and displays of opinion."[9] This account, however, would seem to be even less charitable toward reading than Blofeld's. The text does not say that whatever state Lin-chi had attained that empowered his transcendence of texts was a consequence of the early practice of reading. Lin-chi merely comes to the realization that all study was inessential and gives it up. Yet perhaps Blofeld has a point here. Perhaps, whether Lin-chi realized it or not, his attainment was only possible on the basis of the reading practice that got him there in the first place. The implications of this line of thinking threaten to surpass what Blofeld might want to allot to reading, however. Not only would reading be essential to Zen practice in the early and formative stages, but we might further be forced to admit that if an enlightened mind "originates dependent" upon prior reading, that state of mind would continue to hold within it, and to be supplemented by, the influence and outcome of reading.

One reason Blofeld would very likely have winced at this conclusion is that his own practice of romanticism also included anti-literary images of considerable significance. In this tradition we find the image of the unschooled poetic genius who, lacking the obstructions of culture and training, penetrates to the very heart of the matter whether in music, art, or philosophy.[10] Modern romantics still express considerable anxiety over the possibility that their own creativity might have been influenced and conditioned by others.[11] Insight that is dependent on, or conditioned by, the insight of others is considered to be unoriginal and inauthentic. Surely this element in western romanticism has had some effect on our practices of reading Zen. At the very least it established a connection through which Zen could be appreciated – here we find the truly natural genius beyond anything the romantics had imagined.[12]

[9] T. 47, p. 502c. See Yanagida, "The Life of Lin-chi."
[10] Sources of this image in romantic writers and their precursors can be found in Bruns, *Inventions: Writing, Textuality, and Understanding in Literary History.*   [11] See Bloom, *The Anxiety of Influence.*
[12] John McRae points out an excellent example of this theme in the Zen tradition in Shen-hsiu who, although he had never read the sutras, showed complete mastery of their content nonetheless (*The Northern School*, p. 263).

In light of this coincidence of theme, we can see how both Zen and romanticism conspired to shape John Blofeld's later evaluation of his own years of reading in the English school system. In the midst of auto-biographical reflections on his own religious experience, he writes:

> If I had retained my powers of reflection, I might have been conscious of an almost egoless state, signifying the magnificent victory of Nature over my fine Occidental education; this had so furrowed my mind with "hard facts" and so chopped it into tiny segments with the knife-edge of dualistic reasoning, that two decades of intermittent effort under the guidance of some of Asia's most gifted sages had been powerless to overcome such an immense handicap.[13]

Reading had proved to be an "immense handicap" for Blofeld and, in contrast to his own account of how it functioned for Zen masters, it seemed to be so deeply ingrained that even if he stopped reading, it still remained there in the mind. Yet romantic (as much as Buddhist) that he was, Blofeld still hoped that "Nature" would win out over the education that had perverted it in the first place. Rather than appreciating the edification received through texts "in the preliminary stages" which led him to explorations in Asia and set the stage for his conversion to Buddhism, Blofeld considered himself saddled with the seemingly impossible task of having to eradicate the negative effect of that early practice.

Yet the "preliminary stage" theory, as convincing as it may seem at first glance, does not provide grounds for understanding how reading has figured into the history of Zen practice, not to mention romanticism. Blofeld wrote right up to the end of his life and each work displays the extent and evolution of his reading practice. He never seems to have stopped or even reduced his reading. Always humble, Blofeld might have explained that this was due to his own inability ever to penetrate beyond the preliminary stage.[14] But could he have accepted this judgment about the Zen figures he so thoroughly valorized, like Huang Po and Lin-chi? Doubtful! We have textual evidence to suggest, however, that the great masters were still reading at the end of their careers, just like Blofeld was. Let us examine two such passages.

One, from *The Transmission of the Lamp*, has Lin-chi returning to Huang Po monastery and finding the aging master Huang Po reading a sutra.

---

[13] Blofeld, *The Wheel of Life*, p. 17.

[14] A thorough study of Blofeld's writings on this topic show widespread ambivalence. He seems to have held several variant views without having reconciled them. For example, in *Beyond the Gods*, he says that "it is inherent in the nature of mystical traditions that they cannot be learnt from books" (p. 151). But earlier in the book he had worked the opposite line when he wrote that he had viewed the progress of Zen in the west with "dismay" because "too many people" have seized "blindly" upon the phrase "a doctrine without words" (p. 93).

With typical wit he says: "I thought you were the perfected man, but here you are, apparently a dull old monk, swallowing black beans [words written in black ink]."[15] Accepting Lin-chi's powerful anti-reading point, and the preliminary stage theory which "could" be assumed in it, let us notice one thing – that even in his later years, Huang Po was still engaged in the practice of reading. Therefore, either Huang Po was still in a pre-liminary stage or Blofeld's commonly held theory is jeopardized. A second passage from the *Lin-chi lu* reads as follows: "The one is the three, the three is the one. Gain understanding such as this and then you can read the sutras."[16] If reading is a preliminary means to a later end, or, even more critically, a practice that one later realizes was inessential to the project of enlightenment, then why would anyone suggest that one read *after* having "gained" enlightened understanding?[17]

Moreover, if we take a closer look at this passage, we notice that the height of realization is thought to be encapsulated in a textual passage, a passage which Lin-chi would have learned through his thorough study of Hua-yen Buddhist literature.[18] No doubt Lin-chi is right that under-standing this passage requires more than a simple act of reading the words – much more. The fact, however, that this passage, inadvertently perhaps, locates reading both at the beginning and at the end of prac-tice is significant because, on this reading, that is inevitably where it will be found – everywhere in Zen. So ubiquitous, in fact, were reading prac-tices in Zen that they constantly threatened to overwhelm other prac-tices and, therefore, required regular critique in the form of the anti-textual text aimed at putting reading in proper perspective.

The slogan which was taken to epitomize the anti-reading sentiment in Zen – "no dependence on language and texts" – was thought to have descended directly from the founding figure of the tradition, Bodhidharma. Whatever its origins, it seems to have been entering into wide discursive circulation in Huang Po's time as a distinguishing feature of "Zen." Determining exactly what it meant, however, and how it was to be put into practice was not an easy task.[19] Indeed, it would not be at all far-fetched to

---

[15] T. 47, p. 505c.   [16] T. 47, p. 498c; Sasaki, *The Recorded Sayings of Lin-chi*, p. 16.

[17] Similarly, in response to a question concerning the use of Zen texts, Tsung-mi says that they "serve two purposes": they assist in awakening "those who have not fully awakened," and they assist "those who are already awakened" but who seek even deeper appropriation of the Buddha mind (Broughton, *Kuei-feng Tsung-mi*, p. 107).

[18] Yanagida shows how Hua-yen and Wei-shih influences can be seen in the *Lin-chi lu*: "The Life of Lin-chi," p. 72.

[19] Here I follow Griffith Foulk: "while most channists from the ninth century onward accepted the slogan 'not depending on texts' as orthodox chan doctrine, they could not agree on what it meant" ("The Ch'an School", p. 235).

read this concern as one of the central issues of Hung-chou Zen, as a problem which Zen masters of that time provoked and passed on to later generations of practitioners. Clearly, no unanimity on the meaning of the mandate against "words and letters" existed. Did it mean literally "no reading" in Zen? Or was its meaning more subtle, like "not too much reading," or "only certain texts," or "only certain ways of reading certain texts," and so on? Evidence suggests that a few did indeed take it literally – they stopped reading or used the doctrine to justify a refusal to start. A few even took "no words" to mean no spoken discourse as well; they retreated into the mountains and isolated themselves even from the monastic community, some never to be heard from again. The vast majority, however, went on reading, even though the particular shape of the practice continued to evolve.[20] What could the anti-textual rhetoric have meant to them?

Since the Huang Po literature presents the master Huang Po both as a voracious reader and as an outspoken critique of this same practice, these texts turn out to be a good place to begin the inquiry. In fact, dozens of passages take up reading and study as focal issues. Why? First, because reading and study were perhaps *the* central practices of the Buddhist tradition in China that Huang Po had inherited and, second, because those practices were in the process of monumental transformation. Indeed, Huang Po was one of the primary instruments of this change, although certainly not the only one. The change was not from reading to non-reading. It was rather from the particular kinds of reading practiced in earlier generations of Chinese Buddhism to fundamentally different kinds. Therefore, to understand how we should read Huang Po's admonitions against reading, we need to consider what reading practices set the context for his views on the subject.

It is certainly clear that a variety of literary practices had been central to Chinese Buddhism throughout its history.[21] Monasteries had become

---

[20] For an interesting description of the placement of reading practices within traditional Zen monasteries in China and Japan, see Collcutt, *Five Mountains*, pp. 215–218.

[21] It is worth recalling here the extent to which China, by Huang Po's time in the mid ninth century and by the subsequent Sung dynasty, was a literate culture. Reading and writing had been a part of Chinese culture already for over two millennia. To see the presence of textuality in the world of Zen, we could look past the sutras and sacred texts to see how virtually every dimension of what went on in the day-to-day business of the monastery depended on reading and writing. Records of all sorts were necessary just to conduct daily affairs – leases, rolls, agreements, government decrees, work assignment lists, plaques with Buddhist names and ranks, signs indicating what was what and where things went, and so on. Indeed, one of the very few absolutely essential possessions of every monk and nun was an ordination certificate, a text bestowing their identity as monastic citizens and permitting their practice. Texts were an inextricable part of their everyday environment, and they knew it. Not to be able to read was an enormous handicap.

the primary educational institutions of China and remained so until their partial displacement by Neo-Confucian academies following the Sung. For much of this history, it was widely expected that literacy was one requirement for the Buddhist priesthood, although it is clear that this was not always actualized in social practice. Several times, primarily for economic reasons having to do with the tax base, the Imperial government had acted to reduce the size of this ecclesiastical body by conducting a literacy exam, an examination on sutra mastery. In Huang Po's time, for example, a compulsory examination was to be administered throughout the country.[22] Both monks and nuns were to be tested on their ability either to read sutra text, or to recite it from memory. Reading 500 pages of Chinese sutra text will not be regarded a simple task if we keep in mind that Chinese is not a phonetic script, and that "Buddhist" Chinese was not the language of colloquial discourse. Knowing how to pronounce a word required having memorized the appearance of the written sign to the point of being able to associate it with a sound and the sound, with a meaning beyond the parameters of everyday life.[23] The other option was to recite from memory 300 pages of text, and this was considered to be of roughly equal difficulty. Any monk or nun unable to perform in one of these capacities was to be removed from monastic life and returned to the tax rolls.[24]

It is interesting that scriptural literacy was widely assumed to constitute the essential dimension of ordained life. Why would this have been so? We can certainly imagine other criteria: constancy of meditation practice, faithfulness to the rules of monastic life, knowledge of ritual practice, and so on. Why would sutra knowledge be the *sine qua non* of authentic Buddhist life? Cultural background provides part of the answer as we have seen. China was the world's most textually oriented culture, and the prestige of the Confucian tradition guaranteed that education and reading would continue to be vital to the overall cultural orientation in significant segments of society.

Another equally important reason for the textual orientation in Chinese Buddhism has to do with how the Chinese had come to be

---

[22] See Weinstein, *Buddhism Under the T'ang*, pp. 111–112.
[23] This is not to say that the government, or the Buddhist establishment, required that monks know the meaning of the texts they recited. But as everyone knows in every language, understanding the meaning of the words you recite greatly facilitates the capacity to remember them.
[24] Imagine Huang Po, enormous in physical stature, overpowering in personal demeanor, and prone to scoff at "external," ritualized textual practices, reciting his personal sutra before the local magistrate in charge of conducting the government sutra exam! For the unnerved examiner, fear may have been motive enough to justify an exemption.

Buddhists in the first place. China had inherited Buddhism primarily in the form of a massive corpus of sacred texts which required enormous cultural efforts in the areas of translation, classification, interpretation, and application. Although missionary monks were essential to their conversion, the most important of these were translators, those skilled in showing the Chinese what might be done with all these texts. Buddhist texts called upon the Chinese to rework their most basic habits of thought and daily comportment, and the process of refashioning the culture in light of these texts went on for many centuries. It is therefore understandable that the practices of reading and textual contemplation dominated the early traditions of Chinese Buddhism.

For centuries the most important and best-known monks in China had been scholars. Mastering the massive canon of sutras and commentaries required total commitment, the task of an entire lifetime – and more. There were scholars specializing in philology and translation; there were others who were expert in the history and classification of texts, a major occupation when thousands of sacred texts in variant editions appeared upon the scene. Some specialized in interpreting, comparing, and relating the meaning of texts; others took the meaning of texts as the ground for further reflection and philosophy.[25] Many monks specialized in one particular sutra, typically committing it to memory for the purposes of public recital, ritual intonement, or private meditation. Furthermore, the textual corpus continued to grow: new translations of new texts, better translations of already-translated texts, new classification schemas, and more and more commentaries on what all of this might mean. It is certainly no accident that the technology of printing came to be discovered in the midst of this cultural envelopment in the practices of textuality. It is also not surprising that the Zen movement would eventually appear as a critique of this immersion in the book, and, at the same time, produce by far the largest and most influential canon of texts of any Buddhist movement in East Asia.[26]

What particular textual practices would have been natural targets for the Zen critique of Huang Po and others? Ritual use of sacred texts without regard for meaning and for the purposes of merit procurement was one substantial arena of criticism. For some monks, sutra recital was

[25] See Lopez, *Buddhist Hermeneutics*, for clarification on this dimension of Buddhist textual practice.
[26] Heinrich Dumoulin is insightful when he writes that "the Zen of the Sung period, despite its occasional iconoclastic tendencies, gave China its richest indigenous expression of Buddhist literature" (*Zen Buddhism: A History*, p. 245).

a vocation, a full-time career grounded in the early Buddhist understanding of the merit produced in the propagation of sutras. The sacred-
ness of sutras meant that their ritual employment was widespread. One
practice, called "turning the texts," allowed monks to chant their way
through the entire canon by intoning only the first few lines of a sutra,
and then move on to the next text. This ritual guaranteed that no sacred
text would be left completely out of circulation no matter how irrelevant
its meaning may have become. Another pious textual practice involved
dedicating a decade or more to reading rapidly through the entire
Buddhist canon. Given its sheer volume, speed-reading without regard
to meaning or time for reflection was a necessity for anyone committed
to the successful completion of this meritorious ritual. Sutras could also
be "turned" mechanically, saving the labor of the professional reader by
installing a revolving bookshelf which, like prayer wheels, could be ritually activated regardless of literacy. Some of these practices were based
more on ideas about the "needs" of the sutras themselves, and the
demands of the theistic Buddha, than on the requirements of spiritual
cultivation. Magical conceptions of the sacred texts were widespread in
all Buddhist cultures as they were in non-Buddhist traditions throughout
the world.[27]

Zen critique did not focus here, however. These criticisms were
already obvious to many practitioners, whether literate or not. Instead,
Zen texts dwell on the shortcomings of scholarly reading, the practices
of the dominant and most prestigious Buddhists of the T'ang dynasty.
Their reading was not so easily susceptible to magical misunderstanding.
Indeed, their weaknesses were more closely aligned to sophistication
than to the lack of it. What was the character of scholarly Buddhist
textual practice which drew the ridicule of Zen masters like Huang Po?
This is not a simple question for two reasons: that these practices were
already quite diverse themselves and that they changed over time.
Nevertheless, let us characterize these practices and Huang Po's critique
in terms of the ends or goals for which they were being performed.
Because sutras were thought to be the words of the Buddha, and because
they made available to the Chinese sophisticated but unfamiliar forms
of thought, knowledge of the sutras was taken to be the most worthy

---

[27] A straightforward critique of the magical use of texts can be found in Blofeld's translation of
Hui-hai, where the Zen master responds to a gullible questioner by asking whether "any marvelous efficacy" comes from the text laying there on the table. Instead, he asserts quite sensibly
that "effectual answers come from proper use of the mind by the person who reads the sutras"
(*The Zen Teaching of Hui Hai*, p. 114).

aspiration, the goal of study as a Buddhist. To know the origins of a sutra, its setting, narrative emplotment, primary concepts, and overall position on Buddhist issues was the primary point of their study. The sutras thus became objects of knowledge in and of themselves. Zen criticisms of these practices commonly point out the limitations of "objectification," and of knowledge as an end in itself. Knowing what the sutras say about enlightenment is not the same as awakening.

Tsung-mi's evaluation of scholarly practice works in this direction, but still falls short of the full force of the Zen critique. He has his interlocutor comment that "the important thing is to get the idea and not to value specialization in the texts."[28] Huang Po's orientation to reading would reposition priorities so that the important thing is neither to "value specialization" nor to "get the idea," but rather to look through the sutra and its "ideas" to the realities presented in their light. The point of studying the sutras, therefore, was not to "know" them, or even to "understand" them, but rather to embody their wisdom in such a way as to experience their referent, that to which they point. The texts themselves were to be regarded as "empty" of "own-being," and, therefore, not something worthy of knowledge in and of themselves. This was true of everything, however. Texts were no more (or less) to be derided than anything else in the world. Yet texts had a way, it seemed, of closing one off from precisely what they were meant to disclose. This closure only occurred, however, if one took them as an end in themselves, as something that one masters for the sake of mastery, rather than something through which some other "end" was to be achieved. What seems to be emerging in the texts of Huang Po and other Hung-chou Zen masters was a new way of practicing textuality, and of relating to their texts. This new practice was clearly experientially oriented, and directed toward evoking moments of "awakening."

Anti-textuality was, therefore, not a theory of Huang Po's, nor of other Zen masters, and it was certainly not their practice. Instead, we will be better off reading it as a powerful way of addressing a situation in which what they took to be the "great matter" of Buddhism – awakening – was being obstructed by a certain style of reading practice. Huang Po's instincts seem to have been iconoclastic in this regard. Sutras were being objectified, externalized, in the same way that statues of Buddhist deities had. Reifying the words of the Buddha had the same detrimental effect as reifying the Buddha. Both prevented the possibility

---

[28] Broughton, *Kuei-feng Tsung-mi*, p. 107.

of seeing the Buddha already present and at hand. Iconoclastic acts and seemingly irreverent behavior had the effect of showing the "emptiness" of the Buddha and the sutras in practice, and of reorienting practitioners to these sacred entities in some more helpful way.

Perhaps the best way to characterize the transformation in reading practice suggested by the Huang Po texts is to say that they question the practice of studying the sutras for knowledge, of looking at them and thinking about them, with a strong preference for a practice of reading in which one would look through the text to the reality presented there. The authentic Zen practitioner would not study texts so much as he or she would study reality, in part by means of the texts that purport to present it in its fullness. Let us read carefully one passage in Huang Po where this position on reading is articulated:

> In these days people only seek to stuff themselves with knowledge and deductions, seeking everywhere for book-knowledge and calling this "Dharma-practice." They do not know that so much knowledge and deduction have just the contrary effect of piling up obstacles. Merely acquiring a lot of knowledge makes you like a child who gives himself indigestion by gobbling too much curds . . . When so-called knowledge and deductions are not digested, they become poisons.[29]

In this passage what has been called "book-knowledge" – clearly the practice of sutra study – is related to human desire and read metaphorically through the processes of eating and digestion. Those who pride themselves on knowledge of the sutras are simply following the paths of craving and gluttony. They do not recognize how this practice has the effect of obstructing the point of the text they study – the overcoming of desires and ego. Their insatiable desire to consume the texts leads to "indigestion." This is the crucial metaphor: sutras are susceptible to being "consumed" in inappropriate ways, with devastating consequences. "Undigested" sutras are those from which all we gain and retain is knowledge "about" them. They accumulate in our bodies and minds without being digested or taken into our system. They don't become part of the reader, except as excess weight, an obstruction to actual life functions. They function to restrict one's vision rather than to open it.

The text's rejection of the accumulation of "knowledge about" the sutras is so forceful that it may seem to reject reading altogether. But clearly it doesn't. It backs its arguments with quotes from the sutras – the

---

[29] T. 48, p. 382c; Blofeld, *Huang Po*, p. 56.

Buddha opposed textual memorization and "mastery"; he taught deep appropriation of their meaning. And, as we have seen, in the midst of his teaching practice, Huang Po does not stop reading. Instead, what he teaches is how to read.

One of the greatest who learned from Huang Po was Mu-chou Tao-tsung who was head monk under the master Huang Po. Two passages from the Mu-chou fascicle of *The Transmission of the Lamp* can instruct us here:

When the Master (Mu-chou) was reading the sutras, the Minister Chen Tsao asked him, "Master, what sutra are you reading?" The Master said, "The *Diamond sutra!*" The Minister said, "The *Diamond sutra* was translated in the Sixth Dynasty; which edition are you using?" The Master lifted up the book and said, "All things produced by causation are simply an illusive dream and the shadow of a bubble."[30]

When the Master was reading the *Nirvana sutra*, a monk asked him what sutra he was reading. The Master picked up the book and said, "This is the last one for cremation."[31]

Before we jump to anti-textual conclusions about these passages, notice who is reading on each occasion. Notice also that the story, which is meant to valorize Mu-chou, does not have Mu-chou going up to some other monk who happens to be reading. If the point is simply that one ought not to read, then Mu-chou himself would have been the target of the narrative. Clearly he isn't. Mu-chou is reading in both stories; nevertheless, it is he who comes down upon the other with respect to reading. What is the point? In the first story, the Minister's question sets the stage for a critique of a certain kind of reading. "Which edition of the text are you using?" Response: "All editions and all things 'originate dependently,' they are empty of inherent 'self-nature' and relative to other things. To grasp for the thing in itself – sixth-dynasty text? – rather than peering through the text as though through a 'dream, a bubble'" or shadow, is to terminate one's reading at precisely the point where it ought to begin.

Notice how Mu-chou's metaphors, drawn from the *Diamond sutra*, the very text he was reading, show his own "digestion" of its meaning. Mu-chou learns from the text that all things, even the text itself, are like "bubbles and shadows." In what sense? Bubbles and shadows are not unreal – they are really there. Mu-chou's interest in them is directed, not to their unreality, but rather to the particular character of their reality.

[30] T. 51, p. 291; Chang, *Original Teachings*, p. 111.
[31] T. 51, p. 291; Chang, *Original Teachings*, p. 111.

Like texts, bubbles and shadows are tentative, fleeting, and brought about in the first place by factors beyond themselves. Their reality is provisional, dependent, and thus, in Buddhist terms, "empty" of an independent and permanent "self-nature." How should we read them therefore? Just like we read bubbles and shadows, by seeing what they can show us about the character of the world right before our eyes, and by refusing to attach ourselves to the signs which perform this showing. When Mu-chou reads the *Diamond sutra*, his concern is not with the text itself (which edition?), but rather with the realities to which it can point when properly read and, through them, to the transformation in his own experience that it may make available. Enlightened reading, not just of texts but of things as well, is unattached; it does not objectify or reify whatever is being read.

The second passage from Mu-chou is even more radical in its qualifications on textuality. When reading is practiced in such a way as to obstruct the meaning of the text, when one focuses on the text itself rather than through it to its referent, then the point of the sutra – emptiness – can only be made by calling to mind its own destruction. Since the monk failed to get the point of the sutra by reading it, Mu-chou wonders out loud whether the act of cremating the text would manage to communicate the point. Will burning the text break the grasping for the text that characterizes the monk before him? Only if that act can be properly read as the "shadow" of emptiness, a sign of something not so much in the text as in the world. Occasionally in Zen, such literal acts of destruction or "emptying" were performed, and, when they were, these radical acts served as symbolic, paradigmatic expressions of the very wisdom meant in the Buddhist sutras. The most famous of these is perhaps the monk–scholar Te-shan, who could only come to the true meaning of the *Diamond sutra* and his vast collection of commentaries on it by ripping them to shreds, a ritual sacrifice that still reverberates in Zen today.[32] When the meaning of the text you read is Buddhist "emptiness," the full force of that meaning can only appear in reflexive application, when the text finally shows its own emptiness, and when the reader sees the emptiness of his or her own act of reading.

---

[32] Bernard Faure is right that, although following Kagamishima Genryu, we should understand the origins of the "no dependence" doctrine as a rejection not of texts but of particular textual practices, nevertheless, continued emphasis on this critique inevitably veered off into an unabashed anti-intellectualism (*Chan Insights and Oversights*, p. 218). This tendency is no doubt at least partially responsible for the eventual marginalization of Zen in China and elsewhere. Inability or unwillingness to reflect on what you do eventually leads to naive and narrow practices.

Several challenges, therefore, are placed upon our acts of reading Zen by the texts themselves. Is Huang Po's critique of reading practice applicable to our reading too, and, if it is, how should we judge its validity? One question raised by Huang Po's critique of reading has to do with motivation, and seems well worth asking ourselves: in the final analysis, why are we reading? What is the character of the end toward which our practice is aimed? Goals, like anything else, can vary significantly in character, and are also susceptible to change over time. One point in the Zen critique of reading is that the ends we seek through it are commonly shallow, that they are insufficiently motivated by something that truly matters. They can be transformed, however. We may read a Zen text to discover which edition it is, to learn about reading practice in medieval China, to gain knowledge about Zen, or to entertain ourselves, but unless these "ends" are clearly subsumed under some larger end, they will be vulnerable to Huang Po's criticism. Why be concerned about "editions"; why care about reading in medieval China? Why do you want to know about Zen?

In the Huang Po literature, this central issue or "end" is called the "Great Matter" (*ta-shih*). To read for any reason other than penetration into this matter is to have mistaken the point of the practice, and, therefore, to diminish its benefit. But what is the "great matter," the one matter among the many others? For Huang Po, "mind" is the great matter, and to "awaken" to it is all that really matters. No doubt other things matter as well, but only to the extent that they can in some way serve an authentic pursuit of the "great matter." How we should understand "mind" and "awakening" are matters to be explored in chapters to follow. Nevertheless, let us postulate for now that, however we understand our own enlightenment, this is the only end or motivation that will ultimately justify our practice of reading Zen. Is Huang Po right in that assertion? So it seems, but following Huang Po's stipulations for authentic reading practice, each reader would need to make that judgment honestly on his or her own terms. If we agree with this initial principle, then the further question mediated from Huang Po to us is: when we examine our reading practice, the activity in motion right now, in what way and to what extent is it motivated by whatever we take to be the "great matter?" What is the character and quality of our aim in reading? Can this practice be deepened and improved so that it may truly matter whether we have done it or not?

To consider these questions as we read is to enter into a relationship with the text that draws the reader fully into the activity. If the motive and aim in reading is the first concern of the Huang Po texts, the implication of the reader's "self" is the second. We can easily read in order to discern which edition of the text this is, or even "what Huang Po believed," without getting involved ourselves. In fact we commonly do so when we read to gather information or to describe objectively what the text says. "Objectivity" is by definition and historical practice the sustained effort to hold the text or object at a distance from the self so that no intermingling of one's own beliefs or feelings with those represented in the text occurs. Much has been learned about Huang Po and about Zen through objective methods of analysis that could not have been known otherwise. In fact, historians will tell us quite rightly that we may completely miss the true "matter of the text" if we have not rigorously separated the Huang Po of contemporary romantic projection (our own subjectivity as readers) from the Huang Po of rigorous historical analysis (the exercise of objectivity). Nevertheless, the Huang Po texts insist that authentic reading demands the full presence of the reader's own self in the activity of reading, not its dismissal. And so should we. Objective historical analysis is not an end in itself. It is rather a means of getting to something that may matter. If it doesn't matter, if it has no bearing on our own lives, then what reason would we have to suppose that it might matter to someone else? The truth is that it may not matter whether we know anything about Huang Po or not. It will matter, however, if, in reading the Huang Po texts, we deepen our own sense of the matters about which the texts speak since these matters may be manifest in our lives as well.

Here we can see that Huang Po's first concern about the aim or motive of reading, and the second concerning the implication of the reader in the reading process, are two sides of a single coin. If the aim of reading is directly on what matters, the one to whom it may matter is drawn fully into the activity. Reading the texts objectively as sources of information holds them at such a distance that their point and power are diminished, or canceled; they are not allowed to matter to the only one for whom they could matter – the reader. When what you're reading is Zen, however, be prepared! The self of the reader *is* the "great matter" of the text.

When we read objectively we understand ourselves as outside observers rather than participants. Thus we can watch the action taking place between others – the characters in the story. When Huang Po ridicules a scholar–monk for an inauthentic reading practice, we can, at a comfortable distance, share in the joke. Having set ourselves and our own reading practice aside for the time being, we don't feel threatened by the force of the story. If we consider the point of the text to be directed at others, we have carefully eluded its power and, at the same time, the primary benefit to be gained from having read it. If, on the other hand, we read Zen in the spirit of Huang Po, the true target of the text's criticism is no one but the reader here and now.

But isn't it important, we might ask, to clear away our own pre-conceptions, set aside our own ideas, in order to be able to understand those of the Zen text we read? No, although the fact that it so clearly seems so reveals to us what it means to be a modern western reader. This idea, so carefully considered in early modernity, is by now a very natural preconception.[33] Thinking this thought, we misunderstand who we are as readers. More than an appendage to the reader, ideas and assumptions are constitutive of the reader's own mind. Setting them aside, we eliminate ourselves as readers. If we attempt to clear our minds in this way, we take ourselves out of play before the game of reading even begins. Rather than being set aside, conceptions and pre-conceptions are more fruitfully brought out in the open, made conscious, and thus susceptible to transformation through reconception *in the very process of reading*. This has not been our modern custom in reading, however. Following the lead of modern historical science, we assume that reading the Huang Po texts requires that we suspend our own beliefs, and, through objective method, reconstruct a picture of the thought, practices, and institutions reflected in the texts. We place the text in its own context and assume that, in doing so, we have kept our own context at a critical distance. The mind of the reader is thus pictured as a mirror which reflects Zen as it really was, without itself being implicated or transformed in the process.

Reading Zen, however, will require greater understanding of subjectivity than this, more reflexivity, and thus more thorough "digestion" of the text into the mind of the reader. How so? To appropriate or "digest" the meaning of the text implies that one has taken it, along with whatever can be known of its context, into one's own context so that it can be considered in relation to life as it is inevitably lived here and now. To read otherwise is to read in abstraction from any issue that might really matter, and thus to leave the text there in the mind undigested, as

---

[33] "If it seems that no prejudice can be appropriate precisely insofar as it is a prejudice, if it seems in other words that the whole task of understanding is the elimination of prejudices and not at all their projection, that is because we ourselves still share the prejudices of the Enlightenment" (Weinsheimer, *Gadamer's Hermeneutics*, p. 167).

a memory or a fact that has yet to have any bearing. What Huang Po calls "wise eating"[34] focuses only on what seems eminently usable by body and mind; it shuns mere accumulation in preference for careful appropriation. The text is useful only when taken into the system as food for thought and experience.

"Taking" the text in this way, however, requires some degree of "letting go" as well. The mental agency entailed in Huang Po's practice of reading includes an element of exposure and relinquishment of will. When we think, as we commonly do, that reading is encompassed by a description of the reader's activity and effort in penetrating the text as object, we overlook all of the ways in which the text can influence, persuade, dislodge, and transform the reader. This realization is especially clear in Zen which stands within a tradition of Buddhist critiques of the substantiality of the self and its agency. To say that subjectivity is "empty," or that there is "no self," is to say, among many other things, that the reader "originates" as the one he or she is "dependent" upon whatever texts have been consumed, and is never the sole agent of that change. No clearer example of how this was realized in Zen reading can be found than in *koan* texts. *Koans* were the focal point of Zen meditative practice when they were read, first from the book, and then over and over in the mind, in such a way that their words did indeed penetrate the reader. To read a *koan* authentically one had to share the role of agency or actor, with the *koan* as textual agent possessing the capacity to open up its reader. A standing joke in Zen was based on the reversal that took place when what the practicing subject took to be its object and goal was realized to be a domain to which the subject in fact already belonged.

For the reader or practitioner to be the "object" of this reversal amounted to a kind of "awakening" from the illusory assumption that we are fully in control of the enlightening process. Henceforth, reading ceases to be an "act" of grasping or taking possession of the text – the textual analogue of Huang Po's "sensual eating."[35] Instead it becomes a meditative opening beyond our "desires" to that which the text may disclose to us, and to whatever transformation in the reader this disclosure may enact. Nothing magical need be intended here, Blofeld's statement at the very beginning of this chapter notwithstanding. The truth is that, when we read a text, analyze and work on it, the text may in fact do its work on us. That depends, however. It depends on the posture and practice of the reader, whether he or she is willing to be

---

[34] T. 48, p. 380b; Blofeld, *Huang Po*, p. 39.   [35] T. 48, p. 380b; Blofeld, *Huang Po*, p. 39.

exposed to its challenges and provocations, willing to take a position from which an alteration of mind may very well be the best way through the text.

One crucial question is: does this "willingness" to be exposed to the text and influenced by it require a posture of "belief" in the reader? Is openness to the text the same as the desire to believe that what it says is true? This is an important question, one about which much can be thought. But let us begin with this distinction. Openness to the possibility that truth may be disclosed in one's encounter with the text is quite different from an a priori commitment to its doctrinal position. "Commitment" is a form of closure and stands in sharp contrast to the "openness" of Zen awakening. Many passages in Zen texts ridicule naive belief, and insist that one's encounter with the "dharma" be fully critical. This tradition of critical appropriation goes all the way back to the early sutras where the Buddha encourages personal experimentation to test the truth of Buddhist doctrine.

It is equally naive to suppose that "belief" has no role to play in Zen, or in Buddhism generally. Minimally, one must believe that Buddhist texts are worth reading on some issue that matters before picking them up to read becomes possible. If Zen monks did not believe at the outset that there was something to which they might awaken, no grounds for entering the practice would exist. We always believe something, even though what we believe is subject to denial and transformation over time. Nevertheless, the reader need not, in fact cannot, simply replace prior beliefs by accepting whatever is said in the text. Appropriation of any kind, especially critical appropriation, takes time. At the outset, and even after an initial reading, we typically don't know exactly what the text is asserting, nor what we think about these issues. Coming to this realization and entering into the awakening process of working back and forth between the "mind of the text" and one's own mind in dialogical exchange is a lengthy and difficult process. Realizations may arrive in a flash of insight, but the complexity of their "origination" is so multi-layered as to be unrecoverable.

It is now possible for us to see that one weakness of Blofeld's romantic reading of Zen is his willingness at the outset to believe. Blofeld begins his reading of the text on the assumption that what it says is true, that the ultimate mode of enlightenment is represented there. Reading is therefore simply a matter of recognizing the truth that one knows already to be there. For example, in the introduction to his translation of Hui-hai, Blofeld writes that Hui-hai is "offering us precious Truth, . . .

the gift beyond all gifts – that of immortal wisdom and the peace which blossoms from it."[36] Clearly, Blofeld fulfills Huang Po's criterion of reading by being open to the truth of the text, and is not concerned with anything other than the "great matter." The danger with this posture, however, is that, in one's eagerness to believe, the "otherness" of the text, its radical challenge, may be passed right over. It is all too likely that in one's readiness to believe, what one believes is more closely tied to one's former views than to those presented in the text. The danger is that, on occasion, Blofeld may have been overly prepared to project a meaning for the text that was simply too believable, that is, simply too much a projection of the beliefs that he held beforehand. When this occurs, piety prevents a radical overturning of the mind; no risk or challenge is encountered. By contrast, the value of the text consists primarily in the disruption to the self and its prior beliefs that may occur in the process of reading it. Romantic readings of Zen texts, therefore, differ tremendously from modern, historiographic analyses, but the outcome bears an important similarity. Both manage to find ways to avoid being targeted and challenged by the text: one, the romantic, by projecting one's own relatively safe meaning onto it, and the other, the historiographer, by considering the text to be about someone else in another time and place. How can we avoid these weaknesses in our own reading? Perhaps, initially, by adopting the strengths of both: by critically appropriating the otherness of the text into the context of our own concerns and issues.

The practice of reading, however, can be extended beyond the domain of written texts. Zen reading required much more in fact. The world itself seemed to require reading: facial expressions can be read, gestures can be read; so can movements, signals, sounds, behaviors, minds, contexts, and situations. Indeed, potentially, anything can become a sign, and thus open itself to the insightful reader. This is the reading ability for which Zen masters like Huang Po were best known. In his long career, Huang Po had thousands of disciples, each a complex text to be interpreted, each a set of actions and words whose deeper implications might be deciphered. A Zen master must also read the "times," a set of historical developments and circumstances – political, economic, and cultural – within which the transmission of mind and *dharma* must be performed. Failure to read this text well would eventuate in a failure of transmission. Reading, both in and out of written texts, was and is a continuous activity for any serious practitioner of Zen. Zen

[36] Blofeld, *The Zen Teaching of Hui Hai*, pp. 17–18.

masters were so conscious of the ubiquity of reading that they began to call the world a text: the reality before them was "The Great Sutra,"[37] not an easy text to decipher, but the only one that truly mattered. When "reading" becomes a metaphor in this sense, it is synonymous with "interpretation," and beyond that, with "understanding" itself. Therefore, we extend our reading and ask: what would it mean not just to read the texts of Huang Po but to understand them, and what role did understanding play in Huang Po's Zen?

[37] Blofeld, *The Zen Teaching of Hui Hai*, p. 126.

CHAPTER 3

UNDERSTANDING: *the context of enlightenment*

> The sense [of my Huang Po translation] is strictly that of the original, unless errors have occurred in my understanding of it.
>
> John Blofeld[1]

> If one does not actually realize the truth of Zen in one's own experience, but simply learns it verbally and collects words, and claims to understand Zen, how can one solve the riddle of life and death?
>
> Huang Po[2]

If Huang Po is right that learning Zen "verbally and collecting words" does not constitute an understanding of Zen, then what does? To answer this, and to read Zen with the aim of true understanding, we will need to consider what understanding is, and develop our understanding of it. What is understanding, if not the kind of knowledge criticized above by Huang Po? For the purposes of this chapter, let us take "understanding" to be different than knowing, something more basic to human life. In contrast to "knowing," let us consider understanding to be something that we are always doing in and among all our other activities. No matter what we are doing – eating, working, or thinking – we are always understanding. Understanding what? All of the components and dimensions presupposed by that particular activity. Understanding, in this sense, is our most practical attunement to the world, the way we are embedded in the world, oriented to it, and engaged with it. Although the particular shape of understanding differs from person to person and from culture to culture, it is always there as the essential background out of which we live and work.

A simple example may help to show the universality and character of understanding so conceived. In order to perform his duties, the cook in Huang Po monastery would have understood many things, without

---

[1] Blofeld, *Huang Po*, p. 25. [2] Chang, *Original Teachings*, p. 105.

perhaps ever having thought much about them. He understands clearly enough what it means to be a cook, what he must do, how he must do it, and why. Writing manuals on each of these dimensions of the task could take years and thousands of pages if they were adequately detailed. Nevertheless, the cook holds all of this in his mind, and in his eyes, hands, and bodily movement. Standing in the kitchen, without a moment's abstraction from his task to think, he cooks, understanding everything: where the knives are, how sharp each one currently is, and which are best in which role. He will no doubt have explicit knowledge about some matters, those especially which are amenable to formulae or which require calculation – the ratio of water to rice for each kind of rice or the ratio of uncooked rice to the number of monks served. That knowledge, however, rests upon and is made possible by immense stores of unconscious understanding. What he knows is merely the tip of the iceberg. Beneath the surface is a much broader and more complex understanding – of the physics of hot and cold, of hard and soft, the sensibilities of tasteful or not, "on time" or not, the psychology of inter-action with kitchen helpers, the rationale of the monastery as a whole, and so on in immeasurable complexity. If the cook had to "know" all this to the point of being able to articulate it, and if he had to think about each dimension of the task as he performed it, Huang Po and the other monks would have starved. From this example, we can see how under-standing is the crucial background to all dimensions of human life; it pervades and makes possible all activity. This is no less true of reading Zen than it is of cooking. In each case the particular contours of under-standing shape our relationship to things and contextualize them for us in a more or less meaningful way.

How is the world presented to us in understanding? For one thing, the various elements of the world in which we live are not experienced in isolation from each other. Instead, we understand each thing through its various relations to others, through countless interconnections and juxtapositions. We understand the knife in relationship to carrots and cabbage, not to mention our fingers, the cutting board, the basin, the drawer, and other knives. Numerous expanding contexts encircle the act of cutting with the knife. We use the knife in order to cut vegetables; we cut vegetables in order to prepare the soup; we prepare the soup in order to present a meal; we present a meal in order to nourish the monks; we nourish the monks in order that they may seek enlightenment; they seek enlightenment in order that wisdom and compassion may be dissemi-nated throughout the land. We understand our fingers, not in and of themselves, but through their relations to carrots, knives, books, duties, injuries, and the act of pointing. All these things and thousands more point our fingers out to us, and our fingers point to them. Understanding is the activity of synthesizing all these elements together into an organic and functional whole. Every time we perceive something new, as we do every moment of our lives, understanding locates the new perception in relation to the world as already understood.

It would be best, however, to resist our modern inclination to understand this entire process as subjective activity, what the individual mind does on its own. Although it is indeed performed by our individual minds, there are larger, more complex and more fundamental processes at work in understanding. Consider initially the extent to which understanding is less an individual matter than it is a social practice. Much of what we understand is understood similarly by those around us, the closer they are to us the more we hold in common. We share an understanding of many things: what knives are and how to use them, what books are and how to read them, what elders are and how to relate to them, what injuries are and how to avoid them. Some of this is taught. We are socialized into a vast store of understanding that is culturally established. As children and as adults, we observe the practices of those around us and we imitate them. Very little needs to be, or ever is, discovered, invented, and determined on our own. Far more than we produce understanding, we are immersed in it. We participate in a world already structured and established in particular shapes of understanding. Therefore, this background of intelligibility is "intersubjective," it forms and connects individual subjectivities through common language, customs, institutions, and practices.

Participation in a particular community, like the monastery on Mount Huang Po, requires initiation into the particular forms of understanding and practice which constitute that community. Shared understanding functions as sensibilities held in common, that is, the "common sense" in terms of which everyone in the community can proceed with their various activities. Although we occasionally have reason to question or to reflect upon this background of understanding, for the most part it is too close to us to notice. Instead, we work out of it, taking it for granted and using it to question and to reflect on one issue at a time.

Precisely because understanding stands so much in the background of our daily activities, we can never see it comprehensively or formalize it in a theory. Every effort to do so presupposes the very understanding that it seeks to objectify. Understanding shapes us far more than we shape it.

It is in this sense, then, that we belong to traditions of understanding and engage in them socially, no matter how isolated we are from others.

Considering understanding a fundamentally social practice goes against the grain of our modern habits of thought, and, coincidentally, against the ways in which we have interpreted Zen. To our modern and romantic dispositions, Zen has stood for radical individualism, and for the depths of personal inner subjectivity. It is now becoming possible to see, however, that this reading of Zen tells us as much about ourselves as modern Westerners as it does about Zen. Various critiques of individualism and subjectivism now make possible post-romantic views of Zen, and of human understanding generally. Following these suggestions, we may open the possibility that in studying a deeply communal tradition of understanding like Huang Po's Zen, we might be shown the character of our own modern individualism and subjectivism.

Realizing that a shared domain of understanding supported and made possible the practices which took place on Mount Huang Po, we can begin to appreciate the communal dimension of its Zen practice. "Awakening" was the collective matter to which all activity would ultimately be directed. The very architectural layout of the monastery (as we receive it through Sung dynasty plans of similar institutions), as well as the schedules of practice and duty, all would have embodied an overall sense of "Zen" purposes. We can picture the coherence of communication and silent action in the "monk's hall," where monks slept, kept their few belongings, and sat in meditation. We can imagine the quarters of the Zen master Huang Po himself (*fang-chang*) where he both lived and examined his students in personal interview. We can picture the "lecture hall" (*fa-t'ang*) where Huang Po would have spoken, responded to questions, and engaged in dialogue over issues of thought and practice.[3] We can imagine monks in their daily practice of communal labor, either in the vegetable garden or in some task of maintenance or construction. We can see the monks chanting sutras before dawn and engaging in afternoon textual study. We can imagine their conversations and relations with the local communities of farmers, townspeople, landowners, and government officials, as well as with visiting monks from other monasteries. In all of these activities and relations, a shared understanding or "common sense" would have invisibly structured their world of Zen.

Although all communal activity presupposed understanding, the one activity that would consciously feature it would have been staged in the

---

[3] For more comprehensive background on this, see Foulk, "The Ch'an School", p. 278.

"lecture hall." The earliest extant code of rules for a Zen monastery pre-
scribes the "*dharma* hall" as follows:

The community of the whole monastery should gather in the *dharma* hall for
the morning and evening discussions. On these occasions the Elder "enters the
hall and ascends his seat." The monastery officers as well as the ordinary monks
stand in files and listen attentively to the discussion. For some of them to raise
questions and for the master to answer, which invigorates and clarifies the
essence of Ch'an teachings, is "to show how to live in accord with the *dharma.*"[4]

Talk makes manifest and "shows" "how to live in accord with the
dharma." Even where understanding is not shown, however, as in all
other activities from meditation to eating and labor, its presence is presupposed.

Both the institutional patterns of Zen practice on Mount Huang Po,
and the articulated "dharma" understanding that they internalized,
have larger cultural and historical underpinnings. Understanding was
shared, not just by monks in Huang Po monastery or even by all Zen
monastic communities, but in broader, and, therefore, less precise ways,
by everyone who at a given time participated in Chinese culture.
Although it is true that Zen monastic communities like Huang Po cultivated a certain isolation from, and critique of, society at large, they were
still in constant and active dialogue with this "outer world." Even criticism is a form of dialogue, and dialogue witnesses to the shared understanding that makes it possible. The monks on Mount Huang Po
participated, whether explicitly or not, in the broader culturally established understanding that unified China enough to make it distinguish-
able from other cultures.

If Huang Po's understanding was continuous in fundamental ways
with the larger world of medieval China, what dimensions of culture are
ingredients of this shared background? Language is no doubt a critical
element, perhaps primary. To share a language is to share ways of experiencing and responding to the world. We consider this in the next
chapter. Within language, understanding is collectively cultivated at the
most basic level by fundamental stories like mythic narratives and the
symbols that are active within them. Myth and symbol help set the broad
context of intelligibility within which communities of more specific
understanding like Huang Po can take shape. Preconditions for the
intelligibility of Huang Po's Zen practice are clearly the stories of the
Buddha's enlightenment, of his meditative practice, of his community

[4] See Collcutt, *Five Mountains*, pp. 138–145, and Foulk, "The Ch'an School", pp. 347–353.

of discourse and reflection, as well as all the symbols and paradigms that emerge from these stories. When the monks on Mount Huang Po sat in meditation, they reenacted ritually what the Buddha had done over a millennium earlier in his quest for enlightenment. Even the very idea of the quest for enlightenment comes to Huang Po and his community as an inheritance without which Zen practice would have been unthinkable. Reenacting the practice of "Buddhas and patriarchs," internalizing sacred narratives, the monks of Huang Po formed their lives out of an extended but finite set of traditional patterns. These patterns form the very structure of understanding for participants.

This is true of us as well. Like them, we know who we are and what we are doing through reference, both compliant and critical, to a store of symbols, narratives, and precedents that give shape and context to our lives. One of the great difficulties entailed in "our" understanding Huang Po is that, while the truth of contextuality applies as much to us as it did to medieval Chinese, the fact that our contexts differ so radically complicates the matter. Consider Alasdair MacIntyre's description of the cross-cultural predicament of understanding:

when two . . . distinct linguistic communities confront one another, each with its own body of canonical texts, its own exemplary images, and its own tradition of elaborating concepts in terms of these, but each also lacking a knowledge of, let alone linguistic capacities informed by, the tradition of the other community, each will represent the beliefs of the other within its own discourse in abstraction from the relevant tradition and so in a way that ensures *misunderstanding*. From each point of view certain of the key concepts and beliefs of the other, just because they are presented apart from that context of inherited texts from which they draw their conceptual life, will necessarily appear contextless and lacking in justification. [My emphasis][5]

Although it is a lesson that takes considerable experience to learn, at some point we all realize that to some extent conclusions about what something means will differ to the extent that points of departure differ. Lacking sufficient background understanding, we may easily misunderstand or fail to understand the texts of Huang Po.

When, for example, the texts describe the following dialogue between Huang Po and one of his disciples, we may read it incredulously: "When a monk asked the master 'What is the meaning of coming from the West?' the master hit him with his staff."[6] For those of us not familiar with a Zen context of understanding, these exchanges make no sense. Not

---

[5] MacIntyre, "Relativism, Power, and Philosophy," p. 392.
[6] T. 51, p. 266; Chang, *Original Teachings*, p. 105.

only does the response call for rigorous interpretation and explanation, but so also does the question. Even if one knows that the question literally asks why Bodhidharma, the legendary founder of Chinese Zen, came from the West (i.e. India) to China, one still lacks the background of assumptions and discursive practices that fit the question into the "common sense" of monastic practice in medieval China. Why would anyone ask that question? What do they really want to know? What kind of question-and-answer ritual is this anyway? We need to understand this context along with them to share in their question. Moreover, why was the questioner hit with Huang Po's staff? If this was a meaningful response, and indeed it was, then what must be understood to interpret it?[7]

The same passage goes on to say of Huang Po that "those of medium and low spirituality were unable to understand his Dharma."[8] In addition to "those of medium and low spirituality," we would need to add another group: those, like us, who stand outside the community of understanding within which this exchange made sense. When this background is absent, the necessary framework for understanding is missing. Those of "medium and low spirituality" could at least assume the fundamental intelligibility of the practice as a whole (along with Huang Po). What they lacked was subtlety of interpretation, or depth of realization. Our problem is more substantial. We need to work our way into the language and customs of local practice before we can share in the subtleties of understanding. This is hard work, and typically not even attempted unless it appears that something important is to be gained from it. In our time, romanticism has supplied this justification, and the tradition of historicism has initiated the quest for a background of understanding sufficient for reading Zen.

It is clear, however, that if a Zen text can only be understood against the background of its Zen "context," the same would be true of its context as well. As an object of study, "context" also has a context which requires complex interpretation. Neither text nor context is easy to contextualize, and regression beyond the most immediate context is infinite. This became clear in interesting ways in Derrida's famous exchange with J. L. Austin.[9] One thesis of Austin's immensely influential *How to Do*

---

[7] Bernard Faure describes the most famous Zen example of the importance of context to understanding in Bodhidharma's legendary effort to play Zen language games with the Emperor of China. The Emperor "did not understand the rules" of the Zen game and concluded that Bodhidharma had simply failed at the game of Imperial propriety (*The Rhetoric of Immediacy*, p. 64). [8] Lu K'uan Yu, *Ch'an and Zen Teachings*, p. 138.

[9] Derrida, "Signature Event Context," in *Margins of Philosophy*. In this explication, I follow the lead of Stanley Fish in "With the Compliments of the Author: Reflections on Austin and Derrida," in *Doing What Comes Naturally*.

Things With Words was that utterances can only be understood within actual speech situations where shared assumptions enable interlocutors to make sense of each other. What Derrida's essay pointed out was that the move from utterance to context doesn't alter the difficulty of interpretation. Contexts are no more self-identifying than are sentences. Moreover, a significant difference exists between how context affects understanding when it is an object of analysis and when context constitutes the very structure of subjectivity in the form of the presuppositions that ground and shape experience.[10] This is simply to say that we will be just as much inclined to understand Huang Po's context in ways that he never could have understood it as we are of misunderstanding the intentions of his discourse. Nevertheless, both object-text and context will come to be understood only in relation to each other, and both of these will be understood from the perspective of the context of the one who understands. Understanding this, we will nod approvingly when John Blofeld writes in the introduction to his translation of Huang Po that wherever there were "obscure passages," passages with a "wide variety of different explanations," he sought to interpret them in the "spirit" of the Zen tradition in general.[11] Unlike Blofeld, however, we will more likely see this as a circular process. While particular teachings are best understood in relation to overall "spirit," this spirit is only accessible through particular teachings. Neither is clearer or more obvious than the other.

No matter how we imagine the context of understanding, however, interpretation will be essential to it. How is interpretation related to understanding? A useful distinction can be made here between understanding, which is always operant in our experience, and interpretation, an explicit elaboration of the understanding in which we already stand. In making this distinction, we follow the tradition of "hermeneutics" initiated by Martin Heidegger in section 32 of *Being and Time* where it is said that "interpretation is grounded existentially in understanding; the latter does not arise from the former. Nor is interpretation the acquiring of information about what is understood; it is rather the working-out of possibilities projected in understanding."[12]

The idea that interpretation is based on understanding gives startling reversal to our modern custom of thinking that interpretation is what produces understanding. Heidegger's insight, now basic to all forms of "post-modern" thinking, is that unless the object of interpretation is

---

[10] Fish, *Doing What Comes Naturally*, pp. 52–53.   [11] Blofeld, *Huang Po*, p. 26.
[12] Heidegger, *Being and Time*, p. 188.

understood in some sense already (pre-understanding), there neither would, nor could, be any interpretation of it. Some understanding of the phenomenon must already be in place motivating and guiding our desire for an interpretive elaboration – we would not want to know "more" about the phenomenon unless we already understood something of it. Understanding, in this sense, is more inclusive and more fundamental than interpretation.[13] A particular background of understanding – a pre-understanding – is already there prior to acts of interpretation, guiding and shaping subsequent interpretive acts.

Immersed in the world, we function out of an understanding that is largely unconscious. In interpretation, we make thematic and explicate some aspect of our understanding. Although interpretation does not produce understanding from out of nothing or "from scratch," it does refine, criticize, correct, and cultivate understanding. In interpretation we come to "know" what we have understood, and sometimes to see how it may have been inadequately understood or misunderstood. If interpretation has been fruitful, our understanding of the phenomenon will have changed. The principle that "interpretation always proceeds from its basis in pre-understanding," will be useful to us in at least two ways: on the object side, for reflection on how the articulation of Zen thought in the Huang Po texts stands upon a deeper basis of understanding, and, on the subject side, for reflection on how our interpretation of Huang Po, our reading Zen, is the cultivation of our own prior understanding, both of "Zen" and of the issues it addresses.

Given these two uses, let us develop the idea one step further. Again, following Heidegger, we notice how "that which has been explicitly understood has the structure of something *as* something."[14] The highlighted *as* is the key word. When we interpret something, we interpret it *as* something in particular. The *as* guides our interpretation; it connects the phenomenon under interpretation – the perception – with some concrete image in our already-understood world in terms that make it understandable. Although, to take a simple example, we perceive only rectangular lines on a wall, we understand the phenomenon before us *as* a door, a passage through which we may move to another room. In the absence of prior experience with doors, we would no doubt interpret these lines *as* something else – cracks in the wall, the design of an artist,

---

[13] It is helpful, following David Klemm in *Hermeneutical Inquiry*, to consider understanding as a first-order activity, interpretation as a second-order elaboration on understanding, and hermeneutics as a third-order reflection on the interplay between the first two.

[14] Heidegger, *Being and Time*, p. 189.

who knows? We interpret this *as* a book and its subject matter *as* Zen. Everything present to us at all is present *as* something. For Blofeld, the images in terms of which Huang Po was interpreted derived from his prior understanding of analogous images in romantic literature and thought. Ours may be romantic and "post-romantic," but we too will find local images or figures to give form and shape to our reading of Zen.

When we understand something, we understand it "in terms of" something else already familiar and available within our world. When we first go to the bookstore in search of a book on "Zen," we do so, first, already having an understanding of Zen that makes it of sufficient interest to want further elaboration, and second, already understanding Zen *as* something – *as* "oriental mysticism," *as* a "non-religious way to cultivate centering," *as* the "key to business success in Japan," *as* something. We may later think that we had misunderstood Zen, that it isn't mysticism, focuses on "decentering," and makes for lousy business. Regardless, however, we can see that some form of "pre-understanding" was already there as the basis from which our subsequent understanding emerged.

If interpretation is always based on prior understanding and always articulated "in terms of" some already available image, then it is never a presuppositionless process. Interpretations are exercises in connecting one thing to another, a phenomenon to an image in our minds, and that connection to the totality of our understanding. We cannot heed, therefore, Blofeld's instruction to us as readers "not to read into the text any preconceived notions as to the nature of the Absolute."[15] For it was precisely *because* we would have such preconceptions that Blofeld has considered placing this word into Huang Po's text. His job as translator was to find images in the cultural world of the English language suited to the understanding of Huang Po's world of Chinese Zen. As readers, we understand one in terms of the other; *i-hsin* in Chinese is understood "in terms of" or "as" "the Absolute" in English. If it is found that "the Absolute" is an inadequate image of *i-hsin*, it is because some other image or set of images has emerged in light of which the inadequacy of "the Absolute" can be seen.

To understand something new or foreign, like a Buddhist concept for us or, say, an unanticipated situation for Huang Po, is not to set one's own background of understanding aside in order to grasp the concept or situation on its own terms. On the contrary, it is to draw upon this background "contextually" as a way to make sense of the new concept or

---

[15] Blofeld, *Huang Po*, p. 19.

situation. We do this quite naturally. Conceiving of the process of under-standing in this way, however, is not natural for us. When called upon to discuss the matter theoretically, we turn to the already articulated theory most readily at hand – theories of knowledge characteristic of moder-nity in the west. These theories focus on the necessity of "objectivity" and the elimination of "preconceptions," and this is clearly the source of Blofeld's instructions to us. On this view, "preconceptions" or "pre-understanding" must be eliminated in order to understand truthfully. Post-modern critiques of these theories show us why, without pre-conceptions, we cannot understand at all, truthfully or otherwise. As we have seen, this background to understanding serves as the positive condi-tion for the occurrence of any understanding at all.

Although so far we have used sources in contemporary western thought to interpret "understanding," it may be that nowhere is the rela-tional, contextual, and impermanent character of the human mind given more thorough and sustained reflection than in the Buddhist tradi-tion. Let us consider here, therefore, how these same issues emerge in Buddhist thought by taking up the central Mahayana concept, "empti-ness." The concept "emptiness" derives from, and eventually encom-passes, the key elements in Buddhist contemplative practice: impermanence, dependent origination, and no self. The earliest layers of the Huang Po literature, the *Ch'uan-hsin fa-yao* and sections of the *Wan-ling lu*, make considerable explicit use of the concept "emptiness." But even in later additions to these texts, where its use is not explicit, "emptiness" permeates the meaning of the texts.

What does "emptiness" mean there? Although the original Sanskrit term, *sunyata*, evolves from the mathematical cipher, "zero," the Chinese term that translates it and that is found so frequently in the Huang Po texts, is *k'ung*, "sky" or "space." The sky metaphorically comes to suggest the vacuum, "empty" space, where no-thing can be found. Over time, this symbolic image of "emptiness" gave rise to elaborate conceptual determination. "Emptiness" became the central philosophical concept in the Mahayana tradition. What does it mean? "Emptiness" is a universal predicate; it applies to everything. All things are "empty," everything is "emptiness." For something to be "empty" means that, because the entity "originates dependent" upon other entities, and is transformed in accor-dance with changes in these "external" conditions, the entity therefore lacks "own-being" (Sanskrit: *svabhava*) or "self-nature" (Chinese: *tzu-hsing*). The thing is not self-determining; on its own it would have never come to be what it is. Its existence and its character are attributable to the multiple factors that condition its origin and subsequent transformations. Coming into existence, changing over time, and passing out of existence, empowered by conditions beyond itself, the "empty" thing lacks any trace of "aseity" or permanence.

This "lack," furthermore, this negative dimension at the very heart of the thing which the concept "emptiness" highlights, is the "nature" or "essence" of all things without exception. When Buddhists contemplate anything – an entity, a situation, or an idea – this "dependence," "instability," or "void" within it directs the meditator beyond the thing itself to its determining conditions, other things, situations, and ideas which similarly point beyond themselves to others, *ad infinitum*. Empty things are what they are contextually; their being is relational. Understanding anything, therefore, requires explication of context, as we know very well. This insight, however, goes beyond our common sense on the matter: contexts are contextualized by other contexts, and those by others, and more. Meditations on the interdependent and inter-penetrating character of reality had become fundamental to the Chinese Buddhist tradition prior to Huang Po's time. Their imprint on the Zen literature of his era and thereafter is unmistakable. These were the conceptual and symbolic resources most readily available for under-standing anything, including understanding itself.

The implications of "emptiness" as a point of departure for our reflections on this matter are immense. One of them is the realization that there is always more to something than initially meets the eye; thor-ough understanding requires seeing the thing outside itself in the other things and contexts which make it what it is. Another implication draws the subject who understands into the circle of understanding. It requires "reflexive" meditation on our part and it is perhaps here that we can learn the most from Huang Po.

Not only are entities, situations, and ideas "empty" – that is, relative to conditioning factors and processes – so am "I," the one who encoun-ters these entities, situations, and ideas in understanding. "No self," the assertion that the "self" is "empty," is perhaps the most widely remem-bered "doctrine" of Buddhism. But what does it mean? "No self" means no permanent self; no separable, enduring entity, essence, or soul grounds human existence. It also means, following the description of emptiness above, that, like everything else, human beings are not self-determining. The self does not possess its "own-being"; there is no "self-nature." The self "co-arises" with the world, and, on its own, *is* nothing. Like everything else, we are embedded in the world; we are immersed in an infinitely interconnected context in such a way that "self" and "other than self" interpenetrate. Huang Po takes these meditations through traditional channels: one by one each of the six senses is shown to imply its own respective sense object, and vice versa.[16] Therefore, he concludes, "mind and context are one."[17] If so, it follows that as one correlate in the relation changes so would the other. As the world changes so does the self; as the self changes so does the world. Understanding one necessitates understanding the other.

Given the long tradition of reflection on this issue before his time, the unity of these two – self and world – can be spoken and reflected in Huang Po's Buddhist Chinese without the awkwardness and self-contradiction implied in our language. On this theme in particular, the vocabulary available to Huang Po facilitates realization. Huang Po's discussions of "emptiness" commonly focus on the status of "dharmas," *fa* in his Chinese version. Although this term carries with it a long history and wide range of meaning, in this context the applicable sense derives from Buddhist meditation practice. Here, *dharmas* are locatable on neither side of the subject/object dichotomy. They are objects as encountered by the mind, things as experienced, or "moments of experience" where self and world reflect each other. Meditation practice and its corresponding "*dharma* language" fosters such "non-dual" experience, experience in which the world can be seen to penetrate the self and vice versa. The "emptiness" of each is the inclusion of the other within it.

Neglecting one dimension of the imagery of "emptiness," Herbert Guenther has translated the term into English as "openness."[18] This alternative image in our language corresponds more adequately to the conceptual and experiential dimensions of "interdependence" so emphasized in Chinese and Tibetan interpretations. Things are "open" insofar as other things enter into them, insofar as their boundaries are not fixed or static but permeable and changing. "Openness" also indicates the stance most applicable to understanding. When we open ourselves, or are opened by unexpected factors in our lives, deeper and more wide-ranging understanding may become possible.

Understanding, as we have developed it here, is, like "emptiness," the particular way in which we are contextualized in the world. Through understanding we correspond to situations and to things by making or

---

[16] T. 48, p. 380b.   [17] "hsin ching yi ju," (T. 48, p. 381c).
[18] Herbert V. Guenther, *Kindly Bent to Ease Us* (Emeryville, CA: Dharma Publications, 1975).

recognizing the connections all around us. The principle component of understanding – application – is seeing how things are related, how they fit together into meaningful and applicable patterns within the here-and-now world of the one who understands. Practical wisdom, so prominent in Zen, is understanding how to work and to function effectively in an "empty" world, a world in which relation and movement are the key elements.

The foregoing paragraphs apply "emptiness" to the issue before us. In this situation, "emptiness" is lifted out of its familiar Buddhist context and brought into the service of a concern for which it may not originally have been intended. Prior to this occasion, others have done the same, thousands of times. It is only in the "application" of the concept to new and significant issues that "emptiness" continues to be a functioning concept. It is not necessary for us to have decided whether or not we "believe" in the truth of "emptiness" before we apply it in this way. On the contrary, application is a prior condition of belief. Before we could ever be in a position to decide whether to "believe" a Buddhist idea or not, we would have had to "apply" it in order to understand what it might mean. In the process of application, two closely related critical activities occur simultaneously.

The first is that we expose our understanding of "emptiness" to critical scrutiny. It may be that the interpretation of the concept that we have initially projected is demonstrated to be insufficient. The projected meaning – what we think Huang Po may have meant – turns out to be our own possibility, not Huang Po's; it originates in our mind and in relation to our understanding even though the meaning we seek is that of the "other." No other source for "meaning" is available. But the meaning thus projected is projected as the text's meaning, and if it cannot be reconciled with what is said in the text, then we have not yet understood it. In that case, a revised projection of meaning will be necessary.

Sound interpretations are not to be produced in an abstinence from projection of meaning by the interpreter. That would result in no understanding at all. Truthful interpretation consists not in the avoidance of projection and preconception, but rather in their critical appraisal and confirmation. Inappropriate projections of meaning for the text are not characterized simply by their being projections, but rather by their inability to fit with the text. The crucial question is thus: how is it possible to locate our inappropriate projections so that they can be revised or replaced by better ones?

The second critical activity that occurs simultaneous to our attempt to understand "emptiness" through application is the use of "emptiness" as a means of critique and evaluation of our own understanding. We apply "emptiness" to the question of understanding in order both to see what "emptiness" means, and to see what it may teach us about understanding. This second dimension of the process amounts to self criticism through the use of the Buddhist concept, "emptiness." Thus we open ourselves to having our own minds supplemented, reworked, revised, or reformed by the concept. In this process, our prior understanding of the matter is not set aside or eliminated in order to see what "emptiness" might be able to contribute. Instead, the two are set into relation with one another so that critical questions can be posed and connections can be seen. Application, always ingredient to understanding, is the process of finding relations.

Although application is always going on whether we are aware of it or not, it can be cultivated explicitly as a practice, in which case it occurs more thoroughly and with greater rigor. This point, and one other, can be made by considering the example of foreign travel. When we travel in a foreign land, we notice and understand how things are, not in and of themselves, but in reference to how they are (or aren't) in our own culture. Application, as the practice of seeing relationship, is constantly at work. Aside from its relation to what we already understand, nothing will be noticed, nothing will evoke interest. Only by means of comparison and contrast, by seeing identity and difference, and thus by relation to our own culture's customs and practices, will we be able to see what this foreign culture is. Put this way, application may seem obvious. It is. But it also runs head-on into, and contradicts, our modern ideology on the matter.

If we were asked about the matter, our instincts, shaped by the understanding of modernity into which we have been socialized, would lead us to say that traveling well requires an open mind, that expectations and presuppositions about what we will see and how things ought to be will prevent our seeing things as they are. We might say that we should be "objective" and "nonjudgmental" about what we see. To do this, we might go on, we must temporarily forget about our own culture and just immerse ourselves in this new and foreign one so that we can really see it as it is in itself, without reference (i.e. application) to our own culture. These thoughts are elements of the common sense of modernity. We can now see their limits, however. Not only is it not possible to set aside one's own background of culturally shaped understanding, even if one could, that would render everything one saw in this foreign land uninteresting and not particularly noteworthy. Without this inescapable but constantly revised background of understanding, we could learn nothing, at home or abroad.

Is it possible to discriminate between people more able to learn from "travel" and those less able? Surely, and from this point of view, the basis upon which that distinction should be made is twofold: the extent to which one is grounded in one's own culture and the way in which one relates to that ground. The person who understands most about his or her own culture and is, at the same time, open to its critical assessment and possible transformation, is in a better position to learn from travel. This person is sensitive to issues, customs, and forms of thought in his or her own culture, and, from this basis, will notice analogous dimensions in the foreign culture. He or she will be able to ask good questions, to see what is worthy of reflection or further inquiry. He or she will notice what is lacking, in that culture and in his or her own culture, and will be interested in asking why and to what effect. Difference and otherness come into view only in their relation to identity and the self, and the reverse holds true as well. Aside from such relational application, travel may be "fun," but neither meaningful nor transformative. The same goes for reading Zen.

The first criteria above is not enough on its own; that is, understanding may be impeded if solid grounding in one's own culture is not accompanied by a critical edge and a sensitivity to the "otherness" of the other. In the effort to understand, we project what we take the other to mean and eagerly open ourselves to its possible value and truth. If this eagerness, however, allows us to be complacent in the thought that our original projection is in fact the other's meaning, then we may very well miss its greatest possibility for us. "Otherness" is not easy to discern; it takes time and patience. From our vantage point, some decades later, it is easy for us to catch John Blofeld in the act of projecting issues upon Huang Po in which Huang Po could not have been interested. Although, given our own envelopment in a world of understanding, we can rarely see this in ourselves, it is easily detectable in others. Studying examples of it, and realizing its inevitability, will help us to catch ourselves in the act on occasion, and to locate a posture from which more sensitive means of understanding can be developed.

Before he even decided to travel to China, both Blofeld and his culture were undergoing significant changes as a result of their cultural encounter with the otherness of the larger British Empire. Blofeld had systematically immersed himself in the rapidly growing literature on the "Orient" and, like a few others around him, he was feeling its effects. One issue that had been a topic of considerable discourse and writing in the western world was "tolerance." From Hobbes and Locke to J. S. Mill and the Huxleys, the issue of the character of liberal society was hotly debated. Many of these thinkers either criticized "religion" for its failure to tolerate difference, or divided it evenly between the truly religious who were tolerant and those who were not. "Oriental religions," for some justifiable reasons, were taken stereotypically to represent the possibility of tolerance within religion. This issue was of critical importance in Blofeld's own life, and it was partly on this basis that he would convert to Buddhism. He understood Buddhism to be the epitome of true religion which, although present in all religions, was hidden under a cloak of intolerance and small-mindedness. Intolerance was one trait for which Blofeld had little tolerance.

When, after having become a Buddhist and after years of immersion in Chinese culture and language, Blofeld decided to try his hand at translation, he sought out just the right text. His Buddhist friends and teachers recommended Huang Po, the great Zen master. Reading the text, he agreed – this was the one to transmit back home. Beginning the project with detailed study, as any translator should, he encountered an interpretive problem. Sometimes Huang Po seemed intolerant of other kinds of Buddhism. How could this be? Huang Po was a Buddhist and Buddhists, as Blofeld knew, were famous for their attitude of tolerance. Furthermore, Huang Po was "enlightened," and, as Blofeld understood the matter, tolerance was an inevitable outcome of enlightenment. Given these premises, Blofeld assumed that he had misunderstood the text. Huang Po could not have meant these criticisms of other forms of Buddhism "literally." In several instances, therefore, Blofeld sought allegorical interpretations. Although Huang Po might be indicted on "casual glance," Blofeld wrote, deep study would surely vindicate him: "A casual glance at our text or at some other Zen works might well give the impression that non-Zen Buddhism is treated too lightly." However, "a careful study of this work has persuaded me that Huang Po felt no desire to belittle the virtue of those Buddhists who disagreed with his methods"[19]; "I am convinced that Huang Po had no intention of belittling the 'Three Vehicles.'"[20]

When, in the final analysis, his allegorical readings did not prove to be convincing, Blofeld wrote a prominent section in his introduction

[19] Blofeld, *Huang Po*, p. 21.   [20] Blofeld, *Huang Po*, p. 22.

explaining why Huang Po had criticized others. He had, it turned out, good reasons. "Huang Po's seemingly discourteous references to other sects are justified by the urgency and sincerity of his single-minded desire to emphasize the necessity for mind-control."[21] As Blofeld put it, the "Hinayanists" and Buddhist scholars whom Huang Po seemed to be ridiculing had made some grievous mistakes in doctrinal matters, and the propagation of these errors would lead to widespread spiritual decay among those naive enough to have listened. In spiritual matters at least, being wrong is dangerous. Erroneous views might prevent one's own enlightenment, not to mention the enlightenment of others. Huang Po's "discourtesy," Blofeld finally concluded, could be excused by the "urgency" of the situation, and by the fact that his interpretive position in the dispute was the correct one.

Because of the importance of this issue in Blofeld's own culture and mind, and the vehemence of his stand on it, this was the matter that most troubled his work on Huang Po. In the end, his own background of understanding could find ways to pronounce Huang Po innocent of what, in Blofeld's mind, would have been an inexcusable offence, one that simply could not be reconciled with his understanding of "Buddhism" or of "enlightenment." From that location in understanding, Blofeld could not see that Huang Po had absolutely no interest in the issue of tolerance. It simply was not an issue for him, although, clearly enough, it had been an issue in other eras in the history of Buddhism and in Chinese culture. Moreover, in order to extricate Huang Po, Blofeld attributed to him the very same position that Blofeld's own criticisms of "sectarian" Christianity had denounced: they had taken an immovable stand on doctrinal matters and assumed, presumptuously, that they were correct and the others wrong. This had been problematic for Blofeld because he held firmly to the doctrine of the ultimate unity of all religions "beyond doctrinal difference." Huang Po's sectarian vehemence could be excused, however, because the doctrines that he was defending were the ones upon which all religions were united, whether particular "adherents" of those religions knew it or not.

Clearly, pressing issues in his own mind prevented Blofeld from being able to see the importance and vitality of sectarian and doctrinal issues in Huang Po's historical context. Huang Po was not just defending the faith, he was on the offence, and through his efforts and those of others, his Zen sect won. Although, by the twentieth century, the hollowness of

---

[21] Blofeld, *Huang Po*, p. 24.

its victory was more than clear, Blofeld was nevertheless reading Zen from the perspective of its longstanding East Asian triumph. And, although he wouldn't have put it this way, Blofeld was himself entering Zen as a new combatant in the doctrinal battles that were being staged in his own culture. Huang Po was indeed being put to good use.

Blofeld's "application" of these texts to current issues, and mine, are only the most recent of countless such manifestations. Each of them is an instance or example of the impermanence and "emptiness" of meaning that is made available to understanding. Unless we contemplate this "emptiness" of understanding, we will be unable to consider the history of interpretations of Huang Po as anything but the history of error. As we will see when we contemplate "history" and "freedom," the masters of Hung-chou Zen realized that the tradition could maintain itself authentically only by undergoing change. Aside from transformation and recontextualization, no ongoing life is possible. Like all Mahayana Buddhists before him, Huang Po would call upon the Buddhist concept of *upaya*, or "skill-in-means," to help legitimize these transformations.[22] All "means" of understanding must be "skillfully" molded to the situation at hand, and will thus vary from one time and place (or mind) to another. This application of the concepts of "emptiness" and "impermanence" was difficult to conceive, but nevertheless widespread in the tradition.

Our romantic and historicist inclination to privilege an "original meaning" as the one to which correct interpretation must correspond would have to be seen, from this Buddhist point of view, as an act of clinging to illusory permanence and substantiality – a denial of interdependence and change. Our desire to have the text be intelligible in and of itself, and separate from current understanding, however, can never be fulfilled. We too stand in a long history of interpretation and, like our predecessors, we can only understand in the terms available to us. The fact that for us those "terms" include scientific and romantic ideologies does not alter the fact that we apply what we understand to our own world. Indeed, our practices and customs of interpretation, like everyone else's, exemplify the truths of application, contextuality, and contingency.

Long before Blofeld understood Huang Po "differently," Huang Po had himself understood the Buddhist tradition in ways that had never before existed. No one needed allegory more than Huang Po. When the

---

[22] "The canonical teachings of the three vehicles are just remedies for temporary needs. They were taught to meet such needs and so are of temporary value and differ one from another" (T. 48, p. 382c; Blofeld, *Huang Po*, p. 57).

sutras said irrelevant or naive things, he deepened them: "This is a fable in which the 'five hundred Bodhisattvas' *really refers* to your five senses."[23] When a questioner faced existential crisis because of an inability to interpret broadly, Huang Po would allegorize him into more authentic practices: "Question: But what if in previous lives I have behaved like Kaliraja, slicing the limbs from living men? Answer: The holy sages tortured by him *represent* your own Mind, while Kaliraja *symbolizes* that part of you which goes out seeking."[24]

Only modernists and historicists, who assume that texts from distant contexts will be irrelevant to current needs, don't need allegory. Indeed, no premodern textual practice has received more scorn in modernity than this one. Any tradition that includes sacred texts, however, will at some point in history find that allegory is essential. In a culture where texts aren't sacred, old writings that have become irrelevant are just set aside. The canon shifts and the old texts are simply not read. Where their sanctity is maintained, however, reading practices will be motivated to attain whatever sophistication is required to find ways in which they are, in fact, still relevant.

Due to the self-conscious and critical elements in the Zen tradition, reading practices like allegory would occasionally come under scrutiny. On one occasion, Huang Po's allegory was challenged by the great Nan-ch'uan, a Zen master of equal status.

Another day, our Master, Huang Po, was seated in the tea-room when Nan Ch'uan came down and asked him: "What is meant by 'A clear insight into the Buddha-Nature results from the study of dhyana (mind control) and prajna (wisdom)'?" Our Master replied: "It means that, from morning till night, we should never rely on a single thing." "But isn't that just Your Reverence's own concept of its meaning?" "How could I be so presumptuous?" "Well, Your Reverence, some people might pay out cash for rice-water, but whom could you ask to give anything for a pair of home-made straw sandals like that?" At this our Master remained silent.[25]

Huang Po asks, rhetorically and jokingly, "How could I be so presumptuous as to teach my own concept of the text's meaning, rather than the text's meaning?" Whoever's meaning it is, Nan-ch'uan's retort is that its "cash value" isn't much. At this, Huang Po is left silent. Had the story ended there, it would have never made its way into Huang Po's "discourse record"; after all, "Our Master" didn't emerge looking all that enlightened. So the story proceeds as follows, allegorizing Huang Po

[23] Blofeld, *Huang Po*, p. 115.   [24] Blofeld, *Huang Po*, p. 123.   [25] Blofeld, *Huang Po*, p. 98.

out of the predicament: "Later, Wei Shan mentioned the incident to Yang Shan, enquiring if our Master's silence betokened defeat. 'Oh no!' answered Yang. 'Surely you know that Huang Po has a tiger's cunning?' 'Indeed there is no limit to your profundity,' exclaimed the other."[26]

Wei Shan struggles to interpret the text, but a contradiction looms. It appears on the surface that Nan ch'uan had gotten the better of Huang Po. For Wei Shan in this account, however, Huang Po is, by definition, the one whose vision is so penetrating that he cannot be upstaged. Yang Shan steps in to dissolve the apparent contradiction. Huang Po's silence must be interpreted more carefully, allegory providing the means by which silence can be seen *as* something quite the opposite of discursive "defeat." Given Huang Po's profundity, the task before Yang Shan was simply to locate it, to interpret it and to allegorize it out of obscurity and into the open space of understanding. In this case, Yang's task was relatively easy because there was ample precedent in the tradition to underwrite his reversal of Huang Po's demise. Silence can, on some occasions, be understood as defeat while in other contexts it means victory in the forms of profundity and freedom. Since the protagonist is the great Huang Po, this is clearly a case of profundity. Just in case his readers might miss the text's depth here, Blofeld jumps into a footnote to do his own allegorizing: "1 . . . His silence was deeply significant; it implied that the Master NEVER indulged in concepts; . . . But it took a man of Yang Shan's caliber to penetrate through to his meaning."

Allegory displays quite prominently the reader's involvement in the process of interpretation. As we have seen, however, there is no understanding without projective involvement by the one who understands, and there is no understanding that merely duplicates an original. Therefore, we can interpret "allegory" *as* a metaphor for all understanding. We always understand "this" *as* something else, *as* whatever it is when new light is shed on it. Understanding transforms the object of interpretation by bringing it into a new context of meaning, that of the interpreter him or herself.

There is an important sense, therefore, in which the self who understands is not just the subject of this activity, but its object as well. What the Huang Po texts are finally about – their "Great Matter" – is the self, not just any self but rather "the one right now who seeks to understand."[27] Thus, the primary "intention" of the text is that readers

---

[26] Blofeld, *Huang Po*, p. 98.
[27] I borrow this rhetorical "means" from the Zen texts of Ma-tsu and Lin-chi which continually strive to expose "the one right now who reads this" to the light of critical reflexivity.

understand themselves in and through what is said in it. All texts "intend" this in some sense since understanding and self-understanding are inextricably joined. If we have truly encountered the ideas presented in the text, we have encountered our own ideas on these matters and others at the same time. If we have truly understood the Huang Po texts, we have understood ourselves in light of them. And, going further, if we understand what understanding entails, we will sense our immersion in the open space of language.

CHAPTER 4

LANGUAGE: the sphere of immediacy

And the matter of language is a trifle, not worth your thought.
Dorje Chuncheh to John Blofeld[1]

There arises the possibility that we undergo an experience with language, that we enter into something which bowls us over, that is, transmutes our relation to language.
Martin Heidegger[2]

Whenever language becomes an explicit theme in the Huang Po texts, the verdict appears to be negative. Since the true matter of Zen "cannot be grasped by way of language,"[3] the Zen master's practice must take an alternative course: "The Way resides in Mind awakening. How can it be spoken in language?"[4] This attitude toward language is not a unique feature of the Huang Po texts; it pervades the Zen literature of the era. Lin-chi, who called the sacred texts of his own tradition "worthless dust," belittles students of Zen who "seize upon words," taking language to constitute "the true way."[5] Thus, it was for good reason that Ma-tsu, the founder of this Hung-chou tradition of Zen, was given the posthumous title: "Zen master of Great Silence."[6] What more could be said?

Plenty. The texts do much more than simply proclaim the "wordless *dharma*," they debate it, they exalt it, and they trace its sacred lineage. The "Great Silence" does not begin with Ma-tsu. It can be traced back through sacred history all the way to the Buddha himself. Here is how Huang Po delineates its origins: "In the end we are not able to clarify the 'one mind *dharma*.' Therefore, the Buddha called Kasyapa to join him

---

[1] Blofeld, *The Wheel of Life*, p. 42.
[2] Heidegger, *On the Way to Language* (New York: Harper and Row, 1971), p. 107.
[3] T. 48, p. 381a.   [4] T. 48, p. 384a.
[5] T. 47, p. 499b; Sasaki, *The Recorded Sayings of Lin-chi*, p. 19.
[6] T. 51, p. 245; Chang, *Original Teachings*, p. 152.

on the *dharma* seat, and separately transmitted the one mind to him. Without words, he spoke the *dharma*."[7] Elsewhere, we learn how to fill in the details of this narrative. Zen texts tell how, without speaking a word but holding a flower, the Buddha awakened his disciple, Kasyapa. In response, Kasyapa just smiled, and had nothing further to say. This, along with the story of Vimalakirti's "thunderous silence," set the stage for the understanding of language in the Zen tradition. Huang Po frequently calls upon Bodhidharma to represent this understanding. Bodhidharma's "wordless *dharma*"[8] had initiated Zen in China and, from the legends of Bodhidharma, later Zen Buddhists had received Zen's basic formula:

A special transmission outside the sutras, not dependent on language and texts, pointing directly to mind, one sees the true nature of things and becomes the Buddha.

"Direct pointing" circumvents language and cuts immediately to the heart of the matter, a form of moment-to-moment "presence" in which nothing needs to be said. Therefore,

Ascending the lecture platform in the Dharma Hall, Huang Po said: "The search for numerous kinds of knowledge cannot compare with a life of 'no seeking.' This is certainly the most exalted. A person of the Way is a person 'without concerns' (*wu-shih*). Surely there are not numerous kinds of mind, nor principles of the Way (*tao-li*) that can be spoken. Since we are 'without concerns,' you are dismissed!"[9]

Having come to hear the *dharma*, however, the monks should not have been disappointed. What they heard spoken, in powerfully condensed Zen rhetoric, was Huang Po's best *dharma*. In this case, the *dharma* consists precisely in startling disclaimers of *dharma*. Language is made to bend back upon itself, empowering itself through the act of self-denial. To say, as Huang Po did, that there are no "principles of the Way that can be spoken" is to enunciate a fundamental principle of the Way of Zen. The monks of Huang Po monastery and the authors of our text were clearly aware of this. They did not lack the reflexivity to see what kind of *dharma* they spoke. Therefore, in superb reflexivity, *The Essentials of Mind Transmission* has Huang Po pronounce the principle that "saying that there is no *dharma* that can be spoken is called speaking the *dharma*."[10] Nor was this paradox a matter of embarrassment to the

---

[7] T. 48, p. 382b.   [8] T. 48, p. 381b; Blofeld, *Huang Po*, p. 44.   [9] T. 48, p. 383b.
[10] T. 48, p. 382a. Iriya traces this sentence of Huang Po to the *Diamond Sutra* in *Denshin Hoyo*, p. 54.

tradition. It seemed in fact to indicate something of profundity, and was therefore repeated on important occasions. Bodhidharma "only spoke of one mind, only transmitted one *dharma* . . . This *dharma* is the *dharma* that cannot be spoken."[11]

Not all interpreters have been content to let this paradox stand, however, without calling upon some theory of language to explain it. Most of them, like John Blofeld, have found the instrumentalist view of language most suitable for this purpose. According to this understanding, language is an instrument or tool available for our use in achieving certain specific communicative goals. Language is a means to some other end. The success of this theory, as we will see, turns on the capacity to maintain strict separation between goals and means. Consequently, Blofeld frequently makes a clear distinction between the content of Zen awakening and the particular linguistic form in which it happens to be "clothed" for description. On this theory, although the enlightened mind has transcended language unconditionally, nevertheless, language remains necessary and useful. Its role is instrumental, at elementary levels, in order to help others transcend language. Thus, Blofeld writes that, once enlightenment has been achieved, Buddhists "may employ words to point the way to others."[12] Although language can never "describe" awakening – "something lying infinitely beyond the highest point ever reached by the human intellect"[13] – to the uninitiated, it may still be a useful tool, "as words of some sort must be used in order to set disciples on to the right path."[14] Regrettably, therefore, Blofeld acknowledges that "until intuition arises in your mind, words will have to do."[15]

Why didn't the Buddha just remain silent after enlightenment? Why speak at all? The traditional Buddhist answer matches Blofeld's: the Buddha spoke out of compassion, and skillful means. The suffering needed assistance, and the *dharma* was the tool most suited to overcoming their pain. The Huang Po texts have no less an authority than Bodhidharma make this historical point: "The Buddha spoke the *dharma* in order to eradicate all traces of mind."[16] Linguistic formulation of the *dharma* has a purpose in spite of the fact that the best Zen intuitions are inclined toward silence.

The story of Huang Po's first meeting with his teacher, Pai-chang, follows this same line. When Huang Po asked to hear Pai-chang's interpretation of how the enlightened masters of Zen had taught, Pai-chang

---

[11] T. 48, p. 381b.   [12] Blofeld, *Huang Po*, p. 17.   [13] Blofeld, *Huang Po*, p. 17.
[14] Blofeld, *Huang Po*, p. 18.   [15] Blofeld, *Beyond the Gods*, p. 25.   [16] T. 48, p. 381a.

just remained silent. Huang Po's response calls Pai-chang to task, and to responsibility for the lineage of Zen. "You cannot let the original Zen teachings be lost in the hands of later followers,"[17] he reasoned. Pai-chang has something that needs to be passed on to subsequent generations. How else can this be done except through language? Silent withdrawal will not do. Language, therefore, makes its appearance as an inadequate, regrettable, but nevertheless essential tool of the Zen tradition. It is an instrument, a means to a worthy end. Consider this crucial passage from *The Essentials of Mind Transmission*:

This Way of heavenly truth originally lacked a name or word. Because people of the world did not understand and were confused, Buddhas became manifest in the world to teach a remedy to this situation. Concerned that people would still not comprehend, they expediently established the name "Way." But one cannot come to realization by focussing on this name. Therefore it is said: "Having obtained the fish, forget the fishtrap." When body and mind are spontaneous, the Way is penetrated, the mind understood.[18]

This passage is most easily interpreted as sustaining an instrumentalist view of language in Zen. Let us transcribe it as follows: the "Way" is fundamentally pre-linguistic; it existed on its own prior to language. But when people, in their ignorance, failed to make contact with "the Way," the language of Buddhism was constructed. Words like "the Way" were employed to instruct them. If, however, in the midst of using language, people become too fixated on the medium, they will miss the pre-linguistic point of it all. Drawing on the traditional Taoist text, the *Chuang-tzu*, we see an encapsulated version of the relationship between language as temporary means and enlightenment as goal. Although the trap (language) is there in order to catch the fish (enlightenment), once you've got the fish, the trap is no longer useful and can be forgotten.

On the basis of this understanding of language, the Huang Po texts can reflect back on their own Buddhist language and say: "These teachings are merely expedients to entice people to enter the way. Originally there were not these teachings. Letting go of them, this is the *dharma*."[19] Although linguistic and textual training may have had a preliminary function, once the goal had been obtained, these could be released.

In contemporary contexts of thought, however, several realizations place this understanding of language in doubt, and inspire an effort to ask ourselves how we might conceive of the role of language in Huang Po's Zen in terms other than this. Once this doubt is raised, the Zen

---

[17] T. 51, p. 266; Chang, *Original Teachings*, p. 103.   [18] T. 48, p. 382c.   [19] T. 48, p. 381a.

tradition begins to take on a somewhat altered form, and we begin to notice the centrality of language in Zen. We notice, for example, that fascination with language, as well as discursive experimentation, reach their climax in the Zen tradition. We begin to realize in rereading these classic Zen texts that no tradition in any time or place was more aware of its language than Zen.

To initiate ourselves into these new ways of looking at language in Zen, we might begin by taking a closer look at the modern western view of language that has shaped our view of Zen so far. The instrumental theory of language was so deeply ensconced in Blofeld's romantic heritage that he saw no alternative to it. So natural did this theory seem to him that he did not hesitate in presenting it as the key to understanding Huang Po. In his introduction to *The Zen Teaching of Huang Po*, Blofeld articulates his theories of language and religious experience:

Those who have actually achieved this tremendous experience, whether as Christians, Buddhists or members of other faiths, are agreed as to the impossibility of communicating it in words. They may employ words to point the way to others, but, until the latter have achieved the experience for themselves, they can have but the merest glimmer of the truth – a poor intellectual concept of something lying infinitely beyond the highest point ever reached by the human intellect . . . Usually, it is the utter impossibility of describing the Supreme Experience which explains the paradoxical nature of their speech. To affirm or deny is to limit; to limit is to shut out the light of truth; but, as words of some sort must be used in order to set disciples on to the right path, there naturally arises a series of paradoxes.[20]

We will want to take notice of several assumptions that make this theory possible, as well as some consequences that would seem to follow from it.

First, although "the Supreme Experience" is no doubt far from ordinary, there is nothing about it that is specific to any particular culture or language. The extraordinary person in any culture, speaking any language, has equal access to it because the experience is not linguistically and culturally mediated. Except for its differences from "ordinary mind," "the experience of Zen" has no special "otherness" about it. We (Christians, Jews, secular modernists, and romantics) know "the experience" as well as "they" do, provided that we too have passed beyond cultural/linguistic categories to the bottom of things in pure unmediated experience. Romanticism, as a dominant form of modern liberalism, can thus take a charitable view of others – their "highest" experience is

[20] Blofeld, *Huang Po*, pp. 17–18.

every bit as "high" as ours. The hidden, and less charitable, side of this is that, since we already have direct access in our own culture to the highest and best in "their" culture, we don't really have anything to learn from them. People are essentially the same. The otherness of the text, in this view, is only the otherness of depth to the shallowness of ordinary awareness. We may "express" or "describe" "the Supreme Experience" differently after we have it, but in the experience itself, we transcend those differences. The instrumental, secondary status of language makes this "universalist" theory of religious experience natural and obvious. If, however, experience and language "co-arise" in any sense, and are thus not so easily separable, then references to "the Supreme Experience" are problematized, and we begin to be concerned that we have not attended carefully enough to the distinctiveness of Zen.

Secondly, therefore, when Blofeld writes about "employing" and "using" language, we want to ask whether language is in fact best conceived as an instrument. From Blofeld's point of view, language is a tool separate from the reality on which it may be used. We use it when we must say what we already know pre-linguistically. Blofeld does acknowledge that those of us who are not enlightened and who have not had "the Supreme Experience" may indeed be conditioned by language at the level of experience. Language, in this case, acts as a "filter" or a "veil" obstructing the purity of experience. According to Blofeld, when this occurs, we tend to enter into "disputes over words rather than what they signify."[21] We ignorantly take the particular words spoken as a dimension of the way things really are. The value of "Zen," for Blofeld, and for western interpretation generally, is that through its "means" we come to direct experience and see things for ourselves, without regard to anyone's language about them.

Notice, however, how language is continually hidden from Blofeld's view, even when he is talking about it. When, for instance, Blofeld criticizes those who "have tried to clothe the Ultimate in words,"[22] "the Ultimate" – Blofeld's own "clothing" – is not noticed as language. "The Ultimate" here is simply what he is talking about, the referent itself. While "clothing" it as "God" or "Nirvana" may obscure it, the status and implications of the pronoun "it" do not come into view. The insight that "all thinking about language is already once again drawn back into language"[23] leads toward the further realization that language may be

[21] Blofeld, *Tantric Mysticism*, p. 52.   [22] Blofeld, *Hui Hai*, p. 39.
[23] Gadamer, *Philosophical Hermeneutics*, p. 62.

more than a tool available for "employment." More fundamental than a tool at our disposal, language may be an element within which we reside as humans, in such a way that all of our "employments" always presuppose it.

The adequacy of Blofeld's "clothing" metaphor is a good test case for the instrumental theory of language that is based upon it. In this context its adequacy will depend on whether experience and language are related in the same way as are people and their clothing. We understand the distinction between people and their clothing through the fact that they change clothing; they decide what to wear on any given occasion. Clothing both covers the person and presents the person in particular guises and forms. On occasions when all clothing comes off, the person will see him- or herself directly, rather than through one of the selected guises. If language and experience are analogously related, then we would have independent access to our own unclothed experience. Studying the various ways in which experience might be clothed in language, we would select one such outfit for conveyance to others.

This metaphor, and this account of language and experience, are no longer persuasive in our intellectual context. In the alternative that will be proposed in this chapter, experience always comes fully clothed, and the few occasions where that doesn't seem to be so are more matters of limited wardrobe selection than of sheer nakedness. Where do we find language in everyday experience? Not primarily in abstraction as a system available when we must communicate. Instead, we find it in association with things and situations. We find it already in the world. Language constitutes a dimension of any experience. Although on occasion there are linguistic, rhetorical choices to be made, the overwhelming share of the time we don't decide how to "put" things, we just say how they "are." The words adequate to the experience are already there in association with the experience itself. We make decisions about how to put things only when they are not already in place themselves, that is, when ambiguity is a fundamental part of the experience itself. In these interesting cases, we don't examine the experience on its own terms and then try various linguistic guises on to check their fit. Instead, we experience what is there through the juxtaposition of its multiple language forms. We experience "it," therefore, *in* each of the language forms and *in* the relation between them, but never on "its" own.

Thirdly, when Blofeld assails "a poor intellectual concept of something lying infinitely beyond the highest point ever reached by the human intellect,"[24] he draws upon two more forms of dichotomy familiar to romantic metaphysics, between thought and feeling and between what lies within the bounds of language and what lies beyond them. These are distinctions embedded in modern English common sense, and contemporary thought has problematized each of them. When, in modern Europe, science and philosophy denied the cognitive and conceptual legitimacy of religion, poetry, and myth, the romantic counter claim was that religion, poetry, and myth were not matters of thought anyway. Religion and all other forms of "depth" experience were taken to be experiences of "feeling" as opposed to "thought." This thought/feeling dichotomy still pervades our ways of talking about religion, art, poetry, and music. Religious and poetic language are understood to be always inadequate outer "expressions" of something that makes an inner and nonlinguistic impact on one's feelings.

Post-romantic thinking denies that "feeling" is an autonomous domain of experience, and that it is wholly innocent of the structuring imprint of language. On this account, feelings and thoughts "co-arise" and interpenetrate. They depend on each other. Moreover, both are shaped by language. The parameters of what we can "feel" or "think" are dependent on possibilities inherent in linguistic and historical contexts.

Closely related to the separation of thought and feeling is the distinction between what lies within the limits of knowledge or description and what lies beyond them. This is a question about the limits of language, a distinction essential to modernist and romantic understandings of religious experience. An alternative account of the experience of the inadequacy of language might be sketched out as follows. When we speak of experience that is beyond description, we have already described it. Its distinguishing feature or characteristic is this negative dimension, its being "beyond." This feature is nevertheless constituted and structured by language. Like features of other experiences, it is the one that we put into our linguistic description. If the only thing that can be said about "it" is that it cannot be described, then that language is the stark shape of its form. Rather than being a limit that can be seen from the other side in "experience," language establishes this limit and holds the limit within it.

From this point of view, the only sense in which experience goes beyond language is the extent to which they are not the same – there is more to experience than language. The point here, however, is they are never sufficiently separable that, from the side of experience, we could

---

[24] Blofeld, *The Zen Teaching of Huang Po*, p. 17.

see how language has run up against its limits, without language already being there in the construction of those limits. No matter how quickly we manage to maneuver, language will have arrived at the same time. One reason that this problem has been so recalcitrant to modern thinking is that language has come to be conceived in too limited a domain. Modern thought has located language in the derivative and subsequent roles of description and expression; post-modern thought locates it more primordially, in experience itself. Even before we get around to describing experience, language is already there as the form or forms that the experience has taken.

The model of language that I propose as an alternative to Blofeld's modern, instrumental version hinges on the idea that language is already embedded in the content of our experience. It does not concede a clear demarcation between primary experience and a subsequent interpretation that we piece together out of language and then place upon the raw data of experience. Language is present even in the "direct" perception of an object. Language and perception "co-arise." Although theoretically separable, they are indistinguishable in experience itself. How so? In accordance with the way in which "understanding" was articulated in the last chapter, we always understand what we perceive immediately *as* whatever it appears to be. Awareness of what it is that we perceive is linguistically structured, and comes to us directly in the perception itself. We perceive "this" directly *as* what it is – a book, a sound, a strange situation. These linguistically constituted images arise in the perception itself rather than subsequently. We can test this in our own experience. Try to find a perception that is not already associated with some language in the initial encounter. It is true that we do perceive some things incorrectly, and that subsequently we alter the language through which that perception is understood. What we initially perceive *as* a meditation bell is later understood to have been an ice-cream vendor. But both "perceptions," both "correct" and "incorrect," come to us in the form of language. Language doesn't guarantee accuracy; it just guarantees that all of our perceptions will be understood within the given context of language.

It is also true that we sometimes perceive some things in uncertainty, in sheer perplexity. We don't know how to understand them initially even though we have definitely perceived them. Yet language is already there, setting even this perception in context. We have perceived this state of affairs *as* perplexing, *as* uncertain, *as* mysterious, even if that is all that we initially perceive in it. To the extent that anything more than this has been perceived, language will show its shape, whatever it is – colorless, awesome, multidimensional, beyond description, or *mysterium tremendum*.

Anything not experienced *as* something in particular is simply not experienced. Because this hermeneutical "as" is linguistically shaped, language is always implicated in our experience. Language, and its entire history of involvement in thought and practice, functions to set up a context of significance within which perception occurs. By means of language, the world (the given) is focused and organized in advance of every encounter with entities, persons, or situations. Thus, when we see something, we have already interpreted it – immediately – *as* whatever it appears to be. Assigning it a linguistic form is not something we do after seeing it. It is the very shape that seeing has already taken. Although this language refers to something extralinguistic – something beyond language – that something appears to us *as* the reality that it is through language.

Furthermore, this is not to say that because language resides in all experience, all experience is therefore theoretical. The simple, perceptual seeing something *as* what it is in the midst of our activity in the world does not require our thinking about it. No reflective mediation is required. The point, however, is that the results of past reflection and language use – the formation of concepts – get passed along to all participants in a culture through its language. You don't have to reflect on the concept of a "door," or define it, in order to experience that shape *as* a door and to use it in accordance with its appropriate "sense." Language, therefore, is not to be located only at the level of concept and predication. It is also present at the level of perception in such a way that perception, language, and thinking are all interdependent.

Without this linguistically shaped sense that informs our direct awareness of things, the daily life of a Zen master like Huang Po would be problematic at best. His functioning in the world, like ours, requires that things are seen for what they are, in most cases, immediately, without standing around to ponder which linguistic clothing is most suitable to them. Inability to perceive this sound *as* a question, that sound *as* a meditation bell, or any sound *as* a sound would render basic life functions impossible. Inability to experience a monastery fire "immediately" *as* a fire, *as* a threat, *as* a demand for action, *as* requiring the evacuation of others, *as* extinguishable by water, and so on, would render the Zen master helpless and incapable of spontaneous, Zen-like response. No Zen text disputes this; in fact they all assume it. They assume the everyday function of linguistic distinctions by means of which things are experienced *as* what they are, fully laden with linguistically structured meaning and significance. It is only on the basis of this background of language that distinctively Zen actions can be performed.

The instrumental theory of language that we have criticized here is not wrong in asserting that language functions as an instrument or tool that we use for our own purposes. We do, in fact, use language. But this theory is inadequate insofar as it sees this as the only location of language, and insofar as it understands human beings to have an independent and controlling relation to language. Every act of use or control, whether discursive or not, is already structured for us by the linguistically shaped contours of our cultural inheritance. Moreover, transcending these contours, getting back behind them, is no more desirable than it is possible. Not only are we mistaken when we understand the Zen master to have achieved this state, we also render him incapable of the worldly "function" for which he is famous.

It is interesting that language is almost never noticeable to us in this role. When we experience something or even talk about it, we focus exclusively on the thing and not on the language that mediates it to us. Language seems to disappear behind whatever dominates our experience. Ironically, this is even true when we are talking about language, as we are now. We don't notice the medium of our talk as we focus on its object. When Huang Po criticizes language, he typically does not notice that it is language that is currently making the criticism possible. And when he does notice, we get reflexive paradox, the kinds of language that have made Zen texts famous. Language is a universal and inescapable element in all of our experience, and any account of language or of Zen must now come to terms with this realization. Even – or especially – the "great matter" of Huang Po is experienced as a "matter" at all within the language of Zen. Understanding it will require penetration into this language, not a leap out of it.

It was in the language of Zen that the community on Mount Huang Po had come together around their shared concerns. The language of Zen is a condition without which neither the practice of Zen nor the point of Zen would exist. If this is true, then we would not be well advised to accept Huang Po's account of how Buddhist symbols, like "the Way," came into existence. Recall that this passage explained how "the Way" existed prior to its name, but because people failed to experience it, the Buddhas "expediently" named it "the Way" in order to attract people to the possibility of living in accord with it.[25] On this

[25] T. 48, p. 382c.

account, language is a tool that doesn't really fit its referent. Let us construct another version. Consider reversing the story so that, rather than existing on its own eternally, only to be named later, "the Way" came into existence with its name. Gradually, perhaps imperceptibly, the word for dirt paths through fields and forest (an earlier or "literal" meaning of the word, *tao*) came to suggest something more than that, although related. The word itself began to suggest to some "users" that there are "paths" or "ways" through other affairs as well, even life itself. Beyond that, this symbol suggested, there may be a single unifying "Way" structuring all of reality.

Metaphors like "the Way" are the well-springs of new meaning. Words used in new contexts suggest more than their prior literal sense; they give rise to ideas not previously existent. In Paul Ricoeur's words: "the symbol gives rise to thought," and thought extends the possibilities inherent in symbols like "the Way." Rather than assuming the independent and prior origin of entities which come to be "named" later, it is worth considering how name and referent may "co-arise" through the symbolic, metaphoric initiative of language. When "the symbol gives rise to thought," language speaks suggestively to us, both in our own speaking and in the words of others spoken to us, and we listen.

At the end of Huang Po's meditation on the origin of the language of Zen, the text seems to summarize all of this in Chuang-tzu's fish-trap slogan – literally translated, "obtain fish, discard trap."[26] Rich in suggestiveness, the slogan can be understood in several ways. One Zen reading was clearly "once you have obtained the goal of Zen training – awakening – then you have no further need of the means – Zen Buddhism." Similarly, shifting metaphors, the "raft" of Buddhism is simply a vehicle to "the other shore." "Having arrived, why lug the raft along? You don't need it!" This understanding, however, has three significant problems entailed in it.

The first is that few Buddhists, and few Zen Buddhists, understood the moment of "arrival" or "awakening" to be so unequivocal and final. Although today's catch may be very satisfying now, tomorrow you may wish you had kept the fish trap. Even the most productive fishermen may get hungry again. If, like everything else, "awakening" is "empty," that is, relative to contexts, impermanent, and open to both deepening and further refinement, then abandoning all means may be either premature or foolish.

---

[26] T. 48, p. 382c.

A second difficulty with a literal reading of Huang Po's slogan is that the Mahayana Bodhisattva has taken a vow not to abandon others even if, or especially if, he or she has arrived at the goal. Although you may have all the fish you want, your vow is to teach all others how to use the trap. If Buddhism is a "means" to the "goal" of enlightenment, then the career of a Buddhist *as a Buddhist* is never over; it is just transformed. Dissemination of the means becomes the goal. Not only should you keep the trap, you might want to consider fixing it up, or experimenting with new and more effective versions.

Finally, this point leads us to suspect that the relation between "means" and "ends" is not as transparent as this powerful slogan would suggest. "Means" and "ends" are "empty." They arise together and stand continually in relation to one another. Alterations in one give rise to alterations in the other. Moreover, the adoption of any particular set of "means" by a practitioner has an ongoing and irrevocable effect on the one who shapes his or her life in accordance with them. What and how you practice influences who and what you become. Having chosen "these" Buddhist "means," you become "this" kind of person. If there is "no self" existing permanently and independent of the forces of "dependent origination," then who you are is a function of both the means and the goals you have adopted in practice. Once "awakened" you may opt to cease performing "these" Zen practices, but you will never throw them away. They constitute your very being. By then, fisherman and fish trap have already "co-arisen." Having been a real fisherman and a real Buddhist, how could you seriously maintain that your "true self" retains its "own-being" independent of those practices?

So, what remains of the Taoist wisdom that Huang Po has appropriated? This: that a great deal rides on how you relate to your fish trap and to your Buddhism. The rhetoric of "discarding," of "overturning," of "breaking through," is essential to the particular "means" of Zen. It is also fundamental to the entirety of the Buddhist tradition. Non-attachment, releasement, letting go, and emptying are all fundamental Buddhist practices, and, at the most advanced levels, these acts of distanciation are aimed not at things in the world so much as at Buddhism itself. Having "discarded" or loosened other attachments, only the Buddhist "means" of loosening are now held firmly in hand. "Letting go," however, is a two-sided and "dialectical" motion, as the Taoist Chuang-tzu knew too. We must "discard" while "retaining," "let go" while "holding on." Enlightenment is not a proclamation of nihilism, as Huang Po makes clear in correcting overzealous and literal readings of "emptiness." "Emptiness" can only be valorized to the extent that it can be seen in "form."

The "form" most readily used for the dissemination of "emptiness" was language, and this has been true throughout the history of Zen. The language of Zen gives rise to the "thought of enlightenment." The thought of enlightenment gives rise to the practice of Zen, and the practice of Zen, including its linguistic practices, gives rise to the realization of enlightenment. Nor does the circle stop here. New means, new conceptions of goals, and new ways of speaking the language of Zen "arise" out of numerous "realizations." None of these remain the same; each penetrates to the heart of the other – pure "emptiness."

John Blofeld's modern and romantic reading of Zen gave considerably less room for such entanglements. Modern mentality stresses the importance of separation, of individuality, and of clear distinction. Means are clearly distinct from ends, and ends from means. Tools are separate from the products of their labor. Language and the communal contexts of linguistic training have little to do with Zen awakening. On these bases Blofeld would write:

for I am convinced that any man who searches deeply into the inmost recesses of his own spirit will come upon the same eternal Wisdom proceeding from the indivisible unity of our real minds (or spirit) with the real Mind (or Spirit) which fills the universe, other than which nothing has more than a transient, dream-like reality. A tiny child left upon a desert island to grow up without a single human companion would, if he searched deeply and constantly into his own mind, come upon truths identical with those taught by the Buddha, Jesus, Lao-tse and all the other enlightened sages. If he could communicate those truths in some way, they would be purer than any communication the world has received, for such a child would not attempt to clothe Universal truth in the special terms employed by the followers of some particular religion.[27]

The two "ifs" in this passage are crucial. By focusing our reading on them we can see how the line of thinking represented here turns on the extent to which Blofeld's instrumental view of language will hold. The first "if" says: "if" this child, isolated from, and therefore, unperverted by, human society, "searched deeply and constantly into his own mind." But would he? Could he? Lacking the concept "mind," being without the metaphors "search," "depth," and "constancy," what kind of constant in-depth mental searching would we expect to take place? Without a nuanced language of subjectivity, what kind of experience of self do

---

[27] Blofeld, *The Wheel of Life*, p. 228.

we imagine? On Blofeld's view, language and culture are "particularities" which do not touch upon the deep, and therefore, "universal," "recesses of the spirit." The untrammeled island of romantic imagination is the place where particulars, like religious ideas and practices, won't stand in the way of the Universal Truth hidden securely behind them. If Huang Po's Mahayana tradition is right, however, then the "universal" – "emptiness" – only makes its appearance, and only exists, within the particularities of "form."

Indeed, Buddhists have always assumed that this goal will only be achieved through certain forms – certain subtle, reflexive, and imaginative forms that can only be the products of great cultural achievement. If "enlightenment" is a consequence of simply being left alone, then temples, monasteries, Zen masters, and other institutions would not only be beside the point, they would be counterproductive. Given the problems that accompany human institutions and culture, this was indeed what Blofeld was led to wonder. Institutions inevitably foster greed and perversion. Perhaps their absence would be an improvement. When looking in this direction, what Blofeld could not see is that the concepts of "greed," "perversion," "improvement," and "awakening" are only available within linguistically constructed cultural institutions. Lacking these, we could not see what needed improving, nor that improvement was one among the many possibilities. Blofeld still imagines the child a romantic, striving for deep inner attainment, without the perversions. Romantic ideology, his own, was invisible to him. Its language and doctrines were, for him, the structure of reality itself. Since his own doctrines were transparent *as* doctrines, Blofeld could relegate "doctrine" to the realm of the derivative, of "particularity." Therefore, "doctrine" came to mean, essentially, "false doctrine." But from our perspective, the deserted child would be in a more serious situation with respect to religious and cultural matters. Not only would he grow up without the "false" doctrines that "particular religion[s]" tend to promulgate, he would miss out on the "true" ones too, and the effect of this would be no romanticism, no "search," and no "spirit." In the absence of the culture of Zen, we cannot imagine the abandoned child becoming a Zen master.

According to the alternative view of language being sketched in this chapter, outside a particular linguistic context, "spirit" will not even exist as a possible goal of this child's quest. Far from being the "particular" which inappropriately "clothes" the "Universal," language is as "universal" as anything will ever get. It is only in language, and in the form of understanding that resides in a particular language, that any kind of religious possibility comes forth. We learn about such possibilities as "Spirit" and "Universal Truth" only in the process of learning those languages which have set them forth in word and image as realities. It is not the case, in this view, that learning to speak a language is simply learning how to "use" certain words to describe or point to a reality that we already know and understand in itself. On the contrary, reality becomes the reality that it is for us in language. As H.G. Gadamer puts it: "It is in language games . . . that the child becomes acquainted with the world. Indeed, everything we learn takes place in language games . . . The words we find there capture our intending."[28] Blofeld's second "if" follows similar lines: "If he could communicate those truths in some way, they would be purer than any communication the world has received, for such a child would not attempt to clothe Universal truth in the special terms employed by the followers of some particular religion."[29] On the contrary, without a particular language, these "truths" could not be experienced or known, much less communicated. Without the particular, no universal. From this point of view, Blofeld's interest in the "unclothed universal" was itself neither "universal" nor "unclothed." Interest in such an experience can be located with some exactitude in a particular era of a particular culture, the era in which romanticism established the norms for religious thinking in European culture. The vast vocabulary for the "universal" and its quest were opened up as real possibilities in many of the great nineteenth-century romantic texts. Indeed, it is there that we find in great abundance Blofeld's "clothing" metaphor. These texts had "capture[d]" Blofeld's "intending." Blofeld had listened deeply to what the religious language of his time and place had to say to him. This listening, and the learning that accompanied it, shaped the way in which the Buddhist texts he would read came to have meaning for him. Indeed, it made possible his having any interest in them at all. And as we think these thoughts in English, we must realize that the same applies to us. These same romantic texts, now once or twice removed, perhaps even as unknown to us as our great-grandparents, stand in the lineage of our openness to Huang Po and invisibly shape our reading Zen.

What implications would all of this have for our understanding of Zen? It would mean, for one thing, that the language of Zen (or more precisely, the T'ang dynasty language of this text or the Sung dynasty

---

[28] Gadamer, *Philosophical Hermeneutics*, p. 56.   [29] Blofeld, *The Wheel of Life*, p. 228.

language of that) embodies a particular understanding of reality, and that this background is what has enabled the kind of religious practice and realization associated with it. It also means that we would want to qualify the extent of the universality that we would imagine to be available in Huang Po's Zen. Each time and place, by virtue of its participation in a somewhat different language, would be characterized by the particular kind of experience that was made possible by its language and other dimensions of cultural background. It would therefore not be a mere accident that Zen practices and experiences were born in the Sinitic languages of certain historical periods, rather than elsewhere or at other times. To this way of thinking, "Zen" interests us not because "they" have the "Universal Experience" too, but because they experience something "we" don't, and because their language has opened up a set of possibilities for them that, by our contemporary standards, is extremely impressive. In it we see something perhaps well worth appropriating for our own cultural use. Aside from this difference opened up in the uniqueness of their language and culture, there are no pressing reasons for studying Zen.

The richer and more diverse the language, the greater the reservoir of possibilities it holds open to those who speak and listen to it. Language, as the medium of these possibilities, is, among our many inheritances, the most fundamental.

The language, after all, is the repository of the kinds of meaning and relation that make a culture what it is. In it one can find the terms by which the natural world is classified and represented, those by which the social universe is constituted, and those terms of motive and value by which action is directed and judged. In a sense we literally are the language that we speak, for the particular culture that makes us a "we" – that defines and connects us, that differentiates us from others – is enacted and embedded in our language.[30]

On this account of language, we would want to understand both the Zen monastery on Mount Huang Po and the texts that issued out of it as having, among their primary tasks, the articulation of a distinct language of Zen. The Zen language in which novices would train would gradually bring them to Zen experiences, showing the world to them in its light. Zen concerns and Zen practices would slowly take shape in the novices' minds, replacing or reshaping whatever concerns and practices were there before. The primary words and symbols of Zen do not just name objects and issues that were already there in the novices' minds

---

[30] James Boyd White, *When Words Lose Their Meaning*, p. 20.

pre-linguistically. Instead, they slowly generate these new concerns, new ways of being in the world, that had no previous existence in the practitioner. Hearing new words and new sentences, and then learning to speak them, the novice is initiated into new forms of life. Thus the "experiences" of Zen would only be available through the language and culture of Zen.

Describing any tradition this way, however, raises a pernicious modern intellectual problem. We suspect the possibility of a vicious "relativism" in which we are thought to be captives of our language, closed off from the world and from people in other cultures. This suspicion, however, arises as much from our traditional reluctance to admit the finitude of human understanding as it does from this particular account of it. Understanding, knowledge, and practice are indeed relative to language. That conclusion is unavoidable in our time. Language plays a role in establishing the boundaries of human finitude. This does not mean, however, that we are captives of our language; it does not mean that we are predetermined in some ineluctable way. It also does not mean that we cannot understand what goes on in another culture or another language. Reading Zen well will give rise to understanding. To say that language establishes limits, or a certain range of possibilities, is not to say which of them will or will not be actualized, nor how, when, by whom, in what way, and to what end. It is rather to say that human freedom and understanding are finite, and that language is what, perhaps more than any other factor, shapes that finitude in the particular way that it is. That finite placement in a language is not closure or isolation is further demonstrated by our ability to learn another language. As we learn to speak we learn to understand, and, understanding, we are able to find our way around in a foreign culture.

It also modifies these limits to know that languages are always in the process of change. As old ways of speaking fade and are replaced by new ones, a transformed set of possibilities are opened up for our endeavor and experience. We never simply repeat the language of our ancestors. Language and culture stay alive by the constant process of reshaping and restructuring. As new situations arise, new ways of speaking are established to deal with them. These "new ways" are never totally new, of course. They are always hammered out on the anvil of the preceding discursive practice and mediated through the culture's grasp of its new situation. But linguistic practices and the shape of the culture will nonetheless be transformed. We can see these changes in retrospect, for example, in the advent of "Zen" out of the resources of earlier Chinese

Buddhism, and in the differences between Blofeld's reading of Zen and ours.

It is no doubt due to this limiting dimension of language that several traditions of thought about language have rendered a negative judgment. Language is taken to be a barrier, restricting knowledge and freedom. If this restriction is understood to be severe, then the response may be to search for ways to transcend language altogether. This must be at least part of the motive behind Blofeld's concern to set aside the "clothing" of particular languages in order to get to the universal hidden behind them. And it has certainly been at least a good guess to say that some understanding like this may have been at stake in Zen as well. The critique of language is clearly fundamental to Zen discourse. What is important for our reading, however, is to see the other side of language in Zen. This "other side" can be most easily seen in the fact that, even in the midst of negative judgments, language is a matter of intense preoccupation in Zen.

Having a "concept" of language, and a vocabulary in which to discuss it, is a sign of considerable cultural sophistication. Not all cultures nor all historical epochs have made language a thematic object of reflection. Thinking "language" requires a great deal of abstraction. Ordinarily we think right through language to its objects and concerns without noticing the medium in which we do our thinking. In Zen, however, this medium is the focal point of inordinate contemplation. The Huang Po texts – including layers from quite different historical periods – share this obsession. In *The Essentials of Mind Transmission* alone, there are no less than nineteen different words for or about language. Numerous passages in the text take language as an explicit theme; very few leave it out of the discussion altogether. Some Zen texts are explicitly reflexive: in addition to discussing language in general, they direct attention to the language that is being spoken, written, read, or thought *at this very moment. Koan* meditation may be the most condensed and self-conscious linguistic practice ever devised in any culture. The suggestion being made in all this is that in reading Zen, rather than bracing ourselves to transcend language at the opportune moment, we may be better off focusing meditatively on the language of transcendence itself. Paying attention to Zen rhetoric, we may come to appreciate and to understand that the instruments and devices of the Zen trade are not so far off after all. Therefore, having seen where language may be located behind the scenes of Zen, let us now turn to the discourse of awakening itself.

CHAPTER 5

RHETORIC: the instrument of mediation

"Huang Po is such a grandmother that he utterly exhausted himself with your troubles!" said Ta-yu. "And now you come here asking whether you were at fault or not!" At these words, Lin-chi attained great enlightenment. "Ah," he cried, "there isn't so much to Huang Po's Buddha-*dharma*!"

The Recorded Sayings of Lin-chi[1]

Ts'ui-feng asked: "What words does Huang Po use to instruct people?" "Huang Po has no words," said Lin-chi.

The Recorded Sayings of Lin-chi[2]

Language plays a far greater role in the mind of a Zen master like Huang Po than that of an "instrument," a tool intentionally applied to the carrying out of particular purposes. Nevertheless, when language does function as an instrument in Zen, it is a tool of considerable power and precision. Indeed, in its "golden age" and today, Zen has been best known for its unique instrumental rhetoric, its own counterclaims notwithstanding. The "discourse of awakening" in Zen produces a kind of rhetoric very much unlike anything ever heard or read in East Asia or elsewhere, a way of speaking/writing that is distinctively "Zen." In this chapter we consider both the character of this rhetoric and the role it plays in the quest for "awakening."

The first extract at the head of this chapter acknowledges the possibility of a rhetorical impetus to awakening: "Lin-chi attained great enlightenment," "[a]*t these words.*" Given the principle of "no dependence on language" and the ubiquity of language critique in Zen, who would have thought that enlightenment might "originate dependent" upon "words," or that "words" might be the primary element structuring its

---

[1] Sasaki, *The Recorded Sayings of Lin-chi*, p. 51; T. 47, p. 504c.
[2] Sasaki, *The Recorded Sayings of Lin-chi*, p. 59; T. 47, p. 506b.

occasion? Were Zen Buddhists unaware of this function of language in Zen? Not in the least! Self-consciousness of language use and of its strategic role in the processes of awakening are among the most distinctive features of Zen. Reading Zen, we see it everywhere. Classic Zen texts give ample evidence that advanced practitioners, at least, looked at nothing with more focus and intensity than the rhetoric of Zen. The rationale for their intense focus was simply that nothing was thought to have greater potential to awaken the mind than the rhetorical excursions of the great Zen masters. It would appear, in fact, that, as the tradition developed, what developed most explicitly were rhetorical practices – the abilities to speak, hear, write, and read Zen discourse.

"Awakening" is not always elicited by language. Meditation, or an encounter or perception in the natural world, were also scenes where on occasion enlightenment might occur. But if you read through classical Zen literature where the enlightenment stories of the most famous Zen masters are recounted, you will find that these are surprisingly few. Overwhelmingly, language and rhetoric stand at the threshold of "awakening." The phrase "at these words, so and so was awakened" is among the most common in the classical Zen *Transmission of the Lamp* literature. In one of his recorded lectures, Huang Po narrates his version of one of the most famous of these awakenings, the story of the reception of the "patriarchal robe," a symbol of "mind transmission," by Hui-neng, the renowned Sixth Patriarch of the Zen tradition. In an atmosphere of jealousy and intrigue, Hui-neng has secretly left the monastery with the patriarchal robe, and is being pursued by hostile forces, a Zen monk named Ming. When Ming finally catches up to him on the mountain top, Hui-neng leaps into offensive posture and puts a *koan* to him: "Just at this moment, return to what you were before your father and mother were born!"[3] Then, "even as the words were spoken, Ming arrived at a sudden tacit understanding. Accordingly he bowed to the ground and said. . ."[4]

What he said on that occasion need not concern us. That he said something at the moment of awakening, and that the words of the *koan* are what evoked that breakthrough, are, instead, the objects of our reflection. Not only is Huang Po's Zen rhetoric the medium of the narrative, rhetoric is its content as well. "Words" seem to be everywhere. Words give rise to the experience and then issue from it immediately and spontaneously. "Awakening" has not occurred in the absence of language, but fully

---

[3] T. 48, p. 383c; Blofeld, *Huang Po*, p. 65.
[4] T. 48, p. 383c; Blofeld, *Huang Po*, p. 65.

in its presence. And when it does occur, the natural response is not silence but more words.

Classic Zen texts present the moment of awakening *as* a rhetorical occasion, an occasion where readers or hearers can expect language to be at its very best. There are other such occasions, however. Perhaps the two most important are initial conversion experiences, often presented in the texts as preliminary moments of awakening, and "death verses," the last "words" of the great masters of Zen.[5] Just before dying, each Zen master would present the "words" that would be held by the subsequent tradition as the epitome of his Zen mind. Controlling this moment, and staging it with refined contextual sensitivity, were absolutely essential for any monk who would come to be valorized in the later tradition. With the proper audience carefully gathered at the proper time, the master releases himself into this final rhetorical occasion. His "discourse record," then, narrating the event as if through the eyes and ears of a reporter on the spot, gives one or another slight variant of the following: "Having spoken these words, sitting erect, the Master revealed his Nirvana."[6]

"Words" in the Zen tradition were far from inconsequential. Indeed, they hold a place of startling centrality, a realization which will lead us closer to the question: what is "awakened mind?" To get there, we focus on the character of enlightened language. What kinds of rhetoric were thought to be characteristic of enlightenment, and what kinds of rhetoric were commonly thought to evoke that state of mind? Lin-chi's section in *The Transmission of the Lamp* shows intense focus on every occasion of speech. In one of its reflections on liberating language, the text says: "Each word we say should possess the three mystic entrances, and each mystic entrance must possess the three essentials, manifested in temporary appearance and action."[7] Words establish an "entrance," a "doorway" providing passage into the open space of awakening. "Each word" should contain this potential for breakthrough; each word should possess its own power. Indeed, according to the account given in the Ma-tsu "discourse record," the point is even broader: every word *does* possess this power, whether we know it or not, whether we experience it or not. "The very words I now speak are nothing else but a function of the Way."[8] While language may lead to alienation, thus preventing

---

[5] For an analysis and description of these, see Bernard Faure, "The Ritualization of Death," in *The Rhetoric of Immediacy*.

[6] T. 47, p. 506c; Sasaki, *The Recorded Sayings of Lin-chi*, p. 62. True to form, Lin-chi's final two words were: "Blind ass!"   [7] T. 51, p. 290; Chang, *Original Teachings*, p. 122.

[8] Pas, *The Recorded Sayings of Ma-tsu*, p. 40.

awakening, it may also be experienced *as* the obverse of alienation, *as* the functioning of the Way itself.

The language of Zen in Huang Po's time and place was in a certain sense the language of ordinary discourse, heightened and intensified. The language that was being rejected was the formal language of scholarly Buddhist practice. The masters of Hung-chou Zen, following Ma-tsu, placed heavy emphasis on the transformation of everyday rhetoric so that it might become the "instrument" of Zen. To do this, ordinary words had to be used and understood in extraordinary ways. To hear Ma-tsu's words, not just *as* the words of Ma-tsu but also *as* the function of the Way, would take considerable reorientation, first in Ma-tsu's rhetorical practice and then in the practice of hearers. Once this transformation occurred, however, it was thought possible to hear the Way everywhere in language and in all things *as* signs of the Way. Any word was thought to bear this power. Any word or phrase was potentially a "turning word," a word or phrase capable of turning the mind so decisively that awakening would result.

To function in this way, however, words would need to be taken in unusual ways. And since "usual" words tend not to be taken in "unusual" ways, it was thought that the rhetoric with the greatest potential for breakthrough would be language that was itself unusual, so unusual that it would force itself upon the mind in strange and disruptive ways. These words would simply resist the appropriative tactics of "everyday mind." "Strangeness" and "disruptiveness" would come to be characteristics of distinctively Zen rhetoric. Because the "usual" order of language is located in spoken discourse, masters of Zen rhetoric would develop alternative "signs" of awakening. Huang Po came to be well known for his ability to "speak" without really speaking, through acts of "direct pointing" and through signals of silence. In order to characterize Zen rhetoric, therefore, we divide it into four distinct rhetorical styles: the rhetoric of strangeness, the rhetoric of "direct pointing," the rhetoric of silence, and the rhetoric of disruption.

THE RHETORIC OF STRANGENESS

One day during the group work, Lin-chi was going along behind the others. Huang Po looked around, and, seeing that Lin-chi was empty-handed, asked: "Where is your mattock?" "Somebody took it away from me," said Lin-chi. "Come here," said Huang Po. "I want to talk the matter over with you." Lin-chi stepped forward. Huang Po lifted up his mattock and said: "Just *this* people on the earth cannot hold up." Lin-chi snatched the mattock from Huang Po's grasp and held it high. "Then why is this in my hand now?" he asked. "Today there's a man who really is working," said Huang Po, and returned to the temple.[9]

No doubt, uninitiated bystanders, like us, would be hard pressed to say how the foregoing constitutes "talking the matter over." It is not even clear what the "matter" is, much less what Huang Po and Lin-chi have to say about it. Nevertheless, the intriguing character of this conversation – its strangeness – impressed itself so firmly in the mind of some monk that it eventually found its way into the classic texts of Zen. And there it has stood, for the contemplation of generations of Zen readers. Although this particular narrative never reached the status of *koan*, it did rate subsequent commentary by two of the great Zen masters of another generation. The story goes on to include equally "strange" comments and evaluations from Zen masters Kuei-shan and Yang-shan. No one seems to be concerned about "making sense," at least not "sense" in the usual meaning of that word. Indeed, the rhetoric of strangeness in Zen is a sustained effort to call the entire realm of "ordinary sense" up into conscious awareness where, otherwise, it is rarely to be found.

It may be that the most readily identifiable feature of Zen discourse is its unconventional, unusual character. Zen rhetoric is indeed "strange" when read or heard in alien contexts like ours. But in addition to that, and more importantly, Zen rhetoric is eminently strange in relation to its own cultural context. Moreover, this unconventionality is intentionally cultivated and texts refer to it frequently. The central importance of the rhetoric of strangeness can be seen in the way that it is taken to be the primary sign of "awakening." One Zen text that explicitly displays this link between strangeness of talk and awakening has the monk Shen-tsan returning to the monastery of his former teacher. The old teacher immediately sees that this is not the same Shen-tsan who left to go out on pilgrimage, so he says: "Who did you visit while out on pilgrimage? I notice you've been speaking in unusual ways." Shen-tsan replies: "I was awakened by the Zen master Pai-chang."[10] The teacher can see that Shen-tsan has undergone a significant transformation, and the evidence is to be found precisely in what he says and how he says it. Presupposed in the story, and in numerous other stories, is that ordinary discourse issues from an ordinary mind. Out of the ordinary, unusual discourse flows from, and implies, an extra-ordinary state of mind.

[9] T. 47, p. 505b; Sasaki, *The Recorded Sayings of Lin-chi*, p. 54.   [10] T. 51, p. 268a.

"Awakening" and unconventional rhetoric are closely linked. The latter is minimally a sign of the former.

Rhetorical strangeness was thought to be both a natural consequence of awakening – as we see in the Shen-tsan story – and an enabling power for others in that it functioned to open the minds of hearers or readers by breaking the hold that ordinary discourse has on them. One can imagine the effect that the following story of an encounter between Huang Po and Chao-chou had on anyone who may have witnessed it: "One time Chao-chou went to visit Master Huang Po, who closed the door of his chamber when he saw him coming. Whereupon Chao-chou lit a torch in the Dharma Hall and cried out for help. Huang Po immediately opened the door and grabbed him, demanding, 'Speak! Speak!' Chao-chou answered, 'After the thief is gone, you draw your bow!'"[11] Encountering the unusual discourse of a Zen master like Huang Po was considered to be essential to authentic Zen practice, and thus to the possibility of awakening. It was thought to work on the one who encountered it, transforming the perspective from which language and world are experienced. This change was far from subtle. From the perspective of ordinary discursive custom, one might even question its sanity. Thus the *Transmission of the Lamp* says of Zen master P'u-hua that, after being enlightened by his teacher's "parting words," "he appeared to be mad and spoke without conventional restraint."[12] Discourse that strays from social norms reflects an abnormal state of mind, which in some cases, by some interpreters at least, made it difficult to distinguish the "awakened" from the "insane," since both are defined by freedom from norms and by unusual talk.

From what kinds of norm has the discourse of the Zen master been set free? Primarily, it seems, from the requirement that when we speak, we make conventional assertions about how things are in the world. A movement toward nonrepresentational discourse can be traced through the textual history of the Zen tradition. At a crucial point in the history of Zen (in the late ninth or tenth century perhaps), the genre of explanatory textual commentary begins to be replaced by other textual forms; the transcription of didactic sermon is replaced by a concern to record unusual sayings and actions. Commentary as such is not eliminated, however, just a certain style of it. When narrators or characters in Zen texts such as Kuei-shan and Yang-shan comment on a rhetorical segment from one of the great Zen masters before them, their comments

[11] T. 51, p. 276; Chang, *Original Teachings*, p. 165.   [12] T. 51, p. 280b.

display their own distinct style. As the new forms of commentary mature, they increasingly flaunt their nonrepresentational character, their otherness and strangeness. Comments no longer seek to explain. Arguments are not set forth to persuade the reader. Given this reversal of discursive function, propositional statements cease to be the primary mode of discourse.

Although fully intent on awakening the mind, it can easily be seen that, the later the Zen text, the less it will be inclined to formulate propositions about such matters as "enlightenment" and "emptiness." *The Essentials of Mind Transmission,* among the much larger body of literature about Huang Po, is thought to be the earliest extant text of this Hung-chou style of Zen. The most readily available criteria for sorting out which parts of the Huang Po literature are early and which later is the extent to which they engage in traditional explanatory commentary, and the extent to which, adopting colloquial language, they cease to make graspable assertions at all. For example, early segments of the Huang Po literature take a theory of "mind" as the primary matter of discussion. Later segments, composed perhaps decades and centuries after the life of Huang Po Hsi-yun, never discuss "mind." They narrate stories about the strange and wonderful rhetoric of Huang Po. Although no less concerned about the "awakening of mind," editors and writers cease to imagine Huang Po as having ever proposed true statements about the "matter of Zen." "Reference" becomes more and more oblique, hinting, teasing, denying, challenging, but rarely explaining or stating the facts. Increasingly, the language of these texts embodies the "ungraspability" of the matters about which they speak.

Two basic features place this discursive practice in contrast to other well-developed rhetorical traditions. The early Chinese Buddhist tradition, and the Confucian tradition, were primarily oriented toward persuasion. In the European tradition, in fact, rhetoric itself is defined and constituted as the "art of persuasive communication."[13] By contrast, we have seen that the particular way in which Buddhist principles come to be manifest in medieval Zen practice renders persuasion, by rational or emotive means, irrelevant to their concerns.[14] If "belief" as such has

---

[13] Vickers, *In Defense of Rhetoric,* pp. 1, 318.

[14] It is important to recognize that this lack of emphasis on persuasion would not be true of early Zen texts, which express a very different position within Chinese culture. These texts are ardently "apologetic," and argue hard for the legitimacy of the lineage they represent. Texts of the Sung period, by contrast, presuppose an established and prestigious position in Chinese culture, the work of persuasion having been accomplished already.

been decentered, or placed in the background as a presupposition, then so has persuasive discourse.[15] This first point of contrast leads to a second. Where persuasion is the goal, discourse will seek to conform to the conventions of the addressee. Hence, the western tradition of rhetoric had maintained that "'the . . . cardinal sin' of oratory is to depart from the language of everyday life, and the usage approved by the sense of community."[16] Eloquence, it seems, must be deeply grounded in common sense and conventional discourse. The contrast here, of course, is that eloquence in Zen was defined precisely by just such a departure from the conventions of both natural and scholarly discourse. Without its unconventionality, discourse would not be recognizably "Zen" in character. Recognizably "Zen" or not, we can see from the context of these texts that the strangeness of Zen rhetoric was no less puzzling even when expected. Thus, like us, the Governor Lu Hsuan, an ardent Buddhist, was nonetheless baffled by Nan-ch'uan's "explanation" of Seng-chao's "strangeness":

Governor Lu Hsuan spoke to the Master Nan-Ch'uan, saying, "Seng-chao is very strange indeed. He maintains that all things share the same root and that right and wrong are mutually identified." The Master pointed to the peony blossoms in the courtyard and said, "Governor! When people of the present day see these blossoms, it is as if they saw them in a dream." The Governor could not understand what he was saying.[17]

The fact that the "Governor could not understand" is an important part of the story. Had he understood, the depth of Nan-ch'uan's awakening might have been placed in doubt. Lacking strangeness and adhering to the conventions of common sense, how could it be enlightened discourse? How could it display an order of awareness beyond the ordinary?

This rejection of the ordinary, however, does not place Zen discourse in the realm of the exalted or sublime. No "heights" are sought or

---

[15] Although persuasive discourse is not featured in this Zen literature, it could not have been altogether absent from the monastic setting from which those texts derived. The everyday business of Zen monasteries would have required "normal" representational and persuasive discourse. Disagreement about such daily matters as, for example, how much rice to store or whether to postpone a festival due to unusual circumstances would, no doubt, have called for persuasive arguments. Anyone making an assertion on such matters would have been expected to produce good reasons. What was extraordinary about this monastic context, however, was that, given the overarching monastic focus on "awakening," the rhetoric of strangeness could break out at any time, even in the midst of everyday business as we saw when Huang Po and Lin-chi were out on the labor detail. Classic texts narrate numerous occasions on which normal and strange discourse appear together in juxtaposition. Without the added dimension of unusual rhetoric, however, these episodes would have never made their way into Zen literature.

[16] Vickers, *In Defense of Rhetoric*, p. 21.   [17] T. 51, p. 257; Chang, *Original Teachings*, p. 160.

reached. Instead, words are to penetrate directly into the "marrow" of the ordinary, to borrow Bodhidharma's Zen metaphor. In describing Huang Po, for example, P'ei-hsiu and his monastic editors make a point of conjoining metaphors of plainness and simplicity with others that connote "otherness" and difference. Describing the bearing of Huang Po, the text says: "His words were plain, his pattern direct; his way was precipitous, his practice, solitary."[18] To write that his words were simple means, in this context, that the master Huang Po had set aside the formal and complex diction of Buddhist philosophical prose in preference for the language of everyday life.[19] Zen masters characteristically rejected an "otherworldly" understanding of their practice, preferring instead to experience the "Way" in the midst of everyday life. But by setting academic prose aside and adopting the vocabulary of contemporary slang, they still did not speak "normally." Instead, they twisted the slang of the time out of its particular representational hold. They spoke the common language of the moment in uncommon ways in order to undermine the norms and grounds embodied in it.

This unconventional element so essential to Zen rhetoric can be overstressed, however. Language solidifies even critical communities into new sets of norms; it re-establishes new paradigms on the ruins of the overthrown. We get a glimpse of the development of Zen rhetorical conventions in the off-hand remarks of a monk who, in response to the Zen master's refusal to give explanations, says in exasperation: "All Zen masters speak like this."[20] Even the minimal characterization of "freedom from norms" can constitute a norm and a repeated pattern. One can only be free from linguistic norms in some particular way and with some characteristic style. Gradually, the distinction could be made between specific styles of rhetorical "freedom," all under the overarching "Zen" rubric. These somewhat distinct styles of speaking and teaching came to be described in terms of Chinese lineage or genealogy as "family styles" (*chia fu*). The "children" or monastic novices raised and trained to speak the language of Zen each bore the imprint of their particular family tree. Freedom is not chaos; it must have its own order and form to be recognizable *as* freedom. Far from undoing the Zen claim to freedom from convention, however, the institutionalization of the "unusual" makes this

---

[18] T. 51, p. 379c.
[19] Yanagida Seizan develops this theme of the simplicity and concreteness of Huang Po's Zen in his comprehensive essay on the *Ch'uan-hsin Fa-yao*, in Iriya, *Denshin Hoyo*, p. 169.
[20] T. 51, pp. 246c – 247a.

particular form of freedom broadly possible, and, for that reason, all the more interesting.

THE RHETORIC OF DIRECT POINTING

One day Pai-chang asked Huang Po, "Where have you been?" The answer was that he had been at the foot of the Ta-hsiung Mountain picking mushrooms. Pai-chang continued, "Have you seen any tigers?" Huang Po immediately roared like a tiger. Pai-chang picked up an ax as if to chop the tiger. Huang Po suddenly slapped Pai-chang's face. Pai-chang laughed heartily, and then returned to his temple and said to the assembly, "At the foot of the mountain there is a tiger. You people should watch out. I have already been bitten today."[21]

Although this conversation appears to be about something quite other than what it manifestly says, Huang Po enters the dialogue with two acts of "direct pointing:" a tiger's roar and a slap to the face of his teacher, Pai-chang. These and other nonlinguistic signs became a hallmark of the "rhetoric" of Huang Po. Even though it never replaced the language of spoken discourse in the teaching of Huang Po, the alternative rhetoric of "direct pointing" (*chih-chih*)[22] did, in fact, become an important element of his teaching method as represented in later texts. Fluency in the use of these non-verbal signs, from ritual comportment to "shouting and hitting," was essential to participation in the monastic community. They amounted to a separate language of gesture which ranged from the relatively simple – ritual being the first area of socialization for novices – to complex spontaneous signs decipherable only by the most "awakened." Consider the following example from *The Transmission of the Lamp*:

The master Hsiang-yen asked a traveling monk where he had come from. He replied that he had come from the monastery on Mount Kuei. The master asked: What sorts of things has the master Kuei-shan been saying lately? The monk replied that someone had asked him what it meant that the patriarch of Zen had come from the West, in response to which the master Kuei-shan had simply held up his *fu-tzu* (a whisk symbolic of the station of Zen master or abbot). Hsiang-yen then asked what Kuei-shan's disciples had understood by this gesture. He said it meant that mind is awakened through the concrete; reality is revealed within situations. Hsiang-yen said: Not bad in some sense but why are they so intent on theory? The monk asked him how he would have explained the gesture. The master held up his *fu-tzu*.[23]

---

[21] T. 51, p. 266; Chang, *Original Teachings*, p. 103.
[22] Earlier traces of this practice can be found in the pedagogical technique of "pointing at things and asking the meaning." See McRae, *The Northern School*, p. 93.
[23] T. 51, p. 284bc; adapted from Chang, *Original Teachings*, p. 223.

The language of this narrative points, at its climax, not to the words of the master but rather, to his gesture, which, in turn, is meant to point "directly" to the "great matter" of Zen. As with other signs, this act of "direct pointing" is necessary because that to which it points is not manifest otherwise, in this case not even available within the boundaries of conventional experience. The master's act of "direct pointing" duplicates Kuei-shan's initial effort to direct the monk to a kind of experience that can only be experienced in "awakening." In this story the act of holding up the *fu- tzu* is taken to "speak" more directly toward this referent than any conventional speaking could – it is meant to evoke that to which it refers.

Several more examples of non-verbal answers to the same "*koan-style*" question help show the character of the rhetoric of "direct pointing": "A monk asked: 'What is the meaning of Bodhidharma coming from the West?' The master came down from his elevated lecture seat and stood beside it. The monk asked: 'Is that your answer?'"[24] On the spot it might have been hard to know, but, in asking, the monk at least takes this as a possibility. Once the story becomes a written text, however, the problem is solved. If the coming down is recorded in response to the question, it must have been significant – a sign. To the question, "Is that your answer?" the master replies "I haven't said a word." But he has made a sign. The monk's onerous task, and ours as readers, is to determine – a sign of what? What kind of sign? The unnerving realization in this case, however, is that if we have asked the question we can be assured that we have already irredeemably missed the "point" of the act. "Direct pointing" is a rhetorical act that either communicates immediately or "directly" without reflection, or not at all, leaving the recipient dumbfounded and out of place: "A monk asked: 'Setting aside what the sutras say, what is the message of the patriarch who came from the West?' The master stood up with his stick, turned his body around one time, lifted one leg up, and then demanded an understanding-laden response. [The narrator then reports that] the monk could not reply, in response to which, the master hit him."[25] The monk knew these contorted gestures meant something, but what? No doubt some pointing is so direct that the point is missed altogether. What might go unnoticed in this story, however, is that, having missed the first sign, the monk gets a second chance. The act of hitting is not simply a form of punishment or chastisement for the dim-witted. It too

[24] T. 51, p. 277c; Chang, *Original Teachings*, p. 170.   [25] T. 51, p. 253c.

can be a direct act of signification, concluding, as many stories indicate, in an event of awakening, not just to the specific point of the narrative, but to the point of existence itself – awakening.

This point is made directly for those of us of "mediocre" understanding in the following story of Huang Po: "A monk asked, 'What is the meaning of Bodhidharma coming from the West?' The Master immediately struck him." Then, for those of us who might miss the significance of this, the narrator adds: "The teachings of Huang Po embodied the highest vision, so those who were mediocre failed to understand him."[26] The story of Lin-chi's enlightenment shows that he misunderstood the sense of these signs from Huang Po too, at least initially. Only when another Zen master interprets Huang Po's "blows" does Lin-chi come to "awakening."[27] Huang Po is represented in later texts as having taken enormous risks in his effort to enlighten Emperor T'ai Chung by slapping him. The Emperor's remarks in response question the directness of Huang Po's pointing. Valorizing this blunt and startling rhetoric, however, the text leaves the Zen master undeterred, even at the risk of appearing to undermine political authority.[28]

By calling this practice a rhetoric of "direct pointing," we draw upon a Zen phrase which intends to show how actions, like spoken words, can become events of signification. But surely gestured signals differ from verbal signs. How? One could characterize the difference by means of a simple example. If you ask "Where is the door?" I can respond by saying: "To your left near the fireplace," or, saying nothing, by directing a pointed finger in the appropriate direction. In the first instance, you must decipher the verbal message and follow its directions. In the second, little or no "deciphering" is required (if you have a history of acquaintance with this particular sign). The sign directs you immediately and does not seem to call for interpretation or reflection. Obviously, however, the simplicity of this example hides the complexity of "direct pointing" in Zen, where the referent of the sign, the "great matter," is neither visible nor readily available to ordinary experience. If, like some Buddhists, we conceive of this referent as "emptiness," or the open space of awakening, then no ordinary act of pointing will bring us into its presence. Like other forms of Zen rhetoric, direct pointing will inevitably be strange, as unconventional as its referent, which is not an object at all. It was in fact just because of the "depth" and invisibility of its referent that

[26] T. 51, p. 266; Chang, *Original Teachings*, pp. 105–106.
[27] T. 47, p. 504c; Sasaki, *The Recorded Sayings of Lin-chi*, pp. 50–52.
[28] Blofeld, *Huang Po*, pp. 95–96.

the use of non-verbal signs was considered to be an effective "device." Nevertheless, it is worth noting that all signs, even non-verbal ones, function as mediators. "Pointing" is, by definition, indirection. It may be more direct than other signs, but as long as the referent comes to experience by way of the pointing, mediation has occurred. This is true even when, as in Zen, what is mediated is the experience of "immediacy."

THE RHETORIC OF SILENCE

The practice of silence had a longstanding and distinguished role to play in Buddhism, especially in the Zen tradition for which meditative practices were important. Stories about the practice of silence among the great paradigmatic figures of the Zen tradition – the Buddha, Mahakasyapa, Vimalakirti, Bodhidharma – were extremely influential. So important was the absence of discourse in Zen that silence soon became a sign or "saying" on its own. It began to signify something important. Many Zen stories of "encounter dialogue" describe how a particular meeting between two Zen masters reaches its climax in an expression of silence. Other narratives explicitly figure silence as an understandable response or answer to a question. Huang Po's disciples knew very well that when the master chose to be silent rather than lecture, that *was* his teaching. We can see how widely this was understood in the Zen tradition by noting its occurrences and the interpretations given to them. Zen master Hsueh-feng's biography, for example, ends an episode by saying: "He answered merely by sitting silently in his seat."[29] Indeed, nothing could be more essential to the depth of awakening than to have understood and appropriated the sense of silence.

In many narratives, silence is explicitly conjoined with speech as parallel forms of signification. Huang Po takes this point so far in, fact, that he surprises a monk who has asked about Vimalakirti's silence by saying that "Speech and silence are one. There is no distinction between them!"[30] Silence in these texts is more than the absence of discourse. It fits into communicative interaction by continuing the dialogue and, very often, bringing it to fruition in awakened disclosure. As the complementary "other" to speech, its message is taken to complete the direction and intent of other rhetorical practices in Zen. Not all silence has significance, however. The master remarked: "Unless you understand profoundly, it is no use thinking that you can just keep quiet!"[31] In this

---

[29] T. 51, p. 327c; see Chang, *Original Teachings*, p. 280.   [30] Blofeld, *Huang Po*, p. 121.
[31] T. 51, p. 277b; Chang, *Original Teachings*, p. 169.

instance, silence has significance only insofar as it displays the monk's confusion. Only certain kinds or qualities of silence are profound enough to join in a conversation that satisfies the requirements of Zen rhetoric. Given the interpretive "strangeness" of Zen dialogue, and the opaque character of silence, it isn't always easy to tell when silence is a sign of wisdom and when it is a sign of failure. In one episode, Huang Po's silence is left hanging, far too ambiguous for the editors not to intervene. So they bring in two later Zen masters to pass judgment: "At this, our Master remained silent. Later, Wei Shan mentioned the incident to Yang Shan, enquiring if our Master's silence betokened defeat. 'Oh no!' answered Yang. 'Surely you know that Huang Po has a tiger's cunning.' 'Indeed, there is no limit to your profundity,' exclaimed the other."[32] Huang Po gets the benefit of the doubt here, because he is Huang Po and, after all, this is his text. It is clear, however, that silence, like any other sign, is open to variant interpretation. To different interpreters, it may "betoken" quite different meanings.

It is interesting to note, however, that the dialogues which climax in silence never really end there. The language of silence always seems to require or to provoke explication – translation, interpretation, and then commentary always seem to follow it. Take, for example, the renowned story of Bodhidharma's final transmission to his best disciples.[33] Four students are asked to say what they had attained through Bodhidharma's Zen teachings. The first three tell him, albeit cryptically. The fourth, Hui-k'o, bows and remains silent, an act fraught with historical profundity. The narrative, however, doesn't just end there with the bow of silence. Although silence is the most enlightened response of the group, its point needs pointing out. Bodhidharma breaks the silence by interjecting his interpretation and judgment. Hui-k'o's silence is the winner, but only after verbal language intervenes, abolishing the silence, in order to announce its victory and, having already done so, to solicit the occasion for didactic purposes. The authors of Bodhidharma's text knew better than to be silent about silence. Silence is indeed profound, but only when brought to the foreground and supported by a discourse that articulates its profundity. Lacking that, silence isn't much of anything. No one attends to it. Zen rhetoric has shaped both the doctrine and the experience of silence, and has transformed them into a sign. Silence is clearly meaningful, but only when it stands in the midst of other forms of Zen rhetoric.

[32] Blofeld, *Huang Po*, p. 98.   [33] T. 51, p. 219bc.

In contrast to most modern interpretations, silence in Zen texts is rarely figured as quietude or acquiescence. On the contrary, like other forms of Zen rhetoric, silence is often presented as disquieting and unnerving. Silence is considered to have the critical power to cut through all "form" and to disrupt all talk that derives from conventional awareness. Only the awakened, who have entered into the "emptiness" and "selflessness" of silence, can "hear" it without fear and loss of bearing.

THE RHETORIC OF DISRUPTION

Lin-chi went to Huang Po, the head of the temple, to ask about the cardinal principle of Buddhism. Before he had finished speaking Huang Po hit him . . . I don't understand, said Lin-chi.[34]

Lin-chi could not figure out what to make of Huang Po's response to his important question. It interrupted, indeed disrupted, his inquiry "[b]efore he had finished speaking." All he knew was that this Zen master was "dangerous" to be around. After having introduced the biography of Huang Po's head monk, Mu-chou Tao-tsung, by saying how "unusual" he was, his discursive practice is described in words that had become standard in the text: "His rhetoric was precipitous and dangerous; it did not follow convention" (literally: "did not follow the rut").[35] In what sense was the rhetoric of Mount Huang Po dangerous? Critically and powerfully, this rhetoric called into question, and thus "endangered," the conventional state of mind implied and supported by normal, representational discourse. It is imagined as undercutting and disrupting their interlocutor's ingrained posture as a grasping subject. These words are dangerous and unnerving in that they seem not to share the common vision of how things are set into place: "One day, Huang Po entered the Dharma Hall where all of the monks had humbly gathered. The Master said, 'All of you! What are you seeking?' Thereupon he took a staff and scattered them, and then said: 'You are all idiots! Seeking the Truth through traveling as you do now will only make others ridicule you'"[36] Gathered there piously to receive the *dharma*, Huang Po gives them what they least expect – disruption of the *dharma*. The rhetoric of disruption cuts through ordinary experience, and thus also ordinary linguistic forms. It works toward evoking an experience of disorientation. In order to catch a glimpse of where you are, dislocation is

---

[34] T. 47, p. 504c; Sasaki, *The Recorded Sayings of Lin-chi*, p. 50.   [35] T. 51, p. 291a.
[36] T. 51, p. 266; Chang, *Original Teachings*, p. 104.

essential. When asked about Zen language, master Tzu-man said: "It disturbs heaven; it shakes the earth."[37] Zen rhetoric is designed to disorient one's relation to everything. "The master Yang-shan said: 'Aren't you able to understand that there isn't a single doctrine that is adequate?'" The narrator then adds: "Later when this comment was reported to Kuei-shan, he remarked: 'One word from Yang-shan throws everyone into doubt.'"[38] Here language functions not to answer questions and to settle things, but rather to unsettle and open them to alternate viewing. Here is a religious discourse that, at least in this one significant way, stimulates doubt rather than belief.

How does it do so? First, the renowned Zen master, whose "ethos" had captured the attention of the entire culture, speaks in ways that simply do not fit conventional patterns. This unusual discourse forces one to ask about, and perhaps to seek for, the different kind of placement in the world that might have given rise to this kind of rhetoric, an alternative position from which it might make sense to say such things. Having shifted discursive gears, the whole Zen community seems to be based on just such a re-placement, one that signals a fundamental shift in practice and comportment. Upon entering this discursive world, most unsettling is the realization that, not only does it not make sense, but it won't make sense as long as I remain who I am, that is, a subject self supported by particular conventions of placement in the world. The language of Zen throws into question the self/world relation that supports the reader's position as one who grasps and acts on the world. The text acts to evoke a disorientation, and then reorientation, of the reader's subjectivity. This is clearly the "otherness" of Zen language and Zen experience. To be in accord with this language, one must allow it to transport the self out of the posture of subjectivity – out of the ordinary and into an open space where one's prior socialization is rendered dysfunctional. Beyond disruption, this is truly frightening, and Huang Po does not hesitate to tell us so. His text says, in fact, that the experience is somewhat like being suspended over an infinite void, groundless, with nothing to hold on to.[39]

In order to evoke this experience of dislocation and groundlessness, Zen discourse, including the rhetorics of strangeness, direct pointing, and silence, brought intense pressure to bear on conventional subjectivity. The demand for immediate, prereflective response under the glare of the Zen master was one form this pressure took. The basic pattern

[37] T. 51, p. 249b.   [38] T. 51, p. 283b; see Chang, *Original Teachings*, p. 215.   [39] T. 48, p. 382a.

was to have the master pose an inescapable verbal quandary, and then demand response. When P'ei-hsiu requested an audience with Huang Po and began by setting the context for his question, "the master screamed, 'P'ei-hsiu!' 'Sir,' I answered respectfully. 'Where are you?' . . . no reply was possible to such a question."[40] Suddenly out of context, P'ei-hsiu was lost. Or, to take another example: "The master said: 'When you encounter someone who embodies the Way, you should respond neither in words nor in silence. Now, what will your response be?'"[41] Unable to respond out of conventional speech and behavioral patterns, on the spot the practitioner must push through "ordinary mind" to someplace else, wherever that might be, with all the urgency and seriousness of his position in the monastic community. The monk knows all too well that an appropriate response will not emerge from an ordinary posture. The self who can respond is not the conventional subject, which has been forcefully thrown into question by all forms of Zen rhetoric.

In many classical Zen narratives, disruption and disorientation are hastened through the use of negative language, which disrupts conventional practices and beliefs. Given continual overturning, practitioners of Zen, including readers, are hard pressed to know what to believe. Monks come to the monastery, and we to our texts, believing and knowing a great deal about Zen, not to mention who we are and what we are doing. But the rhetoric of Zen begins to subvert those beliefs and that knowledge from the first moment of exposure. Zen discourse is disruptive, of both itself and its reader, by overturning and undercutting any effort to hold on to it as correct vision or true belief. The *Recorded Sayings of Lin-chi*, for example, ruthlessly breaks out of the reader's grasp when it has the master say: "Followers of the Way, don't believe what I say. Why? Assertions have no foundations. They're just pictures temporarily drawn in the empty sky . . ."[42] Or, "Followers of the Way, don't take the Buddha to be ultimate. As I see it, he is just like a privy hole."[43] If, having come to the great master Lin-chi for wisdom, you cannot believe what he says, nor, groping for something to hold on to, even that the Buddha is ultimate, then what can you believe?

By the time you have read your way through very much Zen literature, few options haven't been explicitly overturned: "Kuei-shan: 'Of the 40 scrolls in the *Nirvana Sutra*, how much is from the Buddha and how

[40] T. 48, p. 387b; Blofeld, *Huang Po*, pp. 100–101.
[41] T. 51, p. 327b; see Chang, *Original Teachings*, p. 277.
[42] T. 47, p. 502c; adapted from Sasaki, *The Recorded Sayings of Lin-chi*, p. 37.
[43] T. 47, p. 502c; Sasaki, *The Recorded Sayings of Lin-chi*, p. 37.

much is the discourse of devils?' Yang-shan: 'It's all devil-talk.' Kuei-shan replied: 'From now on, there won't be anyone who can correct your views.'"[44] When the subjectivity of "viewing" has itself been dislodged, what views remain to be corrected? To say with Huang Po that "there are no principles of the way that can be spoken"[45] is to enunciate a fundamental principle of the way of Zen – that only by being cast out of the security of knowledge and conventional belief will one awaken to the open space of illumination.

Moreover, this open or empty space is not to become a new object of knowledge. We will be unable to determine conceptually what it is since it becomes manifest precisely in the emptiness that opens up when the practitioner is dislodged from the position of the subject who "represents" and "determines." The experience eludes objective representation by overturning the foundations from which representation proceeds. For this reason it seems that the rhetorical practice of dislodging and undercutting is aimed at evoking a corresponding response, that of "release" and "letting go." It would be aimed at replacing one foundation or set of beliefs, not by another, but rather by an experience of groundlessness, emptiness, or openness. I take this to be the impact of the saying thought to have awakened Zen master Fa-yen: the posture of "'not knowing' most closely approaches the truth."[46] This line makes it abundantly clear that "the truth" is not a matter of correct belief, but rather something that is manifest in the absence of grasping. "Knowing" is here figured as an inauthentic form of self-securing and grasping. It represents human "desire" and "craving" more than it does the "openness of things." The rhetoric of disruption intends to overturn this "posture" in the experience of "awakening" from it.

THE DISCOURSE OF AWAKENING

The rationale for this strange and disruptive dimension of Zen rhetoric is the thought that language can enable an awakening from subjective grasping and craving. Although, drawing on Buddhist metaphor, language is at the heart of human "illness," it is also the "cure." Although language "lulled us to sleep" in the first place, it can also wake us up. It is true that some Buddhists, including Zen Buddhists, focusing on the ways in which language can block and obstruct human freedom and

---

[44] T. 51, p. 265a; see Chang, *Original Teachings*, p. 205.
[45] T. 48, p. 383b; see Iriya, *Denshin Hoyo*, p. 76, note 3, for a discussion of variant readings and similar passages. [46] T. 51, p. 398b; Chang, *Original Teachings*, p. 239.

awakening, sought an alternative to it in pre-linguistic immediacy, the transcendence of language. Others, however, set off in the other direction. They sought instead some form of non-objectifying language through which the experience of immediacy might be mediated.[47] They sought a transformed rhetoric of "live words" and "turning words" through which awakening might be evoked. This understanding of Zen rhetoric best accounts for the focus on language in Zen texts. It also best explains why enlightenment narratives in classic Zen texts overwhelmingly feature discursive, rhetorical backdrops to the experience of awakening. When, "at these words", Lin-chi attained great enlightenment under Huang Po, what had changed most was his way of speaking. Once awakened, Lin-chi was anything but silent. His speech is represented in the texts as overpowering, penetrating, and always striking directly to the heart of the matter. So favorably impressed with Lin-chi's rhetoric was Huang Po that he predicted Lin-chi would "sit upon the tongue of every person on earth."[48] Lin-chi's discursive practice is imagined as being so powerful in its critical thrust that virtually everyone "falters" (*i-i*) before it. Overwhelmed by the way in which Lin-chi cuts through convention, interlocutors are left disoriented, unable to respond with insight.[49] The *Lin-chi lu*, which gathers story after story exemplifying this feature of Lin-chi's discourse, asserts very clearly that language and the power of awakening are deeply interfused.

There is an important connection between the image of the Zen master as unhesitating and unflinching and the central Buddhist realization of the emptiness or groundlessness of all things. The Zen master is the one who no longer seeks solid ground, who realizes that all things and situations are supported, not by firm ground and solid self-nature, but rather by shifting and contingent relations. Having passed through this experience of the void at the heart of everything, the master no longer fears change and relativity. The Zen master is undaunted by the negativity in every situation and every conversation. He no longer needs

---

[47] On the idea of language as the sphere of immediacy, I am influenced by Scharlemann, *Inscriptions and Reflections*.

[48] T. 47, p. 505c; adapted from Sasaki, *The Recorded Sayings of Lin-chi*, p. 56.

[49] It is interesting that, when these episodes become written text, faltering responses and the failure to respond at all are included in the text as a way to show the power of Zen rhetoric. For the reader, as for observers and participants in "encounter dialogue," these moments of tension and failure are points of possibility where breakthrough could occur. In *The Northern School*, John McRae reflects on structural and historical connections between classical encounter dialogue narrative and the early Zen rhetorical practice of "pointing at things and asking the meaning" (*chih-shih wen-I*), in which only the master's discourse is recorded and not the lesser interlocutor's response (pp. 93–95).

to hold his ground in dialogue, and therefore does not falter when all grounds give way. What he says is not his own anyway; he has no pre-ordained intentions with respect to what ought to occur in the encounter. Indeed, on Buddhist terms, he has no self – his role in the dialogue is to reflect in a selfless way whatever is manifest or can become manifest in the moment.

Many of the passages that we have examined in this chapter are examples of what have come to be called "encounter dialogue" narratives, stories giving account of what transpires when two or more Zen masters encounter one another. These dialogues were linguistic events that took on such importance in the tradition that they became primary points of focus for Zen practice. Fluency in dialogical encounter was taken to be demonstrative of depth of enlightenment. Perhaps the most important characteristic of true encounter between masters was that the exchange would pass back and forth between the two without reflection and hesitation. Indeed, "immediacy" and "directness" are the highest forms of praise given to the discursive practice of a Zen master. The *Transmission of the Lamp* says of Zen master P'ang-yun, for example, that "he was noted for his eloquence and his quick responses."[50] The text later claims that when he encountered other Zen Buddhists, "he responded to them direct and spontaneous, even as an echo, and his replies were beyond measurement and rules."[51]

The "echo" metaphor is important. P'ang-yun's response was as quick and as natural as an echo. Like an echo, P'ang-yun did not need to ponder what was said or done in order to respond. Response simply bounced back, prereflectively. Not being able to respond, what the texts call "faltering" (*i-i*), signals a failure of openness and insight. Faltering, one has been caught in the act of planning ahead, unable to remain in the present moment of discourse. Unfaltering, one follows what appears as it appears, which requires no pre-established intentions.

What gets said, then, in any true occurrence of "encounter dialogue," is less dependent on the speakers than it is on the situation at hand, which is construed as including the speakers. Zen discourse in its ideal form is fully situational and occasional. What is said in any given situation corresponds to the unique and particular demands of that situation. Thus, Zen language is explicitly related to time, place, and circumstance. It fits into a context of interconnections and is not imposed upon it. This

---

[50] T. 51, p. 263b; Chang, *Original Teachings*, p. 175.
[51] T. 51, p. 263c; Chang, *Original Teachings*, p. 176.

is simply to say that the spontaneity of Zen rhetoric is, ideally, a "responsiveness." It "co-responds" with what is going on at the moment.

This is not to say, however, that rhetorical training was not important in Zen. On the contrary, to enter a Zen monastery meant submitting your mind to rigorous reshaping through the language of Zen. Having trained in this way, improvisation is possible – not before. One can speak the language of Zen freely only after having learned it by submitting oneself to its purposes. Training provides the background out of which free moves can be performed. On these bases, Huang Po and Lin-chi ridicule memorization and discursive pre-planning. When a monk has faltered in Zen dialogue, it is common for the master to apply more pressure, saying, for example, "This guy just memorizes words."[52] When one's words emerge from the stockroom of memory, they are suspected of not being called for by the situation itself. In such cases, what enters discourse is more self than situation.

The "echo" metaphor for discourse carries this theme further. P'ang-yun's responses were described as "direct and spontaneous, even as an echo."[53] Following this image, one might say that P'ang is no more the source of his responses than the walls of the canyon or cave are the source of the echo's sound. He doesn't plan to say what he says. What he says is a function of contextual positioning, not of preordained intention.

This may be what Zen texts mean by the speaking of "non-dual words" (*pu-erh chih yen*),[54] words that bespeak the identity or congruence of self and situation. Dual or divided words derive from and point back to the prior intentions of the speaker. Although they may speak about the situation, they imply and implicate the desires of the self more than the shape of the larger context. To speak "non-dual words" requires one to surrender control, to allow the matter and the direction of discourse to go their own way, and to open oneself to the work of overturning and awakening.

The focal word or phrase that seemed to embody this transformative power in an "encounter dialogue" came to be called a "turning word" (*ch'uan-yu*),[55] the word upon which the point of the encounter "turns" and the word holding the power to turn the mind of participants, audience, or reader. "Turning words" were not simply a set of particularly powerful or efficacious symbols. No list of them could be produced. All

---

[52] T. 51, p. 291b. [53] T. 51, p. 263c; Chang, *Original Teachings*, p. 176.
[54] T. 51, p. 399b. [55] T. 47, p. 503a; Sasaki, *The Recorded Sayings of Lin-chi*, p. 40.

words gained their power from the situation in which they were spoken, heard, or read. Words do not possess this power on their own; they are, according to Buddhist theory, "empty" of inherent significance. Instead, "turning words" are words that fit into a context in such a way that they open that context to view in some revealing way. They do so by virtue of their fit with the context and not on account of their own inherent power. The *Lin-chi lu* calls this "speaking a word apropos of the moment."[56] The task of interlocutors is not so much to produce the turning word intentionally as it is to prepare for its appearance in the midst of dialogue. "Preparation" here is only a renunciation of subjective intention and an opening out from the self such that, when a "turning word" does appear, it will be able to do its work of awakening.

Words like these, which were particularly effective in the process of overturning and opening the mind, were called "live words" (*huo-chu*).[57] Explanatory, analytical words were thought to be "dead" (*ssu-chu*) in this respect: they evoked the need for more explanation but not insight, not an awakening from the deadening spell of everyday talk. Live words, like certain actions, could be "direct pointers." Yet what they pointed to was less a meaning than an opening or fissure in the network of meanings. Discursive forms of meditation (including *koan* practice) required a practitioner to abide with a single word or phrase in so unnaturally focused a way that it would open up out of its common-sense relation with all words and meanings and into an awareness that was described as an awakening from the ordinary hold that language has on the mind. Thus released, one would see things in unusual ways and, at the same time, say "unusual things."

[56] T. 47, p. 506b; Sasaki, *The Recorded Sayings of Lin-chi*, p. 60.
[57] T. 51, p. 389; Chang, *Original Teachings*, p. 296. See also Buswell, "The 'Short-cut' Approach to *K'an-Hua* Meditation," pp. 321–377.

CHAPTER 6

HISTORY: the genealogy of mind

Long ago, Zen master Pai-chang, who was Huang Po's teacher, was scolded by his teacher Ma-tsu with such a loud voice that it almost shattered his eardrums. Huang Po heard this story from Pai-chang and was enlightened. This is what we mean by saying the old masters are still living.

Dogen[1]

A truly historical thinking must also think its own historicity.

H. G. Gadamer[2]

Although John Blofeld assumed that, since Huang Po spoke "from a direct perception of truth" he would therefore take no interest in history, the texts he translated show just the opposite. Huang Po lived in an era in which a new history was beginning to be composed, the history of the "Zen school," a new "school" of Chinese Buddhism which was being created precisely in this act of writing.[3] The framework for this new history was the "transmission of mind," which consisted of stories about how "enlightened mind" had been transmitted from the Buddhas down through "Patriarchs" to the present. These historical narratives function in the texts to bring the Zen issues of "mind" and "enlightenment" to the fore, to make them intelligible and attractive. These stories provide rationale for the whole monastic enterprise and feature the particular style of practice structured into Hung-chou Zen monasteries.

These "Zen" stories continued to develop and to "circulate" throughout China, becoming very influential over the next few centuries after Huang Po. As their influence grew, new authors and editors appeared within the Zen monastic world, interested in systematizing the narratives

[1] Dogen Zenji, *Shobogenzo*, trans. Kosen Nishiyarna (Tokyo: Nakayama Shobo, 1975), volume II, p. 142. [2] Gadamer, *Truth and Method*, p. 16.
[3] One of the earliest appearances of the phrase, "Zen school" (*Ch'an-tsung*) is to be found in Huang Po's *Essentials of Mind Transmission*.

by bringing the individual stories together into a holistic view of Buddhist and human history. Thus, the primary genre of Zen literature, the "Lamp Histories," is historical in its most basic orientation and structure. The most influential of these, partly because of its early appearance, was the *Transmission of the Lamp, Ching-te Era*. Published in 1004, this text absorbed and gathered what there was of the Huang Po literature up into itself. From this point on, for the most part, the Huang Po literature would only exist and circulate as a segment of this larger literature. Naturally, therefore, the legacy of Huang Po would henceforth be interpreted and understood from this more comprehensive historical perspective. From then on, Huang Po would be seen as a crucial link in a vastly larger project. This larger historical vision was already explicit in the Huang Po texts in a rudimentary form. The symbols of transmission and many of its most important stories were already there. In the *Transmission of the Lamp* and subsequent "Lamp Histories," however, we see its systematic outcome. Our inquiry here poses two basic questions: what is the conception of history into which the Huang Po texts have been absorbed, and how does this "historical consciousness" relate to the primary matter of Zen – "enlightened mind?"

The initial difficulty with the first of these two questions is that, although the voluminous *Transmission of the Lamp* text is thoroughly historical in character, no "theory" of history is explicit in the text, nor, for that matter, anywhere else in Zen literature. Nevertheless, the language and structure of the text show us in various ways the understanding of history that is presupposed in Zen transmission practices. The historical intention of this text can be gleaned from its title (*Ching-te ch'uan teng lu*): it consists of "records" (*lu*) of "transmission" (*ch'uan*) as seen from the perspective of a particular historical era – the Ching-te Imperial era within the Northern Sung dynasty. What was being transmitted – a lamp and its light (*teng*) – was the fundamental aim of the tradition, enlightenment or "awakening." The overall narrative structure of the text, therefore, is a story of the origins and dissemination of "enlightened mind" beginning with the ancient Buddhas and continuing through Indian and Chinese patriarchs up to current recipients of transmission.[4] Temporal, chronological structure – earliest to most recent – is maintained throughout the text: Huang Po follows the generation of his teacher, Pai-chang, and is succeeded by the generation of his students, such as Lin-chi, and so on. Within this overarching historical framework,

---

[4] For an elaboration on this historical structure, see McRae, *The Northern School*, p. 75.

the actual content of the text employed to tell the story of mind trans-mission is religious biography.

The historical, narrative structure of the text is, therefore, twofold: biographical histories, themselves individually temporalized in a narra-tive order moving from birth through death, are placed within the over-arching history of human enlightenment. The text's editors venture no reflections on sacred history as a whole – on its meaning, *telos*, or signif-icance. Aside from genealogical charts that serve as periodic tables of content, all interesting detail enters the narrative on the level of indi-vidual history. This detail takes basically two forms. First, we are pro-vided with essential biographical information at the beginning and then again at the end of each account. Typically we get an account of names, origins, early signs of brilliance, circumstances of ordination, and some account of the content of early monastic studies. At the end of biogra-phies we often find a transmission *gatha* or poem, an account of the Zen master's death, and its date, along with subsequent Imperial decrees concerning posthumous names, titles, and pagoda inscriptions.

Between these two extremities, however, is content even more per-tinent to the transmission of mind – that is, narratives recounting par-ticular events in the Zen master's life in which the power and efficacy of his "awakening" are clearly manifest. These occasions are most often rhetorical occasions, discursive events that in one way or another display the character of enlightened mind. These stories, more than anything else in classical Zen, were understood to demonstrate what it means to be awakened. What is important to recognize, however, is the way in which these enlightened events receive their full meaning and significance only when placed within the overarching context of Zen history. Enlightenment is not figured as an isolated and unrelated event, nor simply as an experience of eternity in the present moment. In each case enlightenment is a historical event located in a particular temporal, spatial context. The point here is simple: that the classical Zen interest in history is more central to their concerns than we have taken it to be, and that, beyond the Zen rhetoric of timelessness, we find historical contextualization to be central to their self-under-tand-ing.

In order to specify further the role that history plays in Zen, we turn to the key metaphors and symbols that place people and events into temporal relation. How are historical connections construed in this text? Primarily, it seems, through a complex set of metaphors drawn from the domain of family genealogy. Most basic to this symbolic order is that

Zen itself came to be understood as a *tsung*, a word evolving out of the ancient Chinese sense of ancestry.[5] In the most general and archaic sense *tsung* meant "ancestor," and came by extension to connote anything related to clan or family ancestry. It is clear that throughout the Sung and subsequent epochs, the term continued to carry deep pre-Buddhist religious connotations – ancestral spirits oversee and guide the clan. They are to be revered, followed, and honored; it was they who established the clan and made it what it is. In effect, the clan's identity is a gift of the ancestors; only through them can one understand what it is. Similarly, understanding Zen as a clan-like institution meant conceiving it in genealogical terms. Knowing what it meant to belong to the institution entailed knowing from whom it had been inherited, a historical knowledge transmitted and inculcated by means of narratives like *The Transmission of the Lamp.*

In effect, then, we can think of this text as analogous to a document of family history; it communicates a distinct Zen identity by means of significant family stories. Moreover, we see that family lineage and genealogy provide virtually all significant terms of relation within the Zen clan. Bodhidharma, the founding figure of the lineage, is called the "first ancestor" (*ch'u-tsu*), the patriarch of patriarchs.[6] Subsequent patriarchs are his "*dharma* heirs" (*fa-ssu*), each of whom can be located on distinct branches of the family tree. Relations among later Zen masters are also figured in genealogical terms, basic kinship titles such as "uncle," "nephew," and "cousin," providing the overall framework. Words related to "inheritance" provide the primary symbols for patriarchal succession – the transmission of Zen mind from one generation to the next.

The Transmission of the Lamp pictures the Zen master in constant search of an appropriate heir, someone who is seen as capable of being a "vessel" or "receptacle" of the *dharma*. The Chinese term here is *ch'i*: a sacred, ceremonial vessel used in ancient times to make ritual offerings to the ancestors. A *ch'i* is also a tool or instrument, something that exists for the sake of something else. In this case, the patriarchs exist for the sake of the *dharma* and for posterity. Like the ceremonial vessel, they receive, preserve, and transmit the substance of the sacred. *Dharma* transmission from one generation to the next is also figured as the impression made by

---

[5] For more on the concept of *tsung*, see Yanagida, *Shoki Zenshu Shisho no Kenkyu*; Foulk, The Ch'an School; and McRae, *The Northern School.*

[6] Yanagida traces the Zen history of the term "patriarch" in *Shoki Zenshu Shisho no Kenkyu.* See also Yampolsky, *The Platform Sutra*, pp. 1–23.

a "seal" or "stamp" (*yin*) upon the mind and character of the inheritor. The so-called "mind seal" is imprinted upon the next generation's practice and experience by virtue of long-standing co-practice under the guidance of the master. The Zen practice of issuing certificates of "inheritance" or "authorization" doubles this metaphor of the stamp through the use of an actual seal stamping a document certifying that the holder has in fact received the master's seal upon his mind.

Occasional passages in the text allude to a sense of "debt" that inheritance accrues. Being selected and trained as an heir imposes enormous obligation and responsibility – a debt to be repaid. This responsibility is figured as a form of filial reverence that a descendent owes to the family lineage. "Confession" of this debt is common in the text, where a newly selected successor announces his gratitude and subsequent obligation to others in the lineage. The master warns the recipient not to "neglect posterity," and that "inheriting the *dharma*" imposes an obligation to carry out the transmission as the ancestors had done. Being placed in a genealogy establishes relation not just to the past but to the future as well.[7] In order to feel this obligation to past and future generations, the inheritor must have a working understanding of the history of the lineage, not just knowing it but striving to embody it in act and discourse.

All of the genealogical terms that we see applied to patriarchal succession are applicable to the majority of practitioners who have not succeeded to the abbotship. They too stand in a concrete lineage location, they too inherit the *dharma* and pass it along to the next generation, primarily through the everyday teaching that socializes a new generation of monks. They are all *Ch'an-tzu*, "children of Zen," raised by the family elders and socialized into the lineage. As the offspring of a particular master, raised in this monastic household rather than some other, they all manifest a distinct "family spirit" (*chia-feng*), the particular style of Zen behavior and rhetoric characteristic of the lineage.[8] Given the way in which sense of identity in Zen was structured upon models and terms supplied by family life and lineage, it is not surprising to find that role models, socialization, and mimetic repetition were essential to the way in which Zen practice came to be understood. To practice Zen was to repeat the ancient, ancestral Buddha pattern, and in turn to have its stamp placed upon one's character and comportment.

---

[7] For interesting reflections on themes related to past, present, and future generations, see Ricoeur, *Time and Narrative*, volume III, pp. 109–116.

[8] Ricoeur elaborates on the relation between language and tradition in *Time and Narrative*, volume III, p. 221.9

One of the most important forms of this repetition was the repeated retelling, rereading, and rethinking of Zen narratives like those in the *Transmission of the Lamp*. By means of mental repetition, narrative shapes the participant's self-identity. "Narrative selfhood" here means that who the monk becomes, how he fits himself into the world, is to a great extent shaped by the stories into which he has been socialized. "I can only answer the question 'What am I to do?' if I can answer the prior question 'Of what story or stories do I find myself a part?'"[9] In the case of Zen, this would be to say that personal identity or self-understanding was communicated only partly by doctrines concerning the self, and much more by narratives, models, and precedents. Moreover, the doctrines themselves are integrally tied to the narratives and can be understood only in terms of particular exemplars described in narrative texts. As in other clans, the *Ch'an- tzu*, the "children of Zen," come to understand who they are and what they are doing through the process of hearing and acting out the stories of Zen. Much of this understanding was inculcated through rituals performed in the "ancestor hall" where ancestral tablets and other sacred objects of the lineage were displayed and celebrated.

Prior to the "practice of presence" are stories weaving the concept of "presence" into conscious understanding; prior to the practice of "meditation" are the narratives of meditation telling who did it, how, when, and to what effect. This realization helps us see that narrative, historical identity would have been an essential component of enlightened identity. What this means is that, although the Zen tradition did come to conceptualize and to represent the experience of "awakening" in vocabulary that expresses timelessness and an ahistorical ground, even more prominent in its representation are the genealogical, historical metaphors of relatedness that we have begun to describe here. Furthermore, the ahistorical concept of enlightenment comes to be situated under the overarching structure of genealogy such that belonging to the Zen clan becomes a background, stage-setting factor for the experience of enlightenment – a condition of its possibility. Since "awakening" was figured first and foremost as an "inheritance," the tradition naturally assumed that only well-socialized family members came into its possession. Thus enlightenment and historical understanding were integrally related.[10]

---

[9] MacIntyre, *After Virtue*, p. 216.
[10] Modern interpreters, under the influence of the language of "universality," have ignored this genealogical dimension of "Zen," preferring instead to read it as an excellent example of the transcendence of tradition and history.

What is intriguing about the *Transmission of the Lamp* as a historical document is the extent to which it has been structured as a montage of earlier traditions, a characteristic which reveals something of the historical consciousness presupposed in it. Editors of the text have essentially gathered together all of the legends, stories, and other texts related to the key figures in the lineage. Then through substantial editing, rewriting, and repositioning, they have organized a new text and, through it, a revised understanding of the tradition. Furthermore, while drawing heavily on prior texts, the editors have made no effort at attribution. Innumerable bits and pieces of other texts are woven together into a new one without citation, quotation, or other devices that might credit the appropriate sources. These rewoven texts fail to heed historical chronology (in *our* sense), hence "anachronism," a slip or failure in the chronological order of things, is a common characteristic of the texts. We find, for example, in the early chapters of *The Transmission of the Lamp*, the "ancient Buddhas" speaking in the Zen riddles of the Sung dynasty *koan* tradition, thus belying their antiquity. We find Bodhidharma presiding over a "Zen sect" that wouldn't even be born for several more centuries, and Pai-chang stipulating in the mid-T'ang rules and procedures for Zen monasteries that wouldn't have been feasible until the advent of post-T'ang culture.

Moreover, editors seem very little concerned about the accuracy or legitimacy of their sources. Epistemological concerns – how do we know that this story about Huang Po really did occur? – seem to be subordinate interests at best. From our modern perspective, what we notice is that objective authentication of sources is not the reigning criterion of inclusion. What seems to matter is not where the story came from, but how good it is, and how well it might serve the purposes of transmission.

Although, as a participant in modern romanticism, Blofeld wanted to "believe" against the weight of modern doubt, he could not escape being a "modern," and thus, at times, setting "Buddhism" up for cross-examination. "How do we know," Blofeld found himself asking, "that the Mahayana claim to have preserved the highest teachings, some of them esoterically, is valid? Can we be so sure that these 'teachings' were not put into the mouth of the Buddha by later generations of monks?"[11] Although epistemological questions of this sort were not unknown in the pre-modern Buddhist world, on the rare occasions when they did appear, their purpose was not a denial of the tradition but a defense of

---

[11] Blofeld, *The Wheel of Life*, p. 51.

it by way of refuting a "forgery" which threatened to weaken the "original" tradition. That is to say, skeptical questioning served the particular purposes of the tradition rather than, as in modernity, becoming a universal trait of mind. Blofeld's text shows that, although he could not escape these questions which arose in his modern mind "naturally," as a romantic, he could find good reasons to set them aside, or even to refute them. Thus, in this particular case, when his teacher appealed to "intuitive knowledge of Reality gained by mystics of all ages," and "the experience of the Eternal," Blofeld's critical distance was undercut once again. He "nodded thoughtfully. This argument was impressive."[12] Indeed, it was Blofeld's own argument, and that of a whole generation of young English-language romantics who had come to seek wisdom in the "other" of foreign and past traditions. Blofeld had learned it in England, long before coming to China. In fact, it was the "reason" he came, and it was all he had to hold the modern critical posture of epistemology at bay.

When this "critical posture" of modernity becomes dominant, as it has in the historians of modern culture, a very different sense of "history" emerges. From this perspective, the "Lamp Histories" are not really histories, or, if they are, they are poor ones, weak in objectivity and in methodical procedure. It comes to seem, in fact, that the stories Huang Po and the editors of the "Lamp Histories" told about the origins of Zen are ahistorical, and, therefore, false. For the critical historian, this is not how Zen came to be what it is. Modern historians of Buddhism, therefore, have set out to rewrite this history and, on the basis of critically defined sources, to set straight the historical record on Zen.

Rather than to present these modern conclusions about the history of Zen, our concern will be to look behind both traditions of history to see what differences in perspective can be found there. What is the difference in historical consciousness between the medieval Zen monk who has written a "history of Zen" and the modern western historian who now seeks to rewrite that history? Although the differences between these distinct traditions of historical thought could be shaped in any number of forms and in varying degrees of specificity, we will here characterize the contrast in terms of four basic points.

First, Zen historians see themselves and their own texts as standing in continuity to the tradition. Because they "recapitulate" and "hand down" what has already been handed down to them, their texts stand in

---

[12] Blofeld, *The Wheel of Life*, p. 51.

full continuity with their sources. This continuity is based on a kind of atemporal essentialism, in spite of the centrality of the doctrine of "impermanence" in Buddhist thought. The assumption of temporal unity makes history appear without fundamental transformations. It was assumed that the Buddha lived in a world essentially like that of Sung-dynasty China. From this perspective, the Buddhist past cannot be perceived as foreign to the present, its "pastness" is overcome by the thought of the eternal presence of the unchanged Buddha Nature. Innovations in Zen, therefore, are not seen *as* innovations; they are recapitulations of a timeless identity.

Modern historians, by contrast, draw a line of separation between the object of study and their own text about that object. The modern history of Buddhism is not to be considered a reenactment of that tradition. Their "secondary" works are of an entirely different order than that of the "primary" texts which serve as their data base. A great "historical" distance divides them, which, for the modern historian, means that their natures are not the same. For the critical historian, the past is truly past, that is, fundamentally different from the present, and, therefore, not a likely object of veneration. The modern historian sees that Zen changes in the midst of its denial of change, precisely by claiming its innovations to be timeless and original. "Anachronism," from this perspective, comes to be judged a fallacy, an inability to see that history is dynamic, diverse, and fissured. Each text is to be seen not *as* binding upon the present, but *as* valid and meaningful within its own particular historical location, now past and therefore accessible to objective study.

Second, feeling this sense of continuity, Zen historians act as participants, fully engaged by the stories they transmit. They assume that the literature of the tradition addresses them directly. Stories about past actualities are taken to be current possibilities, fully applicable to current historians in their own context. Prior commitment to Zen and a sense of belonging to it is the rationale for writing its history. Historians in the Zen tradition don't deny that the stories they transmit belong to a past context. What they deny is that this context is categorically different from the one in which they seek wisdom.

Modern historians shift the context of understanding. The text is to be understood, not in relation to the historian in his or her context, but in relation to its original context in another time and place. Bracketing out the present context of meaning, the historian describes what the text once meant to others. Having shifted the relevant context of understanding from the present to the past, the appropriate descriptive terms for the historian's relation to the tradition are not "engagement," "participation," and "commitment," but rather "neutrality," "objectivity," and "critical distance."

Third, Zen historians hope to be freely and thoroughly influenced by the tradition they write about. Because the text at hand, no matter how ancient in origin, is assumed to be fully applicable to their own context, their posture toward it is responsive, not just open but eager to undergo whatever influence it bears. Their ideal is that the language and character of the text have been imprinted upon and joined to their own language and character. Writing the historical text and transmitting it to future generations are acts of Zen practice; they activate the powers of "dependent origination" both in themselves and in others.

The modern historian, by contrast, makes a commitment to avoid that influence on the grounds that it might invalidate the history that he or she has written. The principle of objectivity requires that the historian's voice remain distinct from, and not overlap with, that of the text. The line between what the Buddhist text asserts and what the modern historian asserts about it must in every instance remain clear. While the Buddhist historian strives to learn *from* the text, the modern historian is content to learn *about* it. Although the historian *may* belong to some tradition of thought and practice, this commitment must not affect the way in which the history of Zen is presented.

Fourth, Zen historians assume the overriding truth of the Buddhist tradition and take themselves to be fully accountable for the recapitulation of that truth. Their text is not just a report on what other Buddhists once said, but also what they, the Zen historians, now say. Thus accountable, the stories they transmit must in some way accord with the current "sense of the *dharma*." Whenever they don't, the stories are either edited to highlight allegorical means of understanding, or appropriately altered. In extreme cases, they can simply be omitted from the new text on the pretext that corruption has led to a loss of relevant meaning. No matter what the method, the new text is not just a record of past beliefs, it is a transmission of *dharma*. This is simply to say that it is "true," and every effort must be made by historians to see that it remains that way. They assume that only when the past can legitimately make a claim to truth upon the present is it worth knowing.

The modern historian understands truth primarily as representational accuracy. He or she seeks to know what the text really did say in its own context, and to describe how people in that epoch really did use it. This task requires that he or she bracket, at least for the time being, all opinions about whether what was accurately reported is, in fact, true. The past of Zen is presented as accurately as possible *as* past, *as* having made a claim to truth upon others in another era. The historian assumes that his or her own views on its current truth are irrelevant, and that it simply isn't the historian's job to consider that question. This posture in the author virtually guarantees that it won't be read *as* a source of truth either, although it is always unpredictable what allegorical readers and romantics will do with a text.

From the perspective of the modern historian, the procedures of the Zen historian are flawed to the point of producing "bad history." Lacking sufficient distance from the tradition, the Zen historian fails to describe the tradition accurately because the position from which his text is written conjoins and confuses how it was with how it is or how it should have been from the point of view of current idealization.

The weakness, however, of Zen historical consciousness is not just that it alters or ignores the data available to historical narrative. It is more importantly that its underlying assumptions and desires concerning the continuity, coherence, and idealized form of the tradition, structure for the historian a perspective from which the transformations and "disjunctions" of the tradition, and therefore its own otherness to itself, cannot be seen. If current practitioners model themselves on the ancients *and* the ancients are updated to fit the current image of "awakening," then no fundamental difference remains between ideals past and present. The figure of the ancestors evolves along with the understanding of what "enlightenment" could mean to the extent that each new generation, in the process of practicing "through" the ancestors, projects its highest aspirations onto the ancestors. Thus the ancestors always represent what the current practitioner could conceivably become, even though that conception changes over time, and the height of the ideal as projected makes its actualization virtually impossible.[13] Lacking a way to represent the "otherness" of the tradition to itself (other than through a concept of "fall" which was common in Chinese Buddhism), the Zen historian has no perspective from which the present understanding can be seen as an alteration of the past. One consequence of this is that there is no perspective from which the present can be criticized, other than that of the

---

[13] By this is meant simply that human beings at any stage of development will be able to imagine ideals greater than they can currently achieve, which is essentially what ideals are – something beyond the present, the possible actualization of which will require concerted effort, transformation, and time. Wherever actualization of any kind has occurred, new ideals will have been made possible.

present itself, which can only take the form of chastisement for a failure to live up to current ideals.[14] Practitioners, therefore, live out of a highly idealized and therefore typically "precritical" understanding of their own tradition. What is lost, then, in traditional Zen historiography, when seen from our current perspectives? From the perspective of scientific historiography – the mainstream of current practice – what is lost is accuracy. The facts – what really did happen – have been placed in subservience to the desire for mythic ideals. From the perspective of "postmodern" historiography – the emergent tradition of Foucault and others – what is lost is complexity, "difference," and disjuncture, all hidden from view by the dominant desire for unity and identity in Zen.[15]

Equally possible, however, and even more to the point of reflexive meditation, is to formulate a critique running in the other direction – a critique of current historical consciousness from the perspective of Zen. What can an understanding of the classical Zen sense of history show us about our own practice of historiography and the understanding of history upon which it is based? Two major possibilities come to mind.

First, compared to the Zen tradition, our historical practices demonstrate very little sense of belonging to a tradition. We imagine ourselves tradition-free observers, representing no particular point of view and responsible to no one. On this point, however, we are mistaken. Like Zen

---

[14] This account is overstated in order to highlight one side of a more complex interaction. The texts did in fact serve as an ancient perspective from which the present historical moment could be criticized. This would have been so in several important ways, including the myth of the "degenerating *dharma*." But at least two factors diminished the extent to which this "difference" between past and present could be recognized. The first, suggested above, is that the texts were altered to bring them into accord with the language and thought of the present era. Thus their "otherness" was erased whenever it seemed to protrude. The second is that, even when the text was not altered, the overriding assumption that past and present are in full correspondence sets up the likelihood that whatever the text says will be given a new and current sense, rather than being seen as a "difference" demanding critical judgment regarding former and current points of view. Since, being enlightened, the ancients had to be right, rather than surpassed in the onward surge of history, they had to be interpreted in such a way that they not only were "true," but also continued to represent the highest achievements projectable by current imagination.

[15] The work of Bernard Faure gives the most direct access to this point of view. He writes, for example, that "the complex reality of Chan was gradually replaced by a simplistic image of its mythic past" (*The Rhetoric of Immediacy*, p. 19), and that "The ideological work of the tradition has been to hide the diversity and contingency of its origins behind an apparent consensus of orthodoxy" (p. 16). The same texts which, when interpreted in terms of the Zen symbols of "unity" and "identity", yield the mythic tradition, re-emerge, when interpreted in terms of contemporary symbols of "difference" and "diversity," with quite a different history. Zen points of departure do hide "diversity," and ours do hide "unity." We would only be justified in claiming that the Zen tradition was hiding a unity that it knew very well was there if we were also willing to entertain the correlative point that, behind our faith in "difference," we are hiding a unity that we know very well is there.

Buddhists, we do, in fact, stand within a tradition and write out of a particular context and point of view. Although lack of self-understanding on the issue of standpoint does not mean that we stand nowhere, exempting us from its consequences, it does mean that the quality and depth of our stance in study is significantly diminished. Knowing where you stand is important, as is understanding the relation between where you stand and what you study. In consequence of our view, we weaken the relation to tradition that we do inevitably have, which, in turn, weakens the tradition itself.[16] In the Zen texts under consideration, historical understanding is not regarded as an act of individual subjectivity. It is instead conceived as an act of tradition which places the individual self into the process of history, where past and future are joined to the present. When the tradition is conceived as a generous donor, offering its vast legacy to subsequent generations, then a sense of indebtedness results. Reciprocation, repayment, goes not to the actual donors, the teachers who will no longer be there, but to the tradition itself which they now represent. This sense of gratitude and its corresponding desire for reciprocation in the form of repayment to the future is so prominent in Zen texts, and so impressive, that it would be hard not to sense in the act of reading it some form of lack or deprivation in our own relation to tradition, no matter how conceived.

Second, studying the various kinds of relationship between reader and text in the Zen tradition may bring to our attention a weakness in the extent of reflexivity or self-awareness that we bring to our study. This weakness is a consequence of the modern inclination to take natural science as the model toward which humanistic study should aspire. Valorizing objective disengagement, historical studies of Buddhism tend not to relate the Buddhist text at issue to the context of the interpreter. Thus isolated, Buddhist texts tend not to serve as the impetus to seek a deeper understanding of the positions and assumptions out of which our work proceeds, nor as encouragement to discover what of significance could be learned "from" these texts. We proceed, in effect, as if we aren't really involved. In this respect the narratives we tell about ourselves are underdeveloped.[17] They fail to locate us in a productive relation to the

---

[16] "Modern historical research itself is not only research, but the transmission of tradition" (Gadamer, *Truth and Method*, p. 253). Gadamer's work is the primary source for the concepts of "tradition" and "historicity" operative in this chapter. See also Alasdair MacIntyre, *Three Rival Versions*.

[17] For a critique of modern historiography on this point, see LaCapra, *Rethinking Intellectual History: Texts, Contexts, Language.*

text, one through which we might be provoked by the text, either to understand our own position more deeply, or to rethink, revise, or expand it. A reflexive relation to the text takes advantage of whatever light the text can shed on its reader. When this reflexive relation is lacking or weak, the very rationale for historical study has become obscured. As the Matsu section of the *Transmission of the Lamp* asserts, the most important answers to our questions about Buddhism can be discovered only in self-conscious relation to "the one who is doing the questioning."

Although the deficiencies we have found in both traditions of historiography are, at this level of description, polar opposites of one another, they can also be understood to share a fundamental similarity: both the Zen Buddhist and modern western historical traditions deny implicitly some dimension of the impermanence of history, the radical mutability of temporal movement. Although the Buddhist tradition highlights the deficiency of the present – its unsatisfactory character due to which the ancestral Buddhas need be consulted and imitated – it is neither able to consider critically the deficiencies of the past, nor the possible inapplicability of past truths to present contingencies. And although modern historians understand very clearly the deficiency of the past – the relativity of "out-moded" ideas and practices to their own historical context – they tend to assume the universality and noncontextual truth of their own setting, including modern ideas and practices of historiography. One tradition – the Buddhist – experiences the lack or absence of the present in relation to the fullness of the enlightened past, while the other – the modern – maintains that, whereas the full presence of true historical knowledge is now possible, it appears not to have been so in the past, given that premodern historians, lacking critical methods, seem to have been so often mistaken.

In both traditions, however, one dimension of time stands exempt from the negativity of historical finitude. Locating a kind of historical understanding that overcomes these particular deficiencies is therefore a matter of learning to avoid these exemptions. Working toward this kind of self-awareness in our study would, in effect, constitute work toward the development of new and more encompassing criteria of truth for historical reflection.

Because each style of historiography evolves within its own cultural tradition, and upon the conceptual and practical bases supplied for it by other dimensions of culture, it should not be surprising that each places its focus differently and orients itself to past, present, and future in a distinct way. The possibility of a significant transformation of historical consciousness in each of these cultures is greatly enhanced in the current setting by the availability of different traditions of historical reflection in relation to which each tradition can understand, evaluate, and critique itself.

Already the social, cultural ramifications of the rethinking of both Chinese history and the practice of historiography in China, in light of their encounter with Marxist and other forms of western historical reflection, have been immense. Signs now exist that some form of alteration has begun to occur in western historical thinking as a result, in part, of the twentieth-century encounter with the rest of the world. These signs are promising; indeed, exciting. They push historical imagination to consider possibilities hitherto closed to thinking. It would be a mistake, however (in fact a mistake symptomatic of the modern tendency to exempt its own standpoint from contextualization), to regard this present activity of placing two traditions of historiography in critical relation to one another as itself occupying a position outside and "beyond" those traditions. In a finite, diverse, and historical world, "non-traditional" and all-encompassing theories of history are not possible. What is possible, however, is that, through the encounter with other cultures and epochs, particular traditions of historical reflection will become in some way richer, more comprehensive, more self-critical, and more applicable to cultural ends which are themselves open to similar transformation.

CHAPTER 7

FREEDOM: the practice of constraint

> One must not act as one pleases . . . One must submit to all the restrictions.
>
> *Pure Regulations of Zen*[1]

> The master said to the assembly: "When the great function works, it does not follow rules."
>
> *Transmission of the Lamp*[2]

The obvious tension between the images of Zen contained in the two quotes above provides an intriguing entrance into our theme in this chapter. On the one hand, a thorough reading of Zen literature will disclose the prominence given in the tradition to regulation, hierarchy, authority, and constraint. Living in a Zen monastery requires a thorough-going renunciation of many dimensions of freedom. On the other hand, we can see that Zen masters were widely thought to be rule breakers, free-spirited individuals whose "awakening" enabled them to laugh uproariously in the face of normal social constraint. So, which is the "real" Zen? Or if both images are true to the Zen tradition, how are they to be reconciled?

Freedom is an issue of considerable importance in Zen, and an issue that has been at the forefront of western interpretations of Zen since the very beginning. The background to our interest in this issue is the obvious prominence of "freedom" as a symbol in modern western thought. Western minds, already attuned to the significance of "freedom," have been particularly attracted to this side of Zen.

Writing in the 1970s, and looking back over the brief history of western encounter with "Zen,"[3] John Blofeld, by then one of the best

---

[1] *Pure Regulations of Zen*, trans. G. Foulk, in "The Ch'an School," p. 82.

[2] Lu K'uan Yu, *Ch'an and Zen Teachings*, p. 209.

[3] It is an irony of history that, at the same time that "Buddhist" interpreters in the Maoist-guided Chinese Buddhist Association were developing an understanding of "Buddhist Freedom" that would align with the particular communal demands of Proletarian Liberation, early western interpreters of "Beat Zen" were developing an understanding of "liberation" in radically individualistic terms as the freedom from authority, convention, and "society" at large.

known "transmitters" of Buddhism to the west, could see that "The recent widespread Western interest in Ch'an (Zen) owes much to the appeal of . . . unconventional 'shock tactics' and also to the sect's seeming iconoclasm . . . as exemplified by the anecdote applauding a monk who chopped up a wooden image of the Buddha to provide a fire against the cold of a winter's night."[4] Blofeld's synthesis of western representations of Zen from this period focuses for the most part on the image of the Zen master as having attained a working liberation from social convention and all forms of cultural constraint. Taking their cues from the sacred biographies in classic Zen texts like *The Transmission of the Lamp*, their translations and interpretations imagined the great masters of the "golden age" of Zen as iconoclasts who scoffed at all traditional forms of authority. Their Zen rejection is pictured as radical and thorough-going; true masters repudiate authority in the form of teachers, texts, customs, and traditions. The story perhaps most often called upon to form this image is the account of the return of Lin-chi to Mount Huang Po, where, upsetting all hierarchy and deference, he slaps the abbot and master, Huang Po.[5]

The themes animating this narrative are not unusual in the classical Zen canon; indeed, they are paradigmatic. Enlightenment narratives for most of the great masters of Zen include at least one act in which some form of authority is radically rejected. Many of these are instances of rejecting the tradition, such as Te-shan ripping up the Buddhist sutras, freeing himself from their heteronomous power over him, or similarly, Nan-ch'uan's claims that, at the moment of sudden awakening, he "freed himself from all that he had learned"[6] in several decades of traditional study. More than anything else, however, the power of traditional authority was symbolized in the monastic hierarchy, particularly in the abbot or master from whom the "teachings" would be received. Rejection of any such authority was universalized for western readers by the importance given to the radical Zen admonition that, "if you see the Buddha [the apex of centralized authority], kill him!"

More specific instructions along these same iconoclastic lines are easy to locate in the canon. Huang Po is recorded as instructing monks that, "having listened to the profoundest doctrines, monks must behave as though a light breeze had caressed their ears, a gust had passed away in the blink of an eye. By no means should they attempt to follow such doctrines."[7] True practice,

[4] Blofeld, *Beyond the Gods*, p. 118.   [5] T. 47, p. 504c; Sasaki, *The Recorded Sayings of Lin-chi*, p. 52.
[6] T. 51, p. 257.   [7] T. 48. p. 384a; Blofeld, *Huang Po*, p. 103.

it seemed, required that one ceased "following" altogether; subservience to any form of authority seemed contrary to the image of the great masters' autonomy. The opening "discourse" section of the *Lin-chi lu* is replete with admonitions against dependence on authority: "what I want to point out to you is that you must not accept the deluding views of others."[8] Given their tendencies to just such acceptance, Lin-chi laments that "students nowadays know nothing of Dharma. They are just like sheep that take into their mouths whatever their noses happen to hit against."[9] Contemptuous of monks' failure to be independent, Lin-chi scolds them, saying:

Followers of the Way, you seize upon words from the mouths of those old masters and take them to be the true Way [and say]: "These good teachers are wonderful, and I, simple-minded fellow that I am, don't dare measure such old worthies." Blind idiots! You go through your entire life holding such views, betraying your own two eyes. Trembling with fright, like donkeys on an icy path, [you say to yourselves:] "I don't dare disparage these good teachers for fear of making karma with my mouth!"

Followers of the Way, it is only the great teacher who dares to disparage the buddhas, dares to disparage the patriarchs, to reject the teachings of the Tripitaka."[10]

These iconoclastic themes struck a chord of recognition and agreement among early western readers of Zen texts. Zen monks seemed to reject tradition, authority, and hierarchy in their quest for a form of enlightenment which, like western "enlightenment," incorporated freedom in the form of independence and autonomy into its image of greatness. This correspondence between ideals, however, should give us pause for reflection, allowing us to consider whether this reading of Zen has to some extent served to foster the interests and tastes already in the possession of modern interpreters rather than to bring them into scrutiny. Could it be that the modern western valorization of autonomous reason over authority, personal insight over tradition, and individuality over collectivity has so set the stage and parameters for western interpretations of Zen that the ideals and virtues of that very distant tradition would have been overshadowed by more familiar themes from western thought?[11]

---

[8] T. 47, p. 497b; Sasaki, *The Recorded Sayings of Lin-chi*, p. 7.

[9] T. 47, p. 498a; Sasaki, *The Recorded Sayings of Lin-chi*, p. 12. Note that, although the image of the sheep is a metaphor of uncritical acceptance like the one in western languages, there is a crucial difference. The failure of individual discrimination is seen, not in the sheep's tendency to follow others, but in its failure to eat selectively.

[10] T. 47, p. 499b; Sasaki, *The Recorded Sayings of Lin-chi*, p. 19.

[11] Charles Taylor traces the history of the European concept of freedom as self-determination in *Sources of the Self*.

Several dimensions of the texts give rise to this suspicion.[12] The most important of these reflect the thoroughly collective or communal context within which these texts were studied and practiced. The communal structure of classical Zen life could hardly have encouraged the kinds of radical individualism both valued and assumed by early western practitioners of Zen. By the later T'ang, monasteries of the Zen sect were large, highly structured, and often somewhat isolated institutions. In some cases, like on Mount Huang Po, their relative isolation meant that they operated as a society in and of themselves.[13] Like all other dimensions of Chinese society, Zen monasteries were organized hierarchically – everyone's exact place in the distribution of power, from the newest recruit to the abbot himself, was very clear. Rules and regulations structured all activities and all interaction, both within the monastery and in its dealings with the outside world.[14] Before the Sung dynasty, the traditional Buddhist *vinaya* code of rules as it had been adapted to Chinese society was in effect in Zen monasteries. This code included precepts for ethical conduct, regulations for decision making and

[12] One of these might have been the possession of slaves by monks, nuns, and monasteries during this period of Chinese history. If "freedom" in the sense that we understood it was an important goal of Zen, then how could slavery have been practiced in Zen monasteries? Nevertheless, we are familiar with a similar disjunction in American history. Early colonialists and constitutionalists were singularly focused on the issue of "freedom." Yet that focus did not come into sustained conflict with the institution of slavery until the mid-nineteenth century. Concerning slavery on Mount Huang Po, we know nothing. It is very likely, however, that at least some Zen monks and nuns followed the general Chinese Buddhist practice of slave ownership. At the height of Huang Po's career, in 842, a court decision attempting to reduce the size, wealth, and power of the Buddhist clergy decreed that monks would legally be allowed only one male slave and nuns two female slaves. On this issue see Weinstein, *Buddhism Under the T'ang*, p. 119, and Bols, *This Culture of Ours*, p. 22.

[13] This is not to say, however, that they were independent of the larger socio-economic world of South-central China. Although their projected image of self-sufficient communes, thriving on their own practice of labor, is important, that image does not fit the historical picture that we now have of the majority of these monasteries. While their own labor was a factor in the support of monastery life, dependence on lay patronage grew as Zen became more fully established in China. Monasteries were also enriched by collecting rent on land owned by the institution and by the sale of surplus produce. Since monasteries like Huang Po sometimes housed as many as 1,000 practicing monks, or even more, these required substantial economic bases to keep them going. Interdependence with the larger world of China was inevitable, no matter how much isolation they may have cultivated. See Collcutt, *Five Mountains*, chapter 7.

[14] Foulk suggests the implementation of anthropological theories of "liminality" to understand the purposeful rule breaking and unconventional behavior that occurred in the ceremony of the abbot's "ascending the hall." In this case the rules permit blatant rule breaking within prescribed limits, especially the limits of time and place. Outside these limits, rule breaking becomes simply rule breaking, a punishable infringement rather than an enlightening activity. ("The Ch'an School," p. 36). This may be part of what Faure has in mind when he notes that " a constant dialectic between routinization and nonconformism seems at work in Chan" (*The Rhetoric of Immediacy*, pp. 16–17).

administration, and, in unbelievable detail, rules of behavior, speech, and etiquette for individual monks and nuns.

When the "Pure Regulations" of Zen monastic life (*ch'ing-kuei*) were adopted in the Sung, the collective character of Zen life and these regulations were emphasized further. Collective labor, collective meditation, collective meals, collective *dharma* discussions, collective sleeping arrangements – all of these came to be institutionalized with the new codes, thus possibly giving Zen a more thorough "collective" character than any previous form of Buddhism.[15] Virtually no dimension of Zen monastic life depended upon individual preference and personal decision making. Freedom, in the form of autonomy at least, was not an important consideration. As the *Pure Regulations of Zen* put it: "One must not act as one pleases . . . One must submit to all the restrictions."[16] Nevertheless, in the midst of this "community of constraint," "freedom" came to be an essential defining feature of the community's purpose. This juxtaposition was clearly problematic for early modern interpreters of Zen, and, as a result, English translations and descriptions of "Zen life" featured those stories that seemed to show either lack of constraint or the willful act of throwing off constraint. The union of these two, freedom and constraint, seemed to be unthinkable. Isn't "freedom" the absence of "constraint?" Zen Buddhists must not have thought so; otherwise how could they come to believe that freedom would be the outcome of this life of monastic restriction?

Two brief points will help us begin to work our way beyond this modern stumbling block. The first is that freedom is always "dependent" upon some structure of limitation in terms of which it will come to be defined or understood *as* free. "Acting freely" can only take place against a background of constraints: alternative choices, the possibility of unfree acts, and all the stage-setting features of any context of understanding. We cannot imagine a world without such constraints, without alternative paths and elaborate structures. If we could, we would see that such a world would not include freedom. Freedom is, in an important sense, always a movement in and among constraints. Point 2 follows from the first. If freedom and constraint are always to be found together, we can imagine ourselves, or Zen monks, freely accepting limitations on our individual will in order to make possible forms of freedom beyond those

---

[15] This point is made in an interesting way by Foulk in noticing that monastic structure in India often separated monks into individual cells for meditating and sleeping, and that Chinese monastic style was fundamentally communal ("The Ch'an School," p. 375).

[16] Foulk, "The Ch'an School," p. 82.

surrendered. The choice to accept such limitations is already an act of freedom. Zen monks joining a monastery voluntarily place themselves into a context of severe restraint.[17] Why? Because in this free choice they inherit forms of freedom that would not be "choosable" otherwise. This theme is certainly not absent in modernity. Both "social contract" theory and theory of democracy imply that greater freedom becomes possible through the communal choice of constraint in certain areas. Perhaps closer to the case of Zen is the modern, "Kantian" doctrine that freedom consists precisely in choosing moral constraint – freely adhering to ethical norms lifts you out of causal necessities otherwise determining your existence. In each of these cases we can see that even in "modernity" individualism must be set into some larger context in order to make sense. Nevertheless, the focus of modern thought is on the individual and not on his or her implied relationship to something beyond the self.

We can see these individualist tendencies in the attention given by modern interpreters of Zen to acts and discourses which seem to reject all forms of "following."[18] What these interpretations have failed to notice, however, is that a reflexive paradox informs each such rejection in the text: readers are asked to follow the writer or speaker by accepting the plea to reject "following." Huang Po's discourse record had said: "having listened to the profoundest doctrines, monks must behave as though a light breeze had caressed their ears, a gust had passed away in the blink of an eye. By no means should they attempt to follow such doctrines."[19] Although "following" appears to have been rejected in this passage, the very next sentence calls for a new act of following, one already implicit in the first two sentences. It says: "To act in accordance with these injunctions is to achieve profundity." Release or freedom from authoritative injunctions takes the status of a new injunction, authorized by no less an authority than the monastery's abbot, Huang Po himself. Presupposed in the monastic context of the time was that experiencing the point of Zen practice would require this injunction to be heeded.

---

[17] It is important to recognize here, however, that not all monks in medieval China joined the monastery out of free choice. Various constraints sometimes obligated them; economic vicissitudes, family pressure, and many other factors can be seen to be involved. Some boys were assigned or given to the monastic institution long before they had reached the age of decision making. Nevertheless, the ideal required free choice.

[18] We can see this tendency in early western Zen literature from the "Beat Zen" of Jack Kerouac to the more academic style of Watts and Fromm, but also, and more influentially, in the English language writings of D. T. Suzuki who drew upon Western proclivities in introducing Zen to the west.   [19] T. 48, p. 384a.

Although this injunction against following injunctions might be seen to put the monk in something of a bind, I suspect that this bind was only rarely experienced. For the most part, the act of "rejection" would have had a specific target within the bounds of intra-tradition debate, and would not have been taken to be universally applicable, especially not reflexively. The text, its writer, and the speaker it projects were all seeking a following. This can be seen inconspicuously throughout Zen literature, where, for example, the *Lin-chi lu* has the master say things like: "Take my viewpoint"[20] or, "See it my way."[21] The writing of the text, just like any original speaking of the words that may have occurred, presupposes the propriety of following, or acceptance, and of accord with its version of the tradition. Lin-chi, like the other great creators of the Zen tradition, is a rhetorician – he seeks to be persuasive, to teach, guide, and reveal through various forms of discursive practice. And persuasion always seeks a following.

Moreover, "following" is what Lin-chi himself should be understood as doing. Individualistic connotations ought not to be read into translated phrases such as "my way" or "my point of view." This becomes clear when the text has Lin-chi say: "As for *my* understanding, it's not different from that of the patriarchs and buddhas."[22] Lin-chi follows them; he stands fully within a lineage that he has appropriated into himself through decades of "following." After all, Lin-chi addresses his interlocutors as "Followers of the Way" – *Tao-shun*. The "*shun*" are those who accord, comply, and follow a "way" which is not self-made and which stands beyond any individual participant in the lineage as the ground of the lineage itself. This "way" exists as a standard etched into images of "buddhas and patriarchs." Accord with this standard – an act of following – is quite clearly what the text enjoins, as, for example, when the *Lin-chi lu* says: "If you want to be no different from the buddhas and patriarchs, just see things this way" (*ju shih chien*).[23]

Judging from the perspective of the institutions which produced and sustained these texts, it is unlikely that anyone in this tradition would have understood the charting of this "way" as an individual endeavor. On the contrary, the "way" was that to which all individuality would be subordinated. So when the *Lin-chi lu* has the master gather a following by urging readers to "take my viewpoint," or "see it my way," the "my"

---

[20] T. 47, p. 497b; Sasaki, *The Recorded Sayings of Lin-chi*, p. 9.
[21] T. 47, p. 497b; Sasaki, *The Recorded Sayings of Lin-chi*, p. 8.
[22] T. 47, p. 502a; Sasaki, *The Recorded Sayings of Lin-chi*, p. 32.
[23] T. 47, p. 499c; Sasaki, *The Recorded Sayings of Lin-chi*, p. 20.

is not a formal, personal possessive. Lin-chi understands himself as belonging to the way and not vice versa. For this reason he takes great pains to see that his understanding is "not different from that of the Patriarchs and Buddhas."[24]

If Lin-chi is "no different" than Huang Po and the entire Zen tradition, how could he be said to have "gone beyond" them? Like his predecessors in the lineage, Lin-chi has attained freedom. He is "no different" in that the "seal" placed upon his mind through subordination to the tradition includes, perhaps as its defining feature, the "stamp" of freedom.[25] The content of freedom – what it looks like and what it is – will differ. Each freedom will have "gone beyond" its predecessors. Nevertheless, the focus in Zen was on the ways in which this "stamp of differentiation" occurred through the surrender of "self." In the act of turning yourself over to the tradition, there is "no self." Lacking fixed identity, "going beyond" would be possible. As we saw when we considered Zen "historical consciousness," however, images of previous "transcendence" tend to be erased from the "transmission" histories. When new images of freedom make their appearance, the biographies of past masters were updated to include these previously neglected dimensions of "their" enlightenment. Given *that* they were enlightened, the identities of the "ancients" would be revised throughout history in accordance with current, updated images of what it means to be enlightened. Accordingly, the "ancient Buddhas of India" are pictured speaking Sung-dynasty Chinese *koan* language. Through the practices of textuality, the "Patriarchs and buddhas" came to be "not different" than the recent Zen masters who had "gone beyond" them.

Being "not different," however, is not the image of greatness projected by modern western Zen whose practitioners would turn to Zen in the wake of European romanticism precisely in an effort to differentiate themselves. This twentieth-century tradition could not help but absorb the values of modern individualism and to read Zen from the only perspective available to it. We can see this influence in an extreme form in

---

[24] T. 47, p. 499c; Sasaki, *The Recorded Sayings of Lin-chi*, p. 32.

[25] Two models of this process are attractive. One places identity and difference in sequence. The monk first appropriates the tradition by gaining its identity and then enters into the dialectical process of differing from himself. The past is transmitted as paradigm and challenge. Becoming an instance of the tradition, one then seeks differentiation through challenge and critique. The second model has these two processes occurring simultaneously. Because acts of identification occur in new contexts, critique and differentiation take place all along. It may not be necessary to choose between these models. They may overlap in that, although differentiation is never absent, more important consequences for the tradition follow from it at more advanced stages.

the autobiography of Alan Watts, entitled, appropriately, *In My Own Way*.[26] Although the character Tao is inscribed on the cover of the book, the emphasis in the text is clearly on the word "own." Watts had undertaken to establish his "own way" so that acts of "following" could be avoided altogether. Autobiography – the self's own constructive narrative – is the proper genre for this act of establishment, and a genre absent from the literature of the Zen tradition.[27] "Self establishment" is in an important sense the obverse of central themes in classical Zen literature because there the image of "accord" takes precedence. Overcoming self-assertion, the self is emptied so that accord with a "way" (tao) or a "path" (lu) can occur. Taking this difference seriously, and linking it to different forms of self-understanding, we can begin to get greater perspective on the kind of "freedom" experienced through the Zen rejection of authority and tradition.[28]

A crucial question concerning freedom and authority is posed directly in the *Lin-chi lu*. It asks: "What is meant by 'burning the sutras and images?'"[29] This is precisely what we need to understand – what do iconoclastic acts mean in Zen? The master answers: "Having seen that the sequence of causal relations is empty, that mind is empty, and that *dharma*s are empty – thus your single thought being decisively cut off, you've nothing to do – this is called burning the sutras and images. Virtuous monks, reach such understanding as this, and you'll be free."[30] How should we understand this response and its implied notion of freedom? We can begin by examining a simplified version of its structure. The sentence takes the form of: "Having seen X, Y, and Z, *this* is burning the sutras and *this* yields freedom." What, then, fills in the content of X, Y, and Z? "Having seen or realized that causal relations are empty, mind is empty, and *dharma*s are empty." Rephrasing, we might say: "Having realized 'emptiness' (*k'ung*) – *this* is burning the sutras, *this* is freedom." If we now ask ourselves – what is the point of the Mahayana sutras being burned? – the answer is, quite clearly, "emptiness." So, rephrasing once more, we could say: "Having realized the

[26] Watts, *In My Own Way*.
[27] Although one Zen text, *The Platform Sutra of the Sixth Patriarch*, reads in certain sections like autobiography, it is now clear that the text was not authored by Hui-neng and that its various narratives are better regarded as an early form of discourse record or *yu-lu* literature, which in this case were composed to serve strong political and polemical purposes.
[28] Frithjof Bergmann works insightfully on the necessary link between forms of self- understanding and corresponding forms of freedom in *On Being Free*.
[29] T. 47, p. 502b; Sasaki; *The Recorded Sayings of Lin-chi*, p. 36.
[30] T. 47, p. 502b; Sasaki; *The Recorded Sayings of Lin-chi*, p. 36.

essential point of the sutras – *this* is burning the sutras, *this* is freedom." Freedom from the objective and heteronomous authority of scripture, therefore, results from an in-depth realization of its meaning. Appropriating or "digesting" the sutras into oneself overcomes their authoritarian "otherness."

Interpreted in this light, the famous image of Te-shan ripping up the sutras in liberated ecstasy is the image of Te-shan in the moment of having appropriated and internalized them. Is Te-shan destroying the text and subverting its authority because his realization is in conflict with that projected by the text? Clearly not. Te-shan's realization is understood to be an actualization of the same "way" that gave rise to the Buddha's realization which is written into the sutra, just as Te-shan's realization is imprinted into the textual account of his iconoclastic act.[31] The freedom Te-shan receives *through* the sutra includes within it a dimension of freedom *from* it, and it is in this respect that "going beyond" will have occurred. The second dimension of freedom, however, is acknowledged to be a function of the first.

That iconoclastic acts are not denunciations of an authority that has been broken and overcome is similarly implied in the life of Lin-chi. After having slapped his teacher, Huang Po, thus flaunting his freedom from Buddhist authority, Lin-chi settles down in the monastery to study under the master, possibly for as long as two decades. The liberating act of "casting off" was incorporated into a more encompassing intention directed toward communal practice which included obedience, loyalty, and learning. It is these latter virtues that our early renderings of Zen "freedom" were unable to accommodate.

For those of us who have been raised in a modern European cultural tradition, this co-operation of freedom and obedient subsumption to authority is difficult to conceptualize. Modern western thought has tended to place freedom and obedience in a dichotomous relation. In the wake of Enlightenment-era thinkers, we tend to assume that recognition of and obedience to any authority prevents the free use of one's own autonomous resources. Similarly, from the various forms of romanticism, to which we owe much of our interest in Zen and cultural otherness, we learn that obedience to traditional authority prevents the development of one's own creative, imaginative spirit. These cultural

---

[31] The change here is simply that, for some readers in the epoch of Zen ascendancy, the Te-shan text about text-ripping made for a more provocative narrative than those purportedly being ripped. This would not, however, have authorized anyone in the tradition to claim that Te-shan, or the discourse record of his act, was "more enlightened" than the Buddha or his sutras.

preferences and decisions can now demonstrate to us why our western interpretations of Zen have ignored the monastic institutional setting within which radical, iconoclastic acts of freedom were performed. Our interpretations of these acts have assumed and required a background picture of the Zen masters as individuals free of all communal context, liberated from ties to socially ordained ideals and projects.

As a more complete account of the historical, institutional setting of classical Zen becomes available, a paradox emerges for the western interpreter of Zen. The paradox is this: the pursuit of freedom in Zen was understood to be actualized in the act of surrendering one's freedom to a cultural institution and to those individuals who currently represent it. Not only was it assumed that subsumption to authority is not antithetical to freedom, such subsumption was understood in classical Zen to be the primary condition of freedom's possibility. Recognizing the finitude of his own ability both to conceive of and to achieve freedom, the postulant freely chooses a career of following. This act of subordination requires a set of correlate beliefs – minimally, that the Zen master does embody the freedom he teaches and, through compassion, does in fact seek the postulant's subsequent liberation. Typically, the authority of the Zen master is conceded in proportion to his reputation and image, and commands freely given consent in that same proportion.[32] Moreover, the achievement of freedom by individual practitioners does not terminate their ties to the communal, institutional setting. Indeed, the greater the career, the more those bonds may have been imposed and accepted. The two posthumous names affixed to Huang Po's career show this juxtaposition. The final sentence of his "transmission" biography reads: "The Royal Court bestowed upon him the posthumous name, 'Zen Master Free of Limitations,' and named his pagoda, 'Expansive Karma.'"[33] Karma is "limitation" itself, and it "expands" everywhere. "Freedom" becomes manifest within it. Karma is one limitation from which freedom cannot occur since it makes freedom both possible and available. Huang Po's achievement of freedom, proclaims the Royal Court, will be disseminated throughout the Empire, the expansive realm of karma.

One way to achieve greater perspective on this issue is to consider the role that 'imitation' had in the daily life of Zen practitioners. Understood as a form of submission and renunciation of autonomy,

---

[32] In *Truth and Method*, Hans-Georg Gadamer contextualizes and shows the limits of Enlightenment-era dichotomies between freedom and authority, thus offering ways to conceive of premodern forms of freedom.   [33] T. 51, p. 266.

imitation is often taken in modern western thought to represent an antithesis to freedom. Thus we ask of the Zen texts: to what extent was imitation of the master, or of discursively projected images of masters, thought to entail a renunciation of freedom, and to what extent was the imitation of authority figures assumed to be a means of attaining the freedom already possessed by these masters? What, in brief, was the place of imitation in Zen monastic practice?

Our first response to this issue must be that a potent critique of imitation is ubiquitous to classical Zen texts. Rote memorization and mindless repetition were subjected to heavy ridicule by the great teachers. These passages are particularly interesting and we will have occasion to look at several very closely. But one hermeneutical justification for our interest in them is the fact that western interpretations of Zen have inevitably selected these passages as representative of the best of the Zen tradition. One need not look far for the background to our interest here – enlightenment-era critiques of imitation, arising from both science and its romantic opposition, have sharpened our propensities as moderns to see an act of imitation as "unoriginal," "uncreative," and "unfree." On the basis of those modern critiques we have quite naturally been deeply appreciative of what has appeared to be a forceful statement of a similar sentiment in Zen texts. Once again, the Zen tradition seems to have added justification and sanction to our deepest instincts: those who copy have failed the crucial test of autonomy. Freedom and imitation are mutually exclusive.

Perhaps the most famous passage relative to the theme of imitation is the following which I quote in paraphrase from a *koan* text, the *Wu-men kuan* (*The Gateless Barrier*):

In place of conventional instruction, the master, Chu-chih would guide his disciples to enlightenment merely by lifting a finger. On one occasion, a disciple imitated him. Responding to a question from a visitor, he simply raised a finger the way he had seen his master do it. When Chu-chih heard about this, he took a knife and cut off the disciple's finger. Crying out in pain, the disciple began to run away. The master then called to him and as the young monk turned around, he saw the master lifting his finger. At that moment he was enlightened and realized that simple imitation is insufficient. The experience must appear from within.[34]

Not only does the story assert the inadequacies of imitation, but also, at least by suggestion, it links the critique of imitation with enlightenment

[34] *Wu-men kuan*, case 3.

itself. Experiencing the failure of imitation seems to have evoked an experience of "awakening." In another passage, we find Lin-chi scolding his disciples for their acts of imitation: "Followers of the Way, you seize upon words from the mouths of those old masters and take them to be the true Way [and say]: 'These good teachers are wonderful, and I simple-minded fellow that I am, don't dare measure such old worthies.' Blind idiots!"[35]

Imitation inevitably involves some form of self-deprecation, a subordination which in the case of Lin-chi seems to be under criticism. A story about the master Huang Po, immortalized by its selection for a *koan* collection, finds a metaphor for the imitator. Criticizing his followers for their very act of following, Huang Po drives them out of the *dharma* hall with a stick, yelling: "You're just a bunch of dreg-drinkers."[36] Henceforth, all imitators were to be called "dreg- drinkers," based upon the ancient Chinese belief that those who drink the dregs of the wine bottle partake of leftovers, remains from others who have come first and who have consumed all that is truly worthy of consumption. The dreg-drinking imitator draws upon the resources of others and is not self-sustaining.

Although this textual evidence seems to support a straightforward critique of imitation, other passages complicate the issue, either by enjoining imitation or by failing to notice any conflict between imitation and authentic freedom. In a passage toward the end of the *Chun-Chou Record*, Huang Po is lecturing to his followers on how they ought to perform a meditative practice in the midst of daily activities. While the implication is perfectly clear that they ought to follow his instructions and do as he says, he finally comes right out and says what, from the perspective above, ought not to be said: "Why not copy me," he says, "by letting each thought go as if it were nothing, as if it were decaying wood or stone."[37] Indeed, it is not without good reason that the bulk of Zen texts from this period consist in descriptions of the acts and sayings of the great masters, recorded and codified for mimetic purposes. The image of the Zen master is the image of awakened perfection set out before practitioners for the specific purpose of imitative repetition.

Elsewhere, we find Huang Po honing the critique further while, at the same time, dissolving any necessary conflict between imitative obedience and the way of freedom. The text says: "Furthermore, if one does

[35] T. 47, p. 499b; Sasaki, *The Recorded Sayings of Lin-chi*, p. 19.
[36] *Pi-yen lu*, case 11. This story appears earlier in many Zen collections.
[37] T. 48, p. 383b; Blofeld, *Huang Po*, p. 62.

not actually realize the truth of Zen from one's own experience, but simply learns it verbally and collects words, and claims to understand Zen, how can one solve the riddle of life and death? Those who neglect their old master's teachings will soon be led far astray".[38] Two messages converge here: that one must not "neglect [one's] old master's teachings" by failing to appropriate it in imitative practice *and* that merely memorizing, repeating, and following the script is one way to neglect the teachings. In the latter case, the teachings are neglected through a failure to take them up into one's own experience and self. This is a failure in appropriation, a "digestive" failure. What we find, then, is a distinction made between an authentic practice of imitation and an inauthentic miming that never penetrates to the depths of experiential practice. Imitation itself is not antithetical to freedom, only certain forms of it.

By what implicit criteria has the distinction been made between appropriate imitation and imitation as failure? The scope of valid imitation is suggested in the following advice from Huang Po: "This is not something which you can accomplish without effort, but when you reach the point of clinging to nothing whatever, you will be acting as the Buddhas act. This will indeed be acting in accordance with the saying: Develop a mind which rests on nothing whatsoever."[39] Followers here are enjoined to follow two dimensions of their ideal. First, "acting as the Buddhas act" projects the appropriate model for imitative acts; followers are to be like the Buddha. Second, "acting in accordance with a saying" specifies where one would look to get a glimpse of how Buddhas did, in fact, act. This source is "saying" – the language and discourse of the tradition. Act and saying converge here since the way the Buddhas acted is only available in the linguistically constituted forms of the tradition. Notice, however, what it is in the Buddha's acts and discourse that this passage encourages the reader to grasp and to copy: "Develop a mind which rests on nothing whatsoever"; "when you reach the point of clinging to nothing whatever, you will be acting as the Buddhas act." The one image that continues to stand amidst the various postures of critique and subversion in Zen is the image of the great masters in their liberating act of release – the non-clinging, non-grasping, selfless form of freedom. We return to the character of freedom as release later; the crucial point here is that this freedom is actualized in imitative practice wherein the practitioner learns to put him or herself

---

[38] T. 51, p. 266c; Chang, *Original Teachings*, p. 105.   [39] T. 48, p. 383b; Blofeld, *Huang Po*, p. 62.

into accord with the comportment of the Buddhas who have themselves "let go."[40]

The pivotal Chinese character in the passage above is *"ying,"* "to accord or correspond." The right kind of imitation is taken to put the practitioner into accord, not just with a particular paradigm but also, and more importantly, with the entire lineage of paradigms, each representing to successive generations what "accord" would entail. Moreover, this mimetic model was thought to be most immediately present in the concrete character and behavior of one's personal Zen master – a contemporary instantiation of the lineage. For this reason, no strict separation tended to be made between what the teacher had to teach and his or her particular method and style of teaching it. Consequently, participation in the Zen master's message inevitably included the imitation of its speaker. Through long study and practice under the guidance of the master, monks would indiscriminately appropriate all dimensions of the teaching. Familiarity with the master's words entailed, in addition, a familiarity with his acts, movements, gestures, and bearing. The particular language a master drew upon in his teaching was also, inseparably, what he was teaching and, therefore, what the student was learning. Initiates were initiated, not just into a set of ideas, but also into a certain comportment and orientation in the world that accompanied the ideas.

A specific form of self-understanding supports this emphasis on imitative practice. Imitation implies some form of dependence. Those who imitate understand themselves as dependent on foregoing models rather than as autonomous and unconnected. They experience their own finitude and connection to others. This dependence on others, however, is not thought to inhibit freedom, but rather to make it possible. Implicit in this recognition is the Buddhist doctrine of "dependent origination" in its emphatic Mahayana form: the freedom of each "originates dependent" on the freedom of others. The student receives the transmission of freedom from the teacher in the same way that the teacher had received it. Seen in genealogical terms of successive

---

[40] One story about Huang Po, which eventually made its way into *koan* case number 7 of the *Blue Cliff Record*, displays for our meditation his "post-critical" reappropriation of imitative ritual. Huang Po is bowing before an image of the Buddha when a novice, the future Emperor in retreat, challenges his pious act by asking how it instantiates the "non-attachment" and "non-seeking" he advocated. Huang Po responds that, just like "non-seeking," bowing is his custom. All acts imply some "seeking" and "attachment," aside from which no existence at all would remain. Passing through attachment, the Zen master appropriates new forms of seeking, now critically honed and "emptied." Beyond critique, the criticized practice may reappear, refined and reshaped.

generations of teachers and students in a lineage, imitation is the essential practice. The one who is most able to receive the transmission is the one who will later be most able to give it.[41] Notice, however, that the "form" in which the tradition is received is multiple and various. Zen literature offers an incredible array of models to imitate. Out of this variety, each Zen student must construct a new one. Each must synthesize a certain set of chosen images into one more or less coherent life. New creations, new forms of freedom and selfhood, appear through Zen history as new sets of models are brought together under new historical circumstances.

Having examined the explicit dependencies entailed in the Zen path to liberation, *specifically* those linked to the monastic institution and to communal practice, we can now look from a somewhat different angle at images and figures of freedom which project that goal before the minds of practitioners, and which, at the same time, problematize our earlier representations of Zen freedom. Among these figures is a substantial vocabulary in classical Zen texts which functions to generate an understanding of the human condition, or, in this case, the conditions from which one seeks liberation. The primary structural feature that unifies these metaphors is their common concern with "closure" and "constraint." If we ask, "Emancipation from what?" we find the following key terms: *ai*, to obstruct; *chang*, to screen; *ch'u*, to hold; *chueh-ting*, to fix; *pien*, to enclose; *ke*, to limit; *chien*, to view from a fixed perspective, and numerous metaphors projecting borders, boundaries, and limitations of all kinds. Communicated through this complex of terms is an awareness of a condition of enclosure or bondage. Ordinary human life is enclosed within limitations from which some form of freedom is possible.

Corresponding to the negative form of these constraints is a second vocabulary related to the Zen conception of freedom, which is similarly negative. Overthrowing initial negative obstructions is a second or double negation which manifests the point of the Zen tradition in an experience of "sudden liberation." Freedom is actualized, according to this second set of symbols, through the process of abolishing, *li*; cutting off, *tuan*; destroying, *mieh*; severing, *p'o*; exhausting, *chin*; breaking through, *chueh*; and so on. Each set of verbs is understood in terms of the other. Their mutual dependence implies that the character of

---

[41] For an excellent discussion of the theme of imitation in modern European thought and literature, see Weinsheimer, *Imitation*.

Zen freedom is dependent upon the character of constraint, and vice versa. Reading Zen well requires close attention to both; changes in one "co-arise" with changes in the other.

This act of overcoming through negation is not the same, at our initial level of analysis, as familiar religious structures through which the negative – evil – is overcome in its cancellation by the good. What distinguishes the act of negation in Zen is the extent to which it consists in an effort to break through the existing framework within which good and evil have been dichotomized in the first place. The following two passages from the *Pai-chang kuang-lu* show the character of this effort to overcome duality through the posture of "non-grasping":

Q: What is liberation of mind and liberation in all places? The master said: don't seek Buddha, don't seek Dharma, don't seek Sangha. Don't seek virtue, knowledge, and intellectual understanding. When sensations of defilement and purity are abolished through non-seeking, don't hold on to this non-seeking and consider it correct. Do not dwell at the point of ending, and do not long for heavens or fear hells. When you are unhindered by bondage and freedom, then this is called liberation of mind and body in all places.[42]

When the mind of purity and impurity is ended, it does not dwell in bondage, nor does it dwell in liberation; it has no mindfulness of doing, nondoing, bondage or liberation – then, although it remains in the world of samsara, that mind is free.[43]

In the background of statements like these in Zen texts are doctrines fundamental to Buddhist thought and practice, most notably, the concepts of impermanence, no-self, release from desire and craving, and, subsuming all of these, the Mahayana concept of emptiness. Freedom in Zen develops through the deepening realization of one's own emptiness or groundlessness, of one's constant exposure to the forces of contingency and flux. For this reason, Buddhist freedom is less an acquisition and an attainment than the result of a renunciation. Freedom is less an expression of power than an abdication of power, a letting go and a release of grip. In Huang Po's rhetoric: "Relinquishment is the *dharma!*"[44] Replacing metaphors of ground, assurance, and stability are figures of groundlessness and displacement.

Zen monastic practices, therefore, encourage and foster a renunciation of security and all the various mental acts through which we grasp for it. They seek to undermine the practitioner's deeply reinforced sense

---

[42] *Pai-chang kuang-lu*, found in *Ssu-chia yu-lu* and *Ku-tsun-su yu-lu* (Cleary, *Sayings and Doings of Pai-chang*, p. 81).   [43] *Pai-chang kuang-lu*; Cleary, *Sayings and Doings of Pai-chang*, p. 79.
[44] T. 48, p. 381a; Blofeld, *Huang Po*, p. 40.

of self by de-framing and unsettling fundamental modes of self-under-standing. Submission to this process of displacement is represented in Zen texts as a frightening experience. In the moment of full exposure, freedom is terrifying. Numerous literary figures develop this image of the "void" and the corresponding fear that it can evoke in any human being sufficiently open to experience it. The Huang Po fascicle of the *Transmission of the Lamp* likens the experience of freedom to being suspended over an infinite chasm with nothing to hold onto for security. Common to many Zen texts is the image of the moment of liberation as a letting go with both hands, a leap off a hundred-foot pole. These images of freedom cultivate a sense in the practitioner that liberation entails a fundamental defamiliarization with oneself and the world. Enlightenment sheds a kind of light on things that exposes their obvi-ousness to destabilizing forces. Normalcy comes to be seen as a function of a particular stage-setting or framework, and of a particular complex of relations, that not only could be otherwise but – given impermanence – will be otherwise.

Notice, however, how the process of de-structuring is not a call for abandonment. Unattached, having "digested" the "emptiness" of ritual, Huang Po nonetheless continues his ritual of prostration before the Buddha. Even though the "Buddha" may still be present, this "pres-ence" has been transformed. Although allowed to be thrown into ques-tion, the Buddhist monastic structure and all of its intricate particularities are not abandoned. In Buddhist doctrinal terms, the real-ization of "dependent origination" in practice is not a rejection of what has thus originated, but rather a reorientation of one's relation to it. The "emptiness" of things allows one to let go of things, and thus to be released from one dimension of the hold that things have on us. Displacement reworks freedom by means of replacement, a new orientation, and an ability to move in and among relations. Freedom is thus both finite and relative, a situation in the world that has particular rather than universal form.

Several dimensions of this experience warrant particular mention. First, freedom of this sort is not quite the same as that pictured and ideal-ized by the European Enlightenment, wherein emancipation is the pro-gressive attainment of power and maturity. The European ideal centers on self-possession, consciousness in command of its processes, freeing itself from the repressive forces of authoritative power and the prejudice of immature conceptualization. Zen freedom, by contrast, evokes images of relinquishing autonomy and the will to power in their various forms – the will to explain, the will to certain knowledge, the will to control, the will to security, and so on. It is in this sense that the key to Zen freedom is the figure of renunciation.

Second, the radicality of this act of renunciation is occasioned by the pervasive character of the obstruction that it is intended to overcome. Unlike the modern European focus on epistemological concerns – the concern to attain accurate representation through avoiding error – Buddhists envision a systematic distortion that pervades all human understanding. Rather than establishing a framework for the discrimination of truth and falsity, Buddhists entertain the possibility that the frameworks we employ for the process of securing truth are themselves subject to the distorting impacts of desire and ignorance.

Third, instead of conceiving of "liberation" as an act of appropriation – something that the subject achieves or attains – Zen texts envision "awakening" as something that occurs to us. Sudden enlightenment is an event that befalls the practitioner, beyond his or her control. Indeed, awakening is thought to occur only in the open space of renunciation, wherein control has already been relinquished.

Finally, rather than conceive of liberation as a kind of autonomy that transcends relations and their limiting, defining forces, Zen and Buddhist conceptions focus on ways in which human beings can be awakened to this relatedness. Instead of liberation from the destiny of finite placement in the world, the Zen Buddhist envisions an awakening to this placement and to its inconstancy and multiplicity.

Several of these points would have provided doctrinal dilemmas for early western interpreters of Zen for whom freedom was associated with the autonomy and control of a unified and stable self. From this point of view, freedom entails breaking ties of one form or another, rather than the recognition of relatedness. When early interpreters of Zen applied this view consistently, they understood Buddhist freedom as the transcendence of finitude itself. On this reading, Zen conceptions and practices of freedom are especially interesting when they can be seen as exceptions to this transcendental pattern, when attention to communal, linguistic, and institutional grounds highlights the relational qualities of this freedom. Seen in this light, freedom is not the abandonment of dependencies and connections, but rather a kind of movement in and among relations. Of more interest than freedom from the world is freedom within it. This reverse image of freedom, I would maintain, could be extremely valuable in providing an alternative set of images and point of departure for contemporary reflections on our own concepts of "freedom." Such employment for Buddhist texts, however, requires that we first of all listen to the otherness of their thinking. We must look, not only for how Buddhist freedom corresponds with our own, but for ways in which its differences could transform our freedom, and thus set us free.

CHAPTER 8

TRANSCENDENCE: "going beyond" Huang Po

> Master, You conduct a memorial service for the late Master Yun-
> yen. Are you in accordance with his teaching? Half accord, half
> not, replied the Master (Tung-shan). Why not complete accord? If
> I were entirely in accordance, I would have been ungrateful to him.
>
> *Transmission of the Lamp*[1]

> True masters *go beyond* the highest standards of excellence known to
> their contemporaries. They extend those standards thereby estab-
> lishing their own authority as master practitioners and enriching
> the goods that can be pursued and achieved by their successors.
>
> Jeffrey Stout[2]

The Transmission of the Lamp tells us that when the young postulant,
Huang Po, first came to see the Zen master Pai-chang, the teacher
said to him: "If your 'awakening' is identical to that of your teacher,
your power will be merely half of his. Only when you are capable of
'going beyond' your teacher will you have truly received the transmission."[3] If we accept this understanding of the matter, then Pai-
chang's "transmission of mind" to Huang Po will have been effective
and complete only at the point that Huang Po has transcended Pai-
chang's "mind" in the act of creatively "going beyond" it. If each
"enlightened mind" goes beyond its predecessor, then each would be
more than the replication of a pre-given identity. Can "transcendence" or "awakening" appear in forms that transcend each other
successively? Apparently. The quotes above suggest that receiving
transmission from one's teacher with due respect requires that you
pass beyond and extend the highest achievements of the lineage. By
the time we get to the texts transmitting the mind of Huang Po's disciple, Lin-chi, "going beyond" is greatly accentuated. So, when

---

[1] Chang, *Original Teachings*, p. 62.   [2] Stout, *Ethics after Babel*, p. 268.   [3] T. 51, p. 249c.

Huang Po fully acknowledged Lin-chi's "going beyond," and there-fore his own transmission of mind to his disciple, Huang Po called his attendant to bring the sacred items that he had inherited from his teacher, Pai-chang. Immediately, Lin-chi responded: "Attendant, bring me some fire!"[4] How could the sacred texts of Zen transmit an image of "transmission" in which the successor "torches" the most prized symbols of the lineage? This is a radical image, and, even if it was once said, we can be assured that it was not an act that anyone would have considered actually performing. It does make its point in powerful terms, however. In response to receiving the transmission, Lin-chi demonstrates his realization by refusing attachment to any sign of awakening. He "empties" Huang Po's ritual gesture and his own tendencies to "clinging," to pride, and to status.

At this point in the history of Zen, the idea of "going beyond" had taken a position of considerable importance, and would inevitably rede-fine the consciousness of history available to practitioners. Perhaps we should understand the appearance of the "going beyond" doctrine in Zen as itself a case in point, demonstrating the truth of its own claim. Whoever first articulated this new doctrine[5] was extending the tradition, "going beyond" its previous form by altering in some way what both "awakening" and "mind-to-mind transmission" would mean. A radical understanding of impermanence and a thoroughgoing historical consciousness stand behind this thought. Is this how we should read Zen, or not?

Answering "not" would probably place us more squarely in the main-stream of the Zen tradition. Few texts and therefore few "masters" focus on this idea and play it out to its various and unsettling conclusions. In fact, most of the Huang Po literature articulates a position which contra-dicts the force of the "going beyond" idea. Nevertheless, these two opposing ideas exist side by side in the texts. Our task here will be to read these two sides of Zen off against each other, and to think our way between them in the hope that some "going beyond" will occur in our minds.

"Mind transmission" (*ch'uan hsin*) or "*dharma* transmission" (*ch'uan fa*) is most consistently presented in the texts as the historical repetition of a timeless identity. As we have seen, the mind of the Zen master is trans-ferred to, and imprinted upon, the mind of the disciple who then passes

---

[4] T. 47, p. 505c; Sasaki, *The Recorded Sayings of Lin-chi*, p. 56.
[5] Yanagida claims that this idea was newly introduced into Chinese Buddhist culture in the *Transmission of the Lamp* (Iriya, *Denshin Hoyo*, p. 167).

this same mentality on to the next generation of Zen masters. The appearance of the doctrine of "mind-to-mind transmission" is no doubt historically complex – its "origination" bears numerous "dependencies." Yet one historical factor seems particularly important. This is that the Zen tradition used this doctrine to differentiate itself from other competing forms of Chinese Buddhism. Whereas other schools transmit texts, doctrines, or particular meditative/ritual practices, Zen transmits only the goal itself – enlightened mind – and not its various means.[6] Given this difference, the realization that "means" are "empty," and thus relative to historical context, would not haunt Zen as it clearly had earlier forms of Chinese Buddhism which had come and gone through history in accordance with the relevance of their particular transmitted "means." While the texts, doctrines, and practices employed in Zen would vary, the awakened state of mind transmitted from one generation to the next would not. Instead, the exactitude and identity of transmission would be understood through the metaphor of the stamp or seal. Pressing the inked stamp upon the absorbent surface yields an exact duplication, no matter how many times it is repeated. Thus in Zen, the precise contours of the master's mind and experience of awakening would be impressed or imprinted upon the successor's mind by means of thorough, longstanding co-practice, regardless of means. When this imprinting process – this socialization into the deepest recesses of Zen mind – was complete, "transmission" required only the act of ritual announcement.

The idea of "patriarchs" standing in a historical lineage as the foundation for a "school" of Chinese Buddhism existed prior to Zen. It may be that, instead of "mind-to-mind transmission" giving rise to the recording of historical lineage, it was actually the other way around. Once the need to legitimize the new "Zen school" with a historical lineage was felt within the context of its own doctrinal and practical orientation, "mind-to-mind transmission" may have been the obvious and ingenious consequence. Or perhaps the "co-arising" of all these factors was much more complex: numerous factors thoroughly intertwined. Nevertheless, once articulated, the doctrine of

---

[6] There is considerable irony, and probably historical anachronism, in P'ei-hsiu's claim in the Preface to the *Essentials of Mind Transmission* that this text is an "imprint of mind" (*hsin-yin*). The text itself says that true "mind imprint" occurs without reference to texts – "mind to mind" direct. So although we can sympathize with P'ei-hsiu's desire to claim that his text is an accurate representation of Huang Po, we can also, from the text's own point of view, see how this claim invalidates itself.

"mind-to-mind transmission," along with an eventual consensus on how the historical lineage would be constructed, would bring to Zen substantial persuasive power. It would justify the claim that its "awakening" was an exact replica of the Buddha's "awakening." Lines connecting current Zen masters with Kasyapa, Shakyamuni, and the ancient Buddhas could be demonstrated with precision, thus guaranteeing the quality and authenticity of its transmission of mind in the present and future. Later "awakenings" could be considered precisely the same as the original. Taking this as one of its central points, Huang Po's *Essentials of Mind Transmission* would say: "Since the Tathagata entrusted Kasyapa with the *Dharma* until now, Mind has been transmitted with Mind, and these Minds have been identical . . . Mind is transmitted with Mind and these Minds do not differ."[7] Although the idea of the "patriarchal lineage" was already present in Huang Po's time, it would be at least another century before a method of extending this lineage into the future could be devised. This was accomplished impressively, and decisively, in the early eleventh century when the *Transmission of the Lamp* would absorb the Huang Po texts and many others into a grand vision of enlightened history.

It is against the background of this significant historical doctrine of identity that the radical call for "going beyond" is made. But how can you "go beyond" someone with whom an identity has been established? Any "going beyond" identity is a movement out of identity and into differentiation. For some, no doubt, the tension between these two incompatible doctrines was not noticed. Those who did notice, however, would have required some further adjustment in understanding to hold both of these ideas simultaneously. One strategy, because of its central place within classical Chinese thought generally, occurred to Zen Buddhists right away. The tension between the identity of transmitted mind and the call to "go beyond" the tradition by differentiating oneself could be relieved by calling upon a distinction between the "substance" (*t'i*) of mind and its "functional appearance" (*yung*). While the substance or essence of mind could be said to be identical between equally enlightened masters, the way this "awakening" functions in the world might differ significantly. Thus, while a subsequent master might behave, speak, and teach in ways quite distinct from an earlier master, having in those ways "gone beyond" him in

---

[7] T. 48, p. 382a; Blofeld, *Huang Po*, p. 50.

response to changed circumstances, nevertheless, their state of mind and experience could be held to be identical. Indeed, the character *yung* ("function") soon came to be used to refer more broadly to awakened behavior – in true Zen comportment, one sees the functional manifestation of enlightened mind, a sign of its very essence. Although these signs may change over time, it was thought that what they signify did not.

Had John Blofeld noticed the tension between these two teachings, he too would have sought some form of reconciliation. The repertoire of possibilities available in his own language and culture would have included a metaphysical structure analogous to the Chinese *t'i/yung* dichotomy. Given his background and education, Blofeld might have claimed that, whereas the (Aristotelian) substance or essence of Mind is always identical between Buddhas, its "accidental" manifestation in the realm of history would have been subject to change and differentiation. Therefore, while the essence of Mind is timeless, its temporal or historical "expressions" might be various. Hence, even though a successor's teaching may very well "go beyond" or differ from the predecessor's, this need not thereby cast doubt on the identity of its deeper essential source.

A version of this doctrine appears throughout Blofeld's writing wherever he addressed the question of the identity and difference between religions. Given Blofeld's background – a citizen of the worldwide British Empire and a romantic convert to "universal spirituality" – this question was destined to be of central concern. Rejecting what he perceived to be the excessive exclusivity of English religious traditions and its corresponding dogmatism, Blofeld joined a growing number of English speakers in embracing the Indian doctrine of the ultimate unity of all religions with respect to goals. Persuaded by the Indian model of religions as different paths to the same peak of transcendent experience, Blofeld would argue over and over that the apparent differences between religions are attributable to their employing variant historically derived means to reach the same ultimate end, whether they were able to articulate the matter this way or not.

This line of thinking is easily applicable to the question of apparent differences between Zen masters for whom an identity of enlightened mind had been posited. Although startling differences in language, demeanor, teaching, and practice are evident among the great masters of Zen, these differences are taken to be "accidental" rather than "essential" because they reflect variations in techniques of teaching called forth by variant historical circumstances, but not a divergence in the state of mind from which the teaching issues.

Each of these doctrinal strategies – the Chinese essence/function dichotomy, the classical western substance/accident dichotomy – share a similar essentialist pattern. Each rests upon difficult-to-justify metaphysical grounds, and is thus vulnerable to contemporary anti-essentialist critique. In the wake of contemporary thought, none of these dichotomies now seems persuasive as a perspective from which arguments for the sameness of enlightened mind beyond historical appearances could be articulated. For this reason, the "going beyond" doctrine included in these Zen texts may have considerably more contemporary importance than traditional and modern interpreters have attributed to it. On this reading of Zen, the "mind" transmitted via "mind" would be best conceived, not as a timeless, ahistorical essence, but as a continually evolving, historical realization of successive generations' highest aspirations.

We can begin to make this case by summarizing arguments against substance/accident or essence/function dichotomies, and then take up separately the related but somewhat different strategy of separating enlightenment as a "goal" from its various "means." Our inclination to assume that all sorts of entities in the world – people, ideas, objects, institutions – have a deep structural essence upon which various historical causal factors operate is deep-seated. This is true of many Buddhists as well, in spite of the fact that this tradition was initiated on premises that mitigate against this view, and, moreover, in spite of the fact that forceful critiques of essentialism are found throughout the Buddhist canon. Nagarjuna and the Madhyamika lineage are the primary symbols for this general theme in Buddhist thought. We will return to this heritage shortly. But one of its arguments is still the best against an essence/attribute division. This is that whatever essence we locate can be shown to be dependent upon its various attributes; whatever we designate as central as opposed to peripheral can be dislodged or reversed by altering the angle from which it is seen. Any dependence of "substance" upon "accidents" reverses the figures, giving the posited substance a more "accidental" standing and making the "accidents" appear more substantial. If substance is dependent upon accidents, the tables have been turned, background shifts to the fore. Although in our everyday lives we do separate "essential" features from "peripheral" ones, nevertheless, we do so in finite, contextual, and contingent ways, as, for example, when we isolate what is essential to this particular issue, within this particular time and context, and from these points of view, knowing, in principle, that changes in any of these stage-setting factors will alter the way "essence" appears. In the wake of "deconstruction," arguments like these have become common to our intellectual context – and persuasive. Although this realization in no way eliminates the necessity always placed upon us of finding what is "essential," it does fundamentally alter what we understand essence to mean.

An essence/function dichotomy, like the Chinese *t'i/yung* division, is a version of the same. It maintains that you can separate what something *is* from what it *does*. With respect to Zen, this strategy works to maintain an essence for enlightenment in the face of its changing appearances. The most serious problem that this strategy encounters is that it inevitably pushes the elusive "essence of enlightenment" out of the finite world into a transcendent realm about which nothing can be said because one encounters only its appearances in "the world," which are various and do change. We find Blofeld resorting to this move on numerous occasions. If the "ultimate transcendental experience" is the same in spite of difference in "expression", in spite of the fact that different experiencers in different traditions say and do very different things in response to "it," the only conclusion that remains is that its essence is unknowable. Unknowability, of course, makes claims about its identity and sameness tenuous. Following this track, one can still maintain, of course, as several traditions have in analogous ways, that essence is located elsewhere, in the realm of Ideas, in the mind of God, or in the sphere of nirvana. In a post-Kantian intellectual context, however, the difficulties entailed in legitimizing this metaphysical move appear to be insurmountable. Blofeld manages by ignoring the obstacles and attempting to switch intellectual contexts.

An alternative track, however, and the one being tested in this reading of Zen, is that we not make the initial metaphysical move of positing a timeless, transcendental experience, but rather, consider the possibility that all human experience is finite, historical, and open to transformation. Of all the possible candidates for which "timelessness" might be a tempting attribution, human experience is among the least likely. Just as experiencers change with alterations in context and circumstance, so does "experience." We "experience" in time, temporally, all the time. Temporality and experience are inseparable; neither can be found without the other. Even the experience of "timelessness" occurs or fails to occur in time, its conditions "co-arising" with other factors in history.[8]

The metaphysical inclinations through which John Blofeld read Huang Po have clearly affected how Huang Po has been transmitted to us. The "footnotes" scattered throughout Blofeld's translation of Huang Po provide interesting and excellent clues, indicating places in the text where Huang Po's text has come into tension with Blofeld's metaphysics. Wherever the text is "unclear," wherever what it says must be given considerable allegorical assistance to put it into accord with Blofeld's understanding of "the spirit of Zen," a footnote is appended to straighten things out. Most of these footnotes are intended to keep his readers from following the text too literally down the wrong interpretive road. In the following passage, there may be good reason, given our revised "metaphysics," to prefer a road Blofeld would not have considered:

Since the Tathagata entrusted Kasyapa with the Dharma until now, Mind has been transmitted with Mind, and these Minds have been identical . . . Thus Mind is transmitted with Mind and these Minds do not differ. Transmitting and receiving transmission are both a most difficult and mysterious understanding, so that few indeed have been able to receive it. In fact, however, Mind is not Mind and transmission is not really transmission.[9]

The final line in this passage problematizes everything said before it, so much so that it seems to reverse the very point just made. If "mind" and "transcendence" are somehow not themselves, then the status and character of "mind transmission" will not be graspable in its previous form. Blofeld responds to this interpretive dilemma with the following footnote appended to the troublesome concluding line. He writes: "This is a reminder that All terms used in Zen are mere makeshifts."[10]

This footnote encourages us to read the troublesome passage as saying:

---

[8] An interesting and historically important application of contemporary anti-essentialist history can be found in Foulk, "The Ch'an School." Foulk's thorough study of Chinese Zen institutions through the Sung concludes that, contrary to the many claims of Japanese Zen apologists, no essential, defining feature of Zen can be found. No practice, doctrine, genre, or institution remains to define the essence of Zen over time. Thus the tradition's own radical "going beyond" has abandoned all essences. Nevertheless, Foulk allows one essence to slip away by dividing the whole into historical and "supra-historical" dimensions. According to his understanding, many dimensions of Zen can be studied historically, but enlightenment is "entirely beyond the scope of critical historiography" (p. 32). Although this division of "realms" has its advantages, such as delimiting the range of scientific research, the metaphysics required to make the division are currently untenable. Although Foulk's historical research could hardly be more distinct from Blofeld's romantic theology, nevertheless, both share the same modern metaphysics, on the basis of which history and the "transcendent" can be separated.

[9] T. 48, p. 382a; Blofeld, *Huang Po*, p. 50.   [10] Blofeld, *Huang Po*, p. 50.

"Keep in mind that real transmission and transcendent Mind – the actual referents of our language here – are not the same as, and not determinable by, whatever meaning these two terms may conjure up in your mind." This is so because, in Blofeld's words, "words belong to the realm of flux and illusion,"[11] which is separate from and transcended by the realm of "Mind" and "Transmission." It is not that Blofeld acknowledges no continuity between these two realms. There is an identity between them that Blofeld does see clearly. The connection is severely limited, however, and located in the priority given to the "other" side. The realm of eternity, for Blofeld, encompasses the realm of temporality – our world – but ultimately in such a way as to render it a mistake, an illusion that is subsumed into the overarching reality of timelessness. The two realms are heavily reified and, for the most part, non-dialectically related. They are not characterized by "co-arising," and "mutual penetration" is not their nature. Instead, one subsumes and cancels the other.

As the foregoing comments hint, the metaphysics behind Blofeld's interpretation of this passage are not typically "Buddhist," nor are they attractive in our current setting. In our context, "the spirit of Zen" points elsewhere, the minimal requirement "going beyond" a new set of footnotes. Our lead is supplied by Huang Po in the text's numerous claims that nirvana and samsara are not separate realms at all, and that all existants, including "mind" and the practice of "transmission," "originate dependent" upon other mutually dependent existants. Blofeld's footnote allows too easy an escape from a moment in the text where contradiction might invite our reading to focus. Can our replacement footnote invoke insight, or just further evasion of the power of Huang Po's mind?

Blofeld's gloss on this passage – a reminder that words and referents are distinct – follows his tendency to read Huang Po as a metaphysical dualist. His image of Huang Po has the master living in a transcendent world beyond the realm of time and space. As Blofeld puts it, "The state of Mind of an Illumined Man is independent of time-relationships."[12] On this view his Zen sermons are a hopeless attempt to reach back into our world, pointers which, by metaphysical location, cannot possibly do their job of pointing.

How else might we read the passage from Huang Po which so eagerly subverts the assertions leading up to it? Clues may be found in a better reading of the meaning of the Buddhist concept "emptiness." One plausible rule to consider in reading Zen is that when you find a blatant

---

[11] Blofeld, *Huang Po*, p. 82.   [12] Blofeld, *The Zen Teaching of Hui Hai*, p. 131.

contradiction in the text, consult "emptiness" for guidance. Blofeld has done this. But for him, "emptiness," "The Void," has already been assimilated to his two-world metaphysics.[13] This is accomplished in the Huang Po translation by dividing "emptiness" to fit the metaphysical dualism. "The Void" is divided into two parts, one for each metaphysical realm. Blofeld makes this explicit in a footnote: "A distinction is here made between 'void' in the sense of flux where all forms are seen in dissolution, and the Great Void which overspreads, penetrates and IS all."[14] Blofeld calls upon the English practice of capitalization to clarify what, to his metaphysics, is an untenable ambiguity within the one Chinese word *k'ung*, meaning "void" or "empty." The "void" is samsara – the realm of history, culture, language, religion, philosophy, change, and finitude. The "Great Void" is nirvana – a realm lacking all of these human configurations. Given the Buddhist texts now available to us, however, this reading of Buddhist "emptiness" should no longer be persuasive, nor will it attract our interest in Zen as it did Blofeld's. Taking another line of thought, we can read the two sides of Blofeld's "void" as uniting on the side of the flux – the side on which impermanence and "dependent origination" necessitate a reality "empty" of static essence. As it was defined in chapter 2, the Mahayana concept of "emptiness" means the lack of own-being (*svabhava*) or self-nature (*tzu-hsing*); it calls for a perspective from which nothing – not mind, transmission, or emptiness itself – is reified, made permanent, or conceived to be independent of everything else. Emptiness, on this reading, is the Buddhist principle of finitude. It makes a claim about how things take on form and characteristics, and what this comes to mean over time.

Needless to say, this definition is "empty." Buddhists in different contexts will have defined it differently and perhaps with more insight. Some Buddhists, like Blofeld, preferred something more substantial, with stronger "otherworldly" qualities. Chinese culture alone produced countless variant definitions. Other cultures tended to define it otherwise. From this perspective, however, many of these definitions tend heavily to reify "emptiness," perhaps because, beyond its conceptual use, the experience of "emptiness" came to be identified with "nirvana" and the "Buddha." When Buddhist sutras announce that nirvana is the

---

[13] Naturally, since "non-dualism" was a doctrinal requirement in Buddhism, Blofeld considered himself a non-dualist. He argued, for instance, that the dichotomy between the pure and the impure (*Huang Po*, p. 117) was an illusion that must be overcome, and that the "great mystics of all ages" had done so. Nevertheless, from this perspective, Blofeld maintained other dualistic structures at the basis of his reading of Huang Po.   [14] Blofeld, *Huang Po*, p. 75.

realization of emptiness, several interpretive possibilities are present. We can either subsume "nirvana" under the connotations of "emptiness," or "emptiness" under "nirvana," with results varying, of course, in accordance with how each has been understood. Under the latter conditions, to which Blofeld was a convert, "emptiness" – "The Great Void" – is deified and removed from the flux of this world. "Emptiness" comes to suggest another realm altogether different from this one, where temporality is unknown. We are led elsewhere, however, if we read "nirvana is emptiness" under the former conditions. In this case, "emptiness" leads to the practice of seeing "essences," including the "essence of nirvana," through the lens of their various conditions. In this light, relations, contingencies, and transformations come into view, and with them, the possibility of "going beyond."

With this second possibility in mind, let us reread Huang Po's blasphemous tribute to "mind-to-mind Transmission" along lines not open to Blofeld's view. Following a series of claims about the identity of mind through a differentiated process of transmission, the text says (still in Blofeld's words): "In fact, however, Mind is not Mind and transmission is not really transmission."[15] This formula or pattern is common and central to many Mahayana Buddhist texts. It means: both "mind" and "transmission" are "empty," that is, neither are timeless, transhistorical entities. Like everything else in a contingent and finite world, "mind" and "transmission" arise and take particular shape in particular contexts and in relation to other religious, cultural, and physical factors. "Emptiness is form," as the *Perfection of Wisdom Sutras* have said, and form lacks both permanence and essence. Form continually reforms, "going beyond" its previous shape. If we read this Huang Po sermon as being engaged in the reflexive "deconstruction" of its own religious discourse, an effort to "break through" reification and hardened experience, we link it to the most common rhetorical theme in the *Prajnaparamita Sutras*, the texts which initiated the Mahayana tradition in the first place. Such a reading seems both more suited to that particular religious context, and more attractive to our own current act of reading Zen.

One further strategy of dichotomy still exists, however, by means of which the call to "go beyond" the realization of former Zen masters can be subordinated to the theme of enlightenment as a pure, ahistorical, identity. This dichotomy separates enlightenment as an unchanging "end" from its various "means" which differ according to context. Thus

---

[15] T. 48, p. 382a; Blofeld, *Huang Po*, p. 50.

one might "go beyond" one's predecessor in articulating new strategies for "inducing" or "expressing" enlightenment, while at the same time sharing the same mental state as one's enlightened teacher. Of the various dichotomies discussed here, this one is perhaps the most plausible. It also has the added advantage of accord with the Mahayana principle of *upaya* or "skill-in-means," one version of which stipulates that all doctrines and all practices are "empty means" (that is, contextually dependent strategies) toward the goal of enlightenment. Nevertheless, the means/ends dichotomy collapses as a foundation supporting the ahistorical essence of Mind – it too is "empty." Even means and ends overlap, new means suggesting and making possible new ends and ends endlessly giving rise to novel means. Its "emptiness" here, the failure of each side of the means/ends dichotomy to remain fully separate from its opposite pole, can be articulated in any number of ways. The best-known Buddhist way was Nagarjuna's, which has been restated over and over throughout the Buddhist tradition. This view maintains that if one side of the dilemma can only be defined in terms of its other, then each exists with the other at its very core. Its "essence" turns out to include non-essence, thus "emptying" the structure of polarity.[16]

This is one of logic's ways beyond the means/ends dichotomy. History provides others, vantage points from which interdependence defines ends and means. From this perspective we see that not just the means but the end – enlightenment – has a history. The goals toward which Buddhists in the history of numerous cultures have striven are various and differentiated. Although Buddhist mythology tells us that there have been an "infinite" number of enlightened Buddhas, it is hard for us to think so. Historically conceived, enlightenment has a story of origins, no matter how complex and no matter how little of it we currently understand. The metaphors of "light" and the language of "waking up," when brought together with sufficient cultural conditions, social practices, and proper timing, came to suggest the possibility that the human mind may be capable of more penetrating light, of a greater wakefulness and awareness, and more. As new practices were devised to actualize these possibilities, new conceptions of the goal and new experiences of it evolved. Our "use" of singular nouns like "enlightenment" and "awakening" disguise the cultural complexity of these processes, as does the brief narrative I have just told about "origins." They entice us into reifying the concepts and separating them from the language, prac-

---

[16] See *Mula Madhyamaka Karikas*, section XV.

tices, and histories that surround them. If this reading of Huang Po is helpful, then it is not just, with Blofeld's account, that words are historical and contingent, and therefore do not match reality which is not. It is rather that both are historical and contingent, the gap and boundary between them being structurally illusive. Not only does "reality" "go beyond" words, but also words "go beyond" reality. Of course, neither goes very far beyond the other, however, since "interpenetration" is their "nature."

The point I want to highlight here is that there is a crucial link between goals and means, especially when the goals are the highest aspirations of an entire culture. The link is such that any change in one will bring with it irresistible impetus for change in the other. Neither side can win the argument about which came first. "Enlightenment" came to be the goal of those who were already engaged in certain practices toward some prior goal. Once the goal was "enlightenment," however, certain old practices receded as being less appropriate while others emerged as the ones most capable of enabling its attainment. Changes in practice can in turn provide the context necessary for further articulations of the goal. The point here is that the "skillful means" and "expedient devices" employed by Buddhists to disseminate "enlightenment" into contexts of diversity had the additional effect of forcing "enlightenment" to "go beyond" itself in an accelerated historical development. As is true in every sphere of human culture, what we do in our quest for the ideal will inevitably have some effect on the very process of idealization.[17]

Our initial question was how to reconcile the call to "go beyond" the tradition with the concept of "identical enlightenment." Our conclusion thus far comes to this: this reconciliation cannot easily be made, and, more importantly, it need not and should not be made. The concept of the "sameness" of enlightenment within differentiated history contradicts many of the central concepts of the Buddhist tradition: impermanence, dependent origination, no-self, emptiness. Moreover, this contradiction is unnecessary since enlightenment or "transcendence"

---

[17] "The very process of trying to obtain what one values may change what it is that one values" (MacIntyre, *Whose Justice*, p. 41). MacIntyre helps us see why the issue before us cannot be handled by a "means–ends distinction according to which all human activities are either conducted as means to already given or decided ends or are simply worthwhile in themselves or perhaps both. What this framework omits from view are those ongoing modes of human activity within which ends have to be discovered and rediscovered, and means devised to pursue them; and it thereby obscures the importance of the ways in which those modes of activity generate new ends and new conceptions of ends" (*After Virtue*, p. 273).

can, and has, been conceived through the figures of "impermanence" and "emptiness" without obstructing its transcendent character. Instead, "transcendence" can be redefined in historical, and therefore, finite terms. For Blofeld, transcendence could not be finite, by definition in fact, because what it transcends is finitude itself. Having constructed an absolute transcendence, beyond space, time, causality, language, and history, how could this state possibly be transcended by future practitioners? Blofeld's only option then was to link up with the text's claim about the identity of mind within transmission and to ignore any claims about "going beyond." As an alternative to this, we have explored the "going beyond" theme in Zen in an effort to conceive, in our terms, what a "historical" transcendence could mean, a "going beyond" that nevertheless remains in the world.

If transcendence is a historical phenomenon, found in historically constituted cultures among historical human beings, it would be subject to change and transformation under the influence of alterations in other factors and circumstances. Transmitted from one generation to the next through historical traditions, texts, and teachings, this experience, like any other, would lack an immutable, eternal essence. Taking its point of departure from past experience, any new experience of transcendence might go beyond its predecessor insofar as circumstances, thinking, practices, and human selves have changed. Understood along these lines, tradition is a living medium, every dimension of which grows, changes, and recedes in relation to other dimensions and surrounding historical circumstances. It is the tradition's "nature" always to be "different," to "go beyond" itself by considering each new realization – each "going beyond" – as one historical potentiality contained within tradition itself.[18]

It is possible that the "going beyond" doctrine in Zen is a product of the realization that the tradition had in fact changed in spite of its occasional claims to immutability. It is true that the expectation in the tradition was that "transmission" would occur only at those points where each new Zen master had attained an "original" experience – his or her own – rather than a replication of someone else's. The "transcendence" that is "transmitted" would not be a "repetition" in the sense of a reduplication of historical precedence. It would instead repeat prior transcendence in that an "original" experience is undergone. If the teacher's experience was his own, an original, so must the student's be

---

[18] "It is the tradition's essence always to be different" (Gadamer, *Truth and Method*, p. 110).

in order to equal it. It is perhaps in this sense that Pai-chang tells Huang Po that transmission will occur only in the act of "going beyond" precedent and tradition. Similarly, the *Transmission of the Lamp* has Huang Po say: "[I]f one does not actually realize the truth of Zen from one's own experience, but simply learns it verbally and collects words, and claims to understand Zen, how can one solve the riddle of life and death?"[19]

Attempting to clarify this matter generations later, the text lets Zen master Kuei-shan ask: "'Tell me, how did Huang Po get it (this marvelous awakened character)? Naturally, or did he get it from someone?' Yang-shan said: 'It is both the inheritance of his teacher's bequest and his own communion with the source.' Kuei-shan said: 'So it is!'"[20] Is Huang Po's power an inheritance, or is it an original discovery? Both, since in principle these two sources amount to the same: what the teacher teaches is how to commune with the source on one's own. Since it is "on one's own," however, and since new historical circumstances surround each individual's encounter with the tradition, each new "transcendence" must in certain respects "go beyond" its predecessors. The "tradition," therefore, is not best conceived as an inert deposit, a sealed package passed on from one generation to the next. Such a unilateral conception of history fails to recognize its reciprocal character. The tradition does provide the "pretext," the point of departure from which the text of the tradition of "transcendence" is to be rewritten, but the operation only makes sense "dialectically" as an exchange between the interpreted past and the interpreting present, the old and the new.[21] Perhaps this is how we should understand the explanation given for Ma-tsu's reception of his teacher's "transmission of mind": Nan-yueh says, "Ma-tsu, among all my disciples, deserves my mind, for he excels in the old and the new."[22] To excel in the old, without managing to "go beyond" it, is to fail in the new – the present – where, in fact, we live. The obverse implication is clear as well: you cannot excel in the new aside from deep appropriation of what has been. As earlier Chinese Buddhist thought (T'ien-t'ai and Hua-yen) had made clear, there is no

---

[19] T. 51, p. 266; Chang, *Original Teachings*, p. 105.   [20] T. 51, p. 266.

[21] For this same reason, Yanagida is overzealous in his claims about the "originality" of Zen. He writes that the "Zen school" was "a new creation, based on its own original experience which negates all preexistent organization and values. The formation of the *zenshu* as a 'separate transmission outside the teachings' means that the Chinese cast away the borrowed clothing they had been given by the Indians, and created a wardrobe that fit their own constitution" (*Zen no goroku* vol. II, *Shoki no zenshu*, trans., Foulk, "The Ch'an School," p. 25). The metaphor of "tradition" as "clothing" had led Blofeld to similar conclusions in which tradition, language, and history are removable at will rather than constitutive of the self.

[22] T. 51, p. 241a; Pas, *The Recorded Sayings of Ma-tsu*, p. 49.

dwelling in the present without the full presence there of the past and future.

This reciprocal relationship between past and present is the source of much paradox in the Zen tradition. Paradoxically, Huang Po can be faithful to his teacher and to the tradition only by freely revising their legacies. Only by redescribing what "Zen" means in such a way as to accommodate issues raised by the present can he truly "pass on" the Zen tradition. Given ongoing temporality, only by re-imagining, redescribing, and re-experiencing Zen "enlightenment," will it continue to be considered "enlightening."[23]

Some degree of transcendence, or "going beyond," will occur to us whether we want it or not. History, in effect, hurls us beyond, not so much against our will as by shaping our wills.[24] We can see that John Blofeld was himself one instrument of the relentless "going beyond" of English culture. He and a few others in his generation went beyond the forms of religion previously available in their culture. Why was this; how did it occur? Blofeld's own explanation (like ours) is a symptom of history's effects on him. As a modernist, he understands the matter individually, not collectively or historically. As a romantic, he makes every effort to understand the matter through the categories of the "other,"

---

[23] In an odd form of historical awareness, Zen interpreter Thomas Hoover has written that "in effect, Huang Po laid it all out, cleared the way, and defined Zen once and for all . . . With his death at the midpoint of the ninth century, there was little more to be invented" (*The Zen Experience*, p. 131). In the most important sense, this is clearly false. Zen was just getting going when Huang Po arrived on the scene. Massive development occurred within the tradition beyond this point. There is, however, an interesting truth to Hoover's remarks. There is a sense in which Chinese Zen did become conservative several centuries later, making itself less relevant to current developments in Chinese culture. The tradition seemed to have lost its vibrant capacity to change, to adapt, and to "go beyond" itself. The cultural avant-garde in China moved elsewhere to a resurgent Neo-Confucian tradition and beyond, and Zen ceased to be a major player in Chinese history. This was the situation to which Blofeld was responding when he wrote that we must "hasten . . . to preserve the essence of Buddhism for the West before most of the traditional links are broken or weakened beyond repair" (*The Zen Teaching of Hui Hai*, p. 14). Unless this "essence" includes the capacity to go beyond prior essences, however, it would not be worth preserving.

[24] The "going beyond" of history sometimes takes on radical proportions. Just prior to its famous "Long March," Mao Tze-tung and the "Red Army" occupied the Buddhist monastery on Mount Huang Po which it held as a base of operations for many years, making it, in a sense, a sacred place in an entirely different lineage. This history, however, did not prevent Huang Po monastery from being destroyed decades later in the Cultural Revolution. With its bricks and stones, a new building was erected on the same site to house the newly formed "Huang Po Production Brigade." Red banners now displayed a new lineage of ancestors: Marx, Engels, Lenin, and Mao. With appropriate symbolism, only the well-spring of the original monastery remains. Locals, however, now dream of rebuilding the monastery, seeking Huang Po's help in "going beyond" the deficiencies of the communist present. The story of transformation on Mount Huang Po is far from over.

such as karma, rebirth, and other mysteries of "Oriental wisdom." Therefore he asks: "How could my chosen mode of life or even my presence there in Sikkim, under such circumstances, be explained in the light of my upbringing and family background, except as the logical result of trends stretching back past my birth?" Having included the answer in the question, he goes on to explicate: "During my earliest years there had been outwardly nothing, however tenuous, to connect me with the Path, nothing to link me even remotely with any aspect of Asia."[25]

The explanation that he is experimenting with here is karma and reincarnation. He has found himself in Asia, a converted Buddhist, not for any reasons having to do with family background and other "external" affairs, but rather due to his individual past – previous lives. The experiment is just the one he should have been performing, probing and testing the "other's" cultural proclivities with an openness of mind, a desire to learn. Nevertheless, what it blocks from his view is an important realization, one that might also be attainable and understandable through less individualistic readings of karma and rebirth. What he does not see, given his experiment, is the historical inevitability that when the British Empire expanded to include "Asia," the results would be reciprocal, each converting the other. When Blofeld says that his conversion was "the logical result of trends stretching back past my birth," his meaning – individualized karma – is encompassed by larger historical developments, "trends" which would make "Buddhism" irresistible and persuasive to certain "individuals" in England. Blofeld was not just a convert, he was an instrument of conversion, his writings helping to turn the tide of history just as he had been turned by it. Precisely *in* the writings of Blofeld, English culture "went beyond" itself. No matter how we understand his "past lives," larger developments set the stage for Blofeld's journey to Asia and his conversion to Buddhism, making possible his place in history. This is the "mystery of transmission" that now summons our reflection.

The Zen doctrine of "historical transcendence," or "going beyond" the tradition as received, is based upon radical insight into other Buddhist principles: impermanence, dependent origination, no-self, and emptiness. Although the tradition did not always affirm this doctrine, and often contradicted it, nonetheless, the fact that it is there at all is intriguing, and impressive. Overcoming the tradition, "going beyond" it, differing from it – these are the tradition's own demands, not something

---

[25] Blofeld, *The Wheel of Life*, p. 18.

counter to it or outside its parameters.[26] Simply to agree with the tradition, to obey its current form, is to fail to receive the "transmission." It is to be "ungrateful," as the *Transmission of the Lamp* put it.[27] This form of reflection can only derive from a deep sense of historicity; it implies the radically temporal thesis that who we are as human beings is historical through and through. History is conceived here not so much as a force that acts upon our human essence from outside but rather as something closer at hand, something beyond which we will not go. It is true that only a few exceptional Buddhists were ever willing to face this realization in a thorough-going way. Most preferred that it apply to things of "this world" but not of the transcendent realm of Buddhas, nirvana, and mind-to-mind transmission. Nevertheless, whoever the Master of Mount Huang Po was, he may have been one of these few. "Mind is not Mind and transmission is not really transmission." Reading Zen in this context, therefore, requires that we too raise the question of what it means to live historically. And when we do, we must also ask: how does the call to "go beyond" also apply to us in the context of reading Zen?

[26] The difference, it seems to me, between the Zen doctrine of "going beyond" and the romantic "anxiety of influence" as articulated by Harold Bloom in *The Anxiety of Influence* is that the romantic "horror of finding oneself to be only a copy or replica" leads to a sense that the most significant achievement is to distance yourself from the tradition, that what you overcome in yourself is the tradition. In Zen, precisely because self-overcoming was the tradition's own demand, such overcoming was considered an act of piety, an act of paying off a debt to the tradition which has made transcendence possible. Transcendence derives from the tradition and is posited in history as a reciprocal gift back to the tradition. Transcendence does not require distance if you *are* the tradition and if, through you, the tradition moves ahead with every excursion you make.   [27] T. 51, p. 291.

CHAPTER 9

MIND: the "Great Matter" of Zen

It is equally deadly for a mind to have a system or to have none.
Therefore it will have to decide to combine both.

Friedrich Schlegel[1]

Question: What is the Buddha?
Answer: Mind is the Buddha and No Mind is the Way?

Huang Po[2]

Of all the symbols in the Huang Po texts, and all the issues of concern there, "mind" is clearly primary. Mind is the matter of the text – the "Great Matter" (*ta-shih*) to which all other concerns are subordinated. Therefore, in his Preface, P'ei-hsiu wrote that Huang Po "transmitted only 'One Mind' (*I-hsin*), aside from which, there is no other *dharma*."[3] Given the frequency of the topic, and the extent to which it encompasses all other concerns in the Huang Po literature, we can easily concur with P'ei-hsiu's observation. We can also see why some Zen editor rather early in the history of this text named the first collection of these Huang Po materials *The Essential Teachings of Mind Transmission (Ch'uan-hsin fa-yao)*. If these are indeed the "essential teachings," our meditations must focus here.

The text begins with the following lines: "The Master said to me [P'ei-hsiu]: All Buddhas and all sentient beings are only 'One Mind.' There is nothing else . . . Right before you, that's it!"[4] If, as P'ei-hsiu's Preface claims, Huang Po's only teaching was the doctrine of the "One Mind," we can now see why that is the case – "There is nothing else." The "One Mind" "exceeds all boundaries"[5] and therefore encompasses everything. This sense of the unity of all things, an awareness of the whole of things symbolized by mind, is represented in the text as requiring long-term

---

[1] I Quoted from Hart, *The Trespass of the Sign*, Cambridge University Press, 1989, p. 105.
[2] T. 48, p. 384b.   [3] T. 48, pp. 379b-c; Blofeld, *Huang Po*, p. 27.
[4] T. 48, p. 379c; Blofeld, *Huang Po*, p. 29.   [5] T. 48, p. 379c.

and exacting cultivation. Overwhelmingly, the texts claim, people experience only the diversity of things, their separateness and distinct identities. Only rarely is this ordinary state of mind intersected by awareness of the interconnectedness and unity of all things. Nevertheless, this "identity" is represented as somehow more fundamental and, therefore, more difficult to appropriate. Moreover, the unity and "sameness" of all things is their "Buddha nature": "Since Mind is the Buddha, it encompasses all things from the Buddhas to the most insignificant insect – these all share the Buddha nature. Their essence is the same 'One Mind.'"[6] Although ordinarily we may see only their separateness, all things are nonetheless united in this "essence." To make this point, the text maintains that this essence is "like one container of the element mercury. Although it separates and moves in all directions, it will once again reunite into an identical whole."[7]

The texts' favored image of "mind" is "space."[8] "Mind is like space," the text says, before going on to specify the sense in which that is so. "Mind is like space, limitless and immeasurable."[9] "Mind is like space, lacking even the slightest characteristic or form."[10] "Mind is like space, undifferentiated and undiminished."[11] The "infinity" of "mind" is figured in both spatial and temporal metaphors, however. Mind not only encompasses that which is far off in space, but also the temporally distant, everything that has ever been and will be.

Elsewhere in the text, the image of the "one" is not identity or wholeness, but the unity of "origins": the "One Mind" is the "source," the "well-spring," the "earth,"[12] the "womb," that from which all things have come into being. Nevertheless, the unity of "origins" is understood as an identity in essence – all things are one in that they derive from and return to the same "source." "Mind" is to all things as "earth" is to all earthly entities – their "ground," their "source," that from which they originate and of which they are essentially composed. In this way the text brings together the two images of mind as "source" and as "substance." Thus it says: "In correspondence to 'conditions,' mind becomes things."[13] "It is pure Mind, which is the source of everything and which, whether appearing as sentient beings or as Buddhas, as the rivers and

[6] T. 48, p. 386b; Blofeld, *Huang Po*, p. 87.   [7] T. 48, p. 386a; Blofeld, *Huang Po*, p. 84.
[8] To explore this theme further, see Faure, *Chan Insights and Oversights*, chapter 6.
[9] T. 48, p. 379c; Blofeld, *Huang Po*, p. 29.   [10] T. 48, p. 380a; Blofeld, *Huang Po*, p. 30.
[11] T 48, p. 380a; Blofeld, *Huang Po*, p. 31.
[12] Iriya Yoshitaka traces the symbol of the earth from this text back through the tradition in *Denshin Hoyo*, p. 37.   [13] T. 48, p. 386b; see Blofeld, *Huang Po*, p. 87.

mountains of the world, as the world of form or the formless, it is all one identity, without the characteristics of self and other."[14] These cosmological and metaphysical images are not unique to Zen. Indeed, they are borrowed from earlier forms of Chinese Buddhism, particularly from the Hua-yen[15] and T'ien-t'ai schools.[16] The Taoist inspiration behind them is also unmistakable; meditations of this kind had been deeply embedded in Chinese culture for centuries.

It was only in well-developed stages of Chinese Buddhism, however, that "mind" becomes the central element in this cosmology. Yogacara (*Wei-shih*) – "consciousness only" – reflections stand at the origins of this connection. In what sense is "mind" the source of all things? One sense of this is that whatever makes its appearance, that is, becomes perceivable or conceivable, does so within the mind. Therefore, Huang Po's *Wan-ling lu* says: "The ten thousand *dharmas* all derive from the mind. If my mind is 'empty,' then all *dharmas* are empty . . . they are all the same substance of One Mind."[17] The world appears as it does, in complex differentiation, as an effect of the mind. When the mind "regroups" itself, "unity" is its overriding characteristic. Unity, however, does not abolish differentiation. Instead, unity appears everywhere within differentiated things. Therefore the text says: "*Within* seeing, hearing, feeling and knowing, recognize the foundations of mind. Although the basis of mind is not identical with these forms of knowing, it is also not separate from them . . . Do not seek mind apart from these forms of knowing . . . Mind is neither identical to them nor different from them."[18] One implication of these lines is that "One Mind," or the "Buddha," cannot be experienced "objectively." In this particular case, therefore, "experience" occurs without there being an object of experience. Seeking for anything "objectively" will miss the point. Having set out on the quest, however, it is difficult not "to seek" for something; nevertheless, that is the demand of Huang Po's *dharma*. Hence, the text says: "There is only One Mind and nothing to be obtained. This mind is the Buddha. When students of the Way do not awaken to this fundamental mind, they superimpose mind upon mind and seek the Buddha beyond themselves, grasping for form and striving through practices . . . This is false *dharma*, not the way of enlightenment."[19] "Conceptions" of the

---

[14] T. 48, p. 380b; see Blofeld, *Huang Po*, p. 36.
[15] Iriya Yoshitaka discusses the Hua-yen influence on this text in *Denshin Hoyo*, p. 35.
[16] Biographical narratives about the young monk, Huang Po, as early as the *Chodang chip*, have him journeying to Mount T'ien-t'ai for instruction.   [17] T. 48, p. 384c; see Blofeld, *Huang Po*, p. 72.
[18] T. 48, p. 380b; see Blofeld, *Huang Po*, p. 37.   [19] T. 48, p. 380a; see Blofeld, *Huang Po*, p. 31.

Buddha or of Mind, although clearly required as a prerequisite to the search, may prevent "awakening." Therefore, Huang Po claims that "If you conceive of a Buddha, you will be obstructed by that Buddha."[20] The "One Mind" is not something to which practitioners could be individually related. On the contrary, the understanding required in this case is that every act of relation to something in the world is at the same time a relation to "mind." "Mind" or the "Buddha" is encountered in every presence, not independently as one presence among others. Instead, it is always there within the presence of anything at all. This accounts for Huang Po's rejection of "seeking" in the midst of the "search." "Seeking" for the Buddha is not possible; nor is it necessary, since the Buddha is always already present within every experience. Mind is not a form within the totality of forms, yet it is there as the "formless" background on the basis of which all forms make their appearance. This "background" is essentially "open," "empty." It cannot be conceptually fixed or determined. The effort to place yourself before it necessarily excludes you from it. Therefore, the effort required in Huang Po's Zen is distinct from other acts of agency because it is "not grasping," not an act of "knowing" or determination.

If Huang Po's "One Mind" is not an object of experience, neither is it a subject. Nevertheless, conceiving "mind" as subjectivity itself is clearly a more tempting option. Many Buddhists, including Zen Buddhists, have opted for this conception. "One Mind," on this view, is the subjectivity behind all individual subjectivities – consciousness itself. Throughout his lengthy career, John Blofeld can be seen to have held various positions on this issue. In his Huang Po translation, his uncertainty on the matter guided him between postures such that no definite stand would be obvious. Later, however, when he was translating Hui-hai, he followed the text in identifying "Buddha nature" with sentient beings for whom "consciousness" is the defining characteristic. Objects of consciousness, he thought, were "illusory creations of Mind. Whatever is illusory, such as plants and rocks, cannot share the Buddha-Nature or self-nature which pertains only to Mind."[21] This position has serious weaknesses, however, and the Huang Po texts show every evidence of avoiding them. Rather than isolating "mind" from objects of mind, the text correlates them. The distinction between "inner" and "outer," between the "mental" and the "material," is subjected to repeated critique. No "mind" exists outside the awareness of "objects";

---

[20] T. 48, p. 384c; Blofeld, *Huang Po*, p. 71.   [21] Blofeld, *The Zen Teaching of Hui Hai*, p. 139.

and no objects exist other than those in mind. Thus Huang Po claims that in "mind," there is "no subject, no object, no self, no other."[22] "Mind and objects of mind are undifferentiated."[23] They are "empty," that is, constituted by their essential relation, and inconceivable independently. Mind and world "co-arise" and depend essentially upon each other. This "essence (*t'i*) is One Mind."[24] Early Buddhist meditation theory had conceived of this essential correlation in the theory of the "18 *dhatus*," the senses, their objects, and the relations between them. Huang Po draws upon this well-known doctrine in his effort to say what "mind" is: "The six senses, their objects, and the connections between them are selfless and without a controlling agent – they are all empty. There is only fundamental mind which is all encompassing."[25] This fundamental connectedness of "mind" and "world," their essential unity, is a frequent theme in the texts.[26] Their "reciprocity" is primordial, that is, it constitutes a limit to conception and experience, and is therefore given the name: "emptiness." Mind is just this emptiness.

On the grounds of their essential reciprocity, one common line in the texts is the claim that "mind cannot see mind" because, if it could, the mind seen would be an object.[27] Therefore, the strategy of splitting mind into two parts, subject and object, so that mind can be conceived as grasping itself, fails. Any "mind" thus "seen" is clearly not mind. Therefore, like his student, Lin-chi, Huang Po poses the question: "when we search for mind, who is the one, at that very moment, doing the searching?"

One other theme, communicated in a "saying" basic to all participants in the tradition of "Hung-chou Zen" to the effect that "everyday mind is the Way" (*p'ing ch'ang hsin shih tao*), recapitulates much of the foregoing. This saying brings to mind the paradox of proximity – the truth that the "mind," precisely because it is so close, will elude its seekers. "Dualistic" practices, those that encourage us to turn away from the world in search of religious realization, derive from understandable conceptual mistakes. "Mind" is the open region, the "empty ground" found in and among things, but never as one of them, never an object set over against the one who would experience it. "Everyday mind is the Way" is

---

[22] T. 48, p. 384b; See Blofeld, *Huang Po*, p. 67.   [23] T. 48, p. 384c; See Blofeld, *Huang Po*, p. 72.

[24] T. 48, p. 384c; See Blofeld, *Huang Po*, p. 72.   [25] T. 48, p. 380c; See Blofeld, *Huang Po*, pp. 38–39.

[26] It can also be seen clearly in texts just prior to Huang Po. For example, Tsung-mi writes: "Mind and objects are mutually supportive . . . There has never been a mind without objects" (Broughton, *Kuei-feng Tsung-mi*, p. 177).

[27] Tsung-mi's writing on this theme is difficult to surpass. See Broughton, *Kuei-feng Tsung-mi*, p. 194. Also, see the work on Tsung-mi by Peter Gregory.

posited as a corrective to monastic otherworldliness.[28] The saying works against the tendency to turn "dualistically" away from "samsara" in order to meditate upon its "other," "nirvana," as if nirvana were simply another world more splendid than this one. The reversal demanded in Huang Po's "everyday mind" is significantly more radical a conception than that. It imagines "One Mind" encountering us in all presences, precisely in their relations and not in a relation independent of them. Any rejection of the diverse world of "presences" simultaneously prohibits awareness of mind. Thus the text instructs:

People often desire to escape the world in order to quiet the mind, to abandon activities in order to grasp principles. They fail to realize that this practice uses the mind to obstruct the world; it uses principles to obstruct activities. Just empty your mind and the world will be emptied of itself. Just release your grasp on principles, and activities will themselves be released.[29]

If "everyday mind is the Way," then there is nothing to escape except abstraction from the everyday. There is also nothing to seek since "seeking" cannot avoid positing that which is sought. Instead, "mind" is always already there, prior to all "seeking."

Had Huang Po known that his words on this topic might reach us, however, he might not have been so eager to identify "everyday mind" with the Buddhist Way. After all, "everyday mind" is what people enter the monastery to overcome. Surely, Huang Po does not mean that they should just forget Zen and go back to their villages. Surely he didn't mean that they were doing just fine before they arrived. A powerful critique of "everyday mind" must be the origin and essential point of "Buddhism." The point of valorizing "everyday mind" is highly contextual, the appropriate context being the community of those who have already dedicated their entire lives to penetrating beneath the dull conformities of "everyday mind," to the search for something beyond it. Huang Po's rhetorical strategy here is *upaya*, "skillful means." What he says depends on the character of those to whom he speaks as they are contextualized in the highly focused world of monastic seeking.

This "skill" or "strategy" leads the Huang Po literature to criticize and

---

[28] This point leads me to question Bernard Faure's identification of an "extremism" in Zen with respect to its use of the "two truth" doctrine in Mahayana Buddhism (*The Rhetoric of Immediacy*, p. 58). Faure regards the tradition's "new emphasis on the phenomenal world" as a nondialectical assertion of one realm or one truth, a "unilateral" reinterpretation of Madhyamika. I see much in these texts as just the opposite: a "worldly" play on the "plurality of planes" staked out by Madhyamika's multiple truths.   [29] T. 48, pp. 381c–382a; See Blofeld, *Huang Po*, p. 48.

to undermine its own doctrine of the "One Mind." Having constructed an elaborate theory of "mind," the work of "deconstruction" begins at once: "Mind is in itself no-mind, yet neither is it no-mind. Grasping mind as 'no-mind' turns it into an existing thing. Simply attune to it in silence and let go of your conceptions. Thus it is said: 'The way of words is severed and mental activity eliminated.'"[30] Almost as quickly as concepts of "mind" are posited, they are taken back. Through these means, the Huang Po texts resist conversion into a system; elaborate theories are difficult to derive from them. The point of the theories when joined to their own intentional subversion appears rather to be "release," the act of letting go of concepts once formed. One important line from Huang Po reads: "If there is dwelling in 'views,' this is heresy [*wai tao* literally, "outside the Way"]."[31] "Heresy," on this account, is not the error of holding incorrect views; it is rather holding to "views" at all. How could that be? How is it possible not to hold "views?" Surely it isn't possible, at least not for any form of human life that we might be tempted to valorize. The concern in this case appears to be directed instead to *how* "views" are held. A great deal of the Zen literature from this time adopts a playful and constantly shifting attitude toward particular ways of conceiving the quest. Numerous views are expressed; that is unavoidable. When they are expressed, however, they are soon thereafter withdrawn, or criticized, or in some way placed in alternate light. The standing joke in Hung-chou Zen was that Ma-tsu, the founder of this Buddhist "style," was forever altering his doctrinal stance such that his followers never knew what to "believe":

A monk asked: Master, why do you say "mind is the Buddha?"
Ma-tsu said: To stop children from crying.
The monk asked: When they stop, what then?
Ma-tsu replied: Neither mind nor Buddha![32]

As monks set out on the path of Zen, they retrain their minds to focus, not on the world, but on the Buddha and the *dharma*. Within that context of retraining the mind, Huang Po at some point responds with what must have seemed a shocking redefinition: "One who sees that there is no Buddha and no Dharma is called a monk!";[33] And as to his theory of "mind": "mind is not mind!"[34] Holding either the conception of "mind" or "no-mind" "imprisons" the mind "between two iron mountains."[35]

---

[30] T. 48, p. 380a; See Blofeld, *Huang Po*, p. 34.   [31] T. 48, p. 385a; See Blofeld, *Huang Po*, p. 74.
[32] Pas, *The Recorded Sayings of Ma-tsu*, p. 102, translation adapted.
[33] T. 48, p. 385b; See Blofeld, *Huang Po*, p. 76.   [34] T. 48, p. 383a; See Blofeld, *Huang Po*, p. 59.
[35] T. 48, p. 385a; See Blofeld, *Huang Po*, p. 76.

This stream of negations, however, does not in the end amount to a philosophical affirmation of "groundlessness." Even that possibility has been revoked. Instead, we are best off considering it a meta-philosophical recommendation about how to hold the views that inevitably occupy our minds. As with many other forms of Buddhism, "no grasping" is the way.

One plausible reading of the Zen teachings on "One Mind" and "no-mind," one that, as Huang Po demands, doesn't "objectify" the goal of practice, is that the state of mind sought is simply the "pure presence" of the world as it presents itself to experience, without the distorting lens of concept construction and emotional projection. This way of reading Zen has been immensely attractive, and has several advantages. One of them – the most important – is that it seems to accord with many passages in the Huang Po texts, especially those that recommend the abandonment of conceptual practices and advocate an undivided "openness" of mind. For Huang Po, "no-mind is the absence of various states of mind."[36] Another reason to give this view ample consideration is that it currently represents the "orthodox" view among both Japanese and English-language interpreters of Zen. Enlightened mind is the "pure presence of things as they are in and of themselves without the distortions of language, thought, and human interests."

John Blofeld was attracted to the simplicity and concreteness of this view. Although hints of it appear in his *Huang Po*, he was able to articulate a clearer version a few years later in his *Hui Hai*. There, for example, he wrote that:

> our minds will become like polished mirrors, reflecting every detail of the passing show and yet remaining unstained, perfectly unaltered by reflections of things, whether beautiful or hideous. Gradually we shall achieve utter tranquillity; we shall cease responding to appearances with outflows of will, passion, desire or aversion; when things appear before us, we shall reflect them with our mirror-like awareness; when they have passed by, they will leave no stain and elicit from us not the smallest reaction.[37]

Throughout Blofeld's writing career, however, another position seemed to dominate his mind. Under the sway of this alternative position, Blofeld considered "enlightened mind" "an Ultimate Perfection lying beyond the realm of ever-changing forms."[38] In this version, "mind" is "the Absolute," "beyond the world of flux" and requiring of the practitioner a "Transcendental experience of Reality."[39] These two

---

[36] T. 48, p. 380a; See Blofeld, *Huang Po*, p. 31.   [37] Blofeld, *The Zen Teaching of Hui Hai*, p. 22.
[38] Blofeld, *The Zen Teaching of Hui Hai*, p. 27.   [39] Blofeld, *Huang Po*, p. 55.

views remained in contention in Blofeld's mind throughout his writing career, appearing in his later works just as readily as in the early ones. Following Blofeld, however, other interpreters have developed the view of "mind" as "presence," particularly as Zen has come to be guided in the west by "Soto" interpretations more than the "Rinzai" views of Suzuki's initial transmission. In this later account, "Zen mind" is "pure experience," the immediate, direct apprehension of the objective world as it is on its own prior to the subjective mediation of language and thought. Purified mind witnesses "pure presence" and, adopting a meditative posture of "absolute openness," has no mediating effect on the way in which "presence" is manifest to mind.

As attractive as this pattern of understanding "Zen mind" may be, however, it will not withstand the contemporary scrutiny of Zen reading. It too will come to be seen as an illusory goal rather than as an accurate description of Zen mind. The "illusory" character of this position can be shown from a variety of perspectives, but, before going into further detail, let us see it briefly from two of these. The first is "deconstruction," one line of contemporary western thought. One of the primary themes of deconstruction as developed in the writings of Jacques Derrida and others is that "the dream of full presence," in any form, is a function of the desire to transcend finitude itself, a "theological" desire to abandon the human altogether. This desire, as the argument is developed, cannot be fulfilled and is best overcome. "Presence," rather than being a pure manifestation of the world, is "always already a representation," a function of the "system of signs" that will determine it. From this point of view, there is no sense in which the frameworks provided by human language and understanding can be avoided by those who experience in a "human" way.

Secondly, however, we can see how a thorough reading of several forms of Buddhist thought will also stand in the way of understanding "Zen mind" as "un-mediated, direct awareness of things as they are." From various Buddhist points of view, the search for "solid ground" is an illusory one, the result of desires that are best abandoned. Peeling back the layers of experience, we never arrive at the final layer – no pure experience at the foundations of mind. Instead, on Buddhist terms, we find "dependent origination," impermanence," and "no-self." This is to say that all experience, even experience that has been "reduced" through meditative concentration, will not have arrived at the "lowest common denominator." All experience is "empty," and to say this means that, for finite human beings, there is no "bottom" to the "void."

Whatever we find will come to be seen as interdependent and interlinked with something else, and thus, less than "final." Therefore, when Huang Po claims that "mind is empty," we are at least within the framework of traditional Buddhist interpretation to understand this as undermining our own desires to have arrived finally at the ultimate resting point of inquiry – something absolute and indubitable upon which "the correct mode of human being" can be established. It seems to me that our own meditation on Zen will falter at the point that we succumb to this desire and read "Zen mind" as the perfectly polished mirror.[40]

One contemporary realization that will help us find our way through this issue is that "presence always includes absence."[41] This is to say that present within our field of experience (but not in the foreground and therefore "absent" or unknown) are always background factors which shape the experience to be what it is. What factors? First, clearly, all the innumerable elements upon which the objects of experience depend in order to be what they are. Here we mean simple "causal" elements that have brought these things into the world as what they are at precisely this moment of experience. Second, we can specify various background factors that constitute the "horizon" or "context" of any experience. This includes everything within the horizon of the senses of which we are not directly aware when we focus our attention, but which, nevertheless, sets the stage for the objects upon which we do focus. When we see a car moving toward children playing on the street our awareness is focused there. We don't notice the street itself, the trees, power lines, buildings in the background, the roar of a distant lawnmower, an airplane, a barking dog, or even the children's playful talk. But all of these non-focal elements "ground" our experience of that scene. Third, in the background of any experience is the "mind" of the experiencer, constituted as it is by specific "structures," past experiences, memories, predilections, emotions, tendencies, genetic traits, dietary preferences, and on and on, so far removed that specific articulation is impossible. No matter how "pure" the mind of the Zen master, these remain. Indeed,

---

[40] For those experienced in reading Zen, the image of Hui-neng's poem denouncing the doctrinal metaphor of the "polished mirror" will come to mind (and if it does you will be able to see that *your* mind is not a polished mirror but a "storehouse" of memories that you would not want to do without). Many historically contextualized motives for this narrative can be articulated. Nevertheless, it is also true that Hui-neng's poem does mean that the understanding of the mind *as* a polished mirror is "empty," that is, relative to specific contexts and by no means "universally true." On this account, we would be mistaken to take literally the story that "Zen mind" is "pure presence."

[41] This statement, which comes to Derrida through Heidegger via other earlier sources, is also an excellent working definition of Buddhist "emptiness."

in sum, these *are* the Zen master. Awareness always includes these background factors even when, as always, they are not the center of attention and we are not aware of their presence. The human mind is not a "blank slate," the *tabula rasa* sought in philosophy and science.[42]

Recall that this account of mind is not just applicable to "thinking," but to "perception" as well.[43] "Meaning" is not something secondarily attached to what we see and hear. Perception already includes meaning in the moment of its arrival. We see cars and hear children's voices, not just abstract shapes, colors, and tones. Shapes, colors, and tones can be elements of awareness too, but only in abstraction, only when what initially appears has been reduced to something else. Perception always proceeds on the basis of understanding. As we saw in chapter 3, we always experience things "*as*" what they appear to be. This is true even when we are later determined to be wrong, and when, in confusion or ambiguity, we don't know what to understand them *as* except as "confused," "ambiguous," or "unknown." Can we conceive of any perception that is not grounded in understanding? If it were possible to "purify" our mind of all language, understanding, and past experience, is there any way we could function in the world or even be in the world? Not in any way that we would be inclined to consider a "human" way. The ideal of "pure experience" as it has been conceived by western interpreters of Zen appears now to be neither possible nor desirable.

If we reject the doctrine of mind as "pure experience," or give it extensive qualification as we will continue to do in this chapter, what

---

[42] It is important to recognize that one of the reasons that the interpretation of "Zen mind" as "pure presence" has been as attractive as it has been is that it aligns with the western tradition of "epistemology" at the basis of science and modern philosophy. We have all learned that "objectivity" is to be valued, and that both truth and justice depend on our willingness to set aside our own interests and prejudices so that things can be seen as they are on their own. The fact that this same language, as well as specific means of actualization, were mirrored back to us from "Zen" made it naturally attractive. "Post-modern" philosophy of science, however, has qualified the claims of modern epistemology. Science does not require the kinds of "objectivity" once thought necessary in order to proceed with its practices. This is fortunate since it is now widely realized that "objectivity" of this kind is systematically impossible because it conflicts with human finitude. No set of practices leads to the "pure presence of things as they are in themselves," whether scientific or meditative. "Things" are always present to "minds" and minds are always complexly cultivated.

[43] Notice, however, that this entire set of questions about how to understand Zen is a matter of thinking, a highly theoretical and conceptual matter. None of us has "direct perception" of these matters. All of us, even the Zen master, has to think them out. Therefore, all of us, even the Zen master, could be wrong. The distinction between "immediate" and "mediated" experience is itself a highly "mediated" abstraction. It is clearly a "doctrine" about which conceptual "errors" can be made, and upon which new light can at any time be cast. For elaboration on the relation between "perception" and "conception," refer back to chapters 3 and 4.

options remain for understanding the element of "enlightenment" in Huang Po's mind? Plenty! Lacking full presence, the "absence" or "void" can be experienced as "mystery." Lacking secure and solid ground, the freedom and contingency of finite existence can be experienced. Lacking the closure of certainty, "openness" becomes the primary feature of the cultivated mind. These themes will constitute the "matter" of concern in the next chapter. Before they can be properly contextualized, however, we must ask ourselves what else Huang Po might have had in mind. If we cannot conceive of his mind as devoid of language, understanding, time, and thinking, what roles would each of these mental elements play in Zen experience?

We have already "rethought" the role of language in Zen. Drawing upon that reading, we can now place "language" in the context of "mind." Language and the particular character of the human mind "co-arise." While not identical, they are inseparable. If "mind," for Huang Po and for our meditation on Zen, includes "objects of mind," then we can extend the correlation: language and our experience of the world are inseparable. Each informs and structures the other.[44] If this is true, then "we have erased the boundary between knowing a language and knowing our way around in the world generally."[45] From our first socialization into the world to the very end of life, language gives us worldly orientation. This insight directs us to the character of Zen language. If we describe the Zen master as having an exceptional ability to function in the world, this would have a great deal to do with the development of an exceptional relation to language. It is not that the Zen master has access to a greater vocabulary to describe experience, nor that, unlike the rest of us, he or she has experiences that lie beyond the realm of description. These ways of conceiving language and experience are deeply "dualistic." They assume that language and experience are each separate and distinct realms on their own that combine occasionally and inadequately when language is called upon to "capture" or "describe" experience. The problem here lies in the metaphor of "capture," and in the assumption that the primary job of language is "description." Huang Po's sermons go on page after page without describing anything; they rarely intend to capture anything beyond the discursive context. They instruct, inform, define, command,

---

[44] Readers of Derrida will be reminded here of the conclusion in *Of Grammatology* that "the thing itself is a sign" because the "transcendental signified" dissolves into the bottomless network of signifiers (p. 50). This amounts to a decision to treat "signifier and signified," or word and thing, as a correlated unity.   [45] Davidson, *Truth and Interpretation*, p. 446.

challenge, ridicule, prod, probe, and inquire, but expend very little energy in "describing."

Moreover, to the extent that we experience something *as* anything at all, it is already deeply enveloped in the mental context of language – it has already been implicitly "described" to us. Language and experience are carefully woven together in understanding. Although it is clear that John Blofeld and other romantics underwent dramatic new experiences in language, both in their travels to foreign lands and in their explorations of unusual experiences, they could only draw upon the discourse of modernity and its corresponding understanding of language to articulate their experience. For Blofeld, language was the "tool" of "representation," useful for description and communication. And this is the understanding through which he would read Huang Po's Zen. Therefore, in his introduction to *Huang Po*, he wrote:

The text indicates that Huang Po was not entirely satisfied with his choice of the word "Mind" to symbolize the inexpressible Reality beyond the reach of conceptual thought, for he more than once explains that the One Mind is not really MIND at all. But he had to use some term or other, and "Mind" had often been used by his predecessors.[46]

This description of the process has it backwards; it places the experience of "mind" first and the language of "mind" second. First, Huang Po experienced "the inexpressible Reality beyond the reach of conceptual thought," and then, subsequently, in the process of deciding what to "name" it, chooses "mind" because his predecessors had "used" that name before. In fact, however, the word "mind" would have symbolized the quest and its goal from the very beginning of his career as a monk. The word "mind" would have led him to the experience of "mind." Huang Po would have heard sermons on mind, read texts on mind, been instructed in how to meditate on mind: "mind" was what he was after, and consequently, "mind" is what he obtained in experience. Although it does symbolize them, it should not surprise us that the word "mind" does not "capture" all of the intricacies of these sermons, texts, meditations, and experiences. It was also clearly in language that Huang Po and John Blofeld came to learn that there was an "inexpressible Reality beyond the realm of conceptual thought." Language suggests, concepts conceive, and experience seeks those very limits. The language of "inconceivability" for Blofeld, and its corresponding language in Chinese for Huang Po,

---

[46] Blofeld, *Huang Po*, p. 18.

were especially significant in the formation of Zen experience. A few other "symbols" in Zen language carry equally powerful effects. The word "silence" is a violation of silence that brings silence into the mind. Without this linguistic form, monks would never have practiced the silent meditation that they did. The word "formlessness" is a specific form that shapes a specific form of experience. The word "emptiness" is both an obstruction and a construction of its referent – "emptiness," and hence it can be seen to perform both negative and positive linguistic functions. It is far from the case that language tags along behind experience. This can easily be seen where, on Blofeld's account, it should not be seen: in the language of meditation. Language brings up the topic and the possibility of meditation in the first place. Language directs meditation and provides the necessary instructions. Language encourages meditation, sets the stage for it, inspires it, informs it, gives intentions for it, justifies it, defines it, broadens it, changes it, criticizes it, applauds it, improves it, and provides ways to understand it. Although language occasionally "describes" meditation, it never "captures" it. Given these other tasks, capturing is clearly beside the point. Even in the midst of silence, "Zen mind" is inconceivable apart from the language of Zen.

Closely linked to the presence of language in "mind" is the background of "understanding" that allows experience to take the particular shape that it does. "Understanding" here, as we have developed it, includes, but goes far beyond, our specific "beliefs" and "ideologies." Understanding is largely preconscious; it is shaped by and contained in long-forgotten memories of past experiences, stories we have been told, and actions we have performed. Our bodily movements show the presence of understanding within them; specific rituals, customs, and forms demonstrate how we have come to be shaped as we are. The early Mahayana conception of a "storehouse consciousness" seems to express this background of understanding very well, beyond other functions that the concept has performed for Buddhists. In reference to Hui-hai's use of the phrase, "The Great Sutra," Blofeld writes in a footnote that "The Great Sutra is another term for Mind."[47] Mind encompasses everything that can be said in all the sutras, even though, like the library of sutras, we don't really know exactly what's there. This enormous background of prior experience, mostly unconscious, structures the framework of our current experience, including "Zen" experience. Although some interpretations of Zen maintain that these specific cultural patterns

---

[47] Blofeld, *The Zen Teaching of Hui Hai*, p. 147.

prevent authentic Zen experience, it seems to me that, in another more important sense, they make it possible. They provide vantage points on the world rather than barriers. "Enlightened Zen mind" cannot be thought to lack this understanding. Without understanding, we are left without functional abilities, and without experience.[48]

As we have seen, the individual shape of "understanding" can be interpreted through the figure *as* and its various correlates. We understand this *as* a book and therefore know what to do with it. We understand that *as* meditation and therefore understand why we might want to do it. This figure of understanding can be seen throughout Blofeld's translation of Huang Po, and mine. Blofeld writes that Huang Po recommends that we regard sentient beings *as* shadows, doctrines *as* dreams, all minds *as* One, the world *as* formless, ourselves *as* no-self, and the mind *as* empty. Without this figure to inform our experience and to give it linguistic shape, we don't know what we experience, or that we experience at all.[49]

This claim, however, does not include the further assertion that all experience is "theoretical," a matter of reflection and thought. Most experience is not, including most "Zen" experience. Clearly the Huang Po texts project a form of pretheoretical and prediscursive experience. We can see that, while the Huang Po texts draw us into a great deal of conscious intellectual activity, their goal is a form of experience beyond that activity. However, let us add to this three important points of qualification. First, the purpose of saying that Zen experience is prior to thought – pretheoretical – is to avoid its reduction to intellectual or rational exercise as, in Huang Po's opinion, it had been in earlier Chinese Buddhism. "Enlightenment" is not sophisticated thinking and, as Huang Po says, anyone who thinks it is won't get it. This "purpose," however, is specific and contextual. It does not mean, secondly, that "understanding" is not embedded within Zen experience. No human experience is devoid of understanding. Understanding both shapes Zen experience and results from it. Third, it is not true that intellectual thinking is something separate from and altogether uninvolved in enlightened

---

[48] It is commonly thought that "intuition" is prior to understanding or even an alternative to it. Learning from Heidegger on this point, however, I think not. Intuition is made possible by the particular shape of the world as it exists in understanding. "By showing how all sight is grounded primarily in understanding," Heidegger writes, "we have deprived pure intuition of its priority, . . . Intuition and thinking are both derivatives of understanding, and already rather remote ones" (*Being and Time*, p. 187).

[49] The issue of "frameworks" of understanding is one of the primary themes of discussion in Charles Taylor, *Sources of the Self*.

experience. Huang Po's sermons are exercises in conceptuality, practices of the mind. They implore us to think this way rather than that. They teach us how to conceive of all things as "mind," among other things. These intellectual exercises set the stage for Zen experience and make it a structural possibility. They may even evoke or elicit this experience. We return to the role of intellectual activity shortly.

In addition to the constituent elements of language and understanding, we cannot conceive of "mind" apart from "time." Yet such is the demand made in some Zen doctrine. Although it was not clear to him how it might be so, John Blofeld's reading of Zen would lead him to insist that the Zen master's "mind" transcends time. Entering a "timeless" realm, the Zen master functions by means of access to a mode of understanding that is independent of all temporal considerations. Thus Blofeld would claim that "the state of mind of an Illumined man is independent of time-relationships."[50] Little reflection on this claim can be found in Blofeld's writing, however, in spite of the existence in the Buddhist canon of an impressively sophisticated "philosophy of time." Although "temporality" is not a central issue in the Huang Po texts, an occasional allusion to earlier Buddhist reflections on time does appear. Reading these from the context of this background literature, it is easy to see how Blofeld might have come to the conclusion that he did. For example, at the very end of the *Wan-ling lu*, Blofeld translates Huang Po as follows: "Avoid the error of thinking in terms of past, present, and future."[51] The next sentence, however, goes on to make that very same "error": "The past has not gone; the present is a fleeting moment; the future is not yet to come."[52] Huang Po is here thinking "time." Although no doubt these thoughts are intended as reasons why one ought not to think in temporal terms, they also demonstrate the impossibility of doing that.

As an example of the necessity of "time" to "mind," consider the basic Buddhist realization of "impermanence." In his experience of enlightenment, the Buddha realized that all things are impermanent, that is, all things change *over time*. Time is presupposed in the experience of change. You cannot recognize that things change unless you can juxtapose in your mind their present condition with some past state of affairs and project that difference as a principle into the future. Unless his "enlightenment" included the awareness of temporality, the Buddha

[50] Blofeld, *The Zen Teaching of Hui Hai*, n.20, p. 131.   [51] Blofeld, *Huang Po*, p. 131.
[52] Blofeld, *Huang Po*, p. 131.

could not have announced the doctrine of "impermanence," nor any other.

The point here is not simply that "minds" share the characteristic of "impermanence" with all other entities in the world, although that would be true as well. It is rather that minds are "in time" in a way that distinguishes them from entities and objects. Temporality is more than impermanence of mind because human minds temporalize things experienced. Mind functions as it does through the structures of temporality so that experience, all mentality, is eminently temporal. The signs of this temporalizing process, and its structures, are etched into language and, therefore, into all understanding (anyone who has learned a language significantly different from their own, however, will recognize that these structures differ between cultures, although all languages distinguish past, present, and future in some way). Every experience arises out of what came before it and shades off into whatever comes after it, forming the continuum of past, present, and future that shapes the mind's awareness. Aside from relations to "before" and "after," the presence of the present moment would not appear as it does. Each element of time is embedded in the others as their presupposition. Huang Po would have received the transmission of these thoughts and much more from the Hua-yen and T'ien-t'ai literature that had made "time" an abundant theme of discourse.

Yet more basic than the fact that we can find a "theory of time" in the texts is the realization all of Huang Po's discourse, whether "about" time or not, is already temporalized. Temporal distinctions and continuities are etched within it both as assertion and presupposition. Without the presence within it of both recollection and anticipation, past and future, the present would lack the kind of reality required for Huang Po to have taken up the Zen concerns that he did. Given past experience of human inadequacy, Huang Po takes up the present practices of the Bodhisattva, aimed at relieving future suffering and ignorance. The more wisdom of "experience" learned from the past a Zen master has appropriated, the more he or she will be able to adopt "skillful means" in the present. Presupposed throughout Buddhism is that in finite human life there is something unresolved and incomplete. Something remains to be done; something not yet the case is called for by the way past and future work together to construct the present. The Zen master, above all others perhaps, acts out of an understanding of the "pro-spective" contribution that discourse and actions may make on behalf of a transformed present and future.

Although it is certainly true that we can imagine a life beyond this one where "eternity," rather than "temporality," reigns, no content for this "life" can be supplied; only that it is "other than what we know," "out of time." Theologies of "eternity" share the experience that temporalized life is pain, and that the divine is "wholly other" than this. These motives inspire the effort to conceive of a realm of timelessness beyond all suffering. Yet, although we can without difficulty find these tendencies in Zen texts, what is most distinctive about this tradition is its effort to forgo the "otherworldly" metaphysics that posits any realm beyond this temporal one. An adamant "this worldly" character is clearly definitive of the Zen tradition as a whole, regardless of specific instances to the contrary. It seems to me, in fact, that this feature of Zen is the one most responsible for its following in the west. It is certainly true that one need not turn to Zen or to Buddhism if an otherworldly metaphysics of eternity is of primary interest. It is probably also true that among these theologies, the Zen literature that projects "eternity" is of relatively little value and interest. Zen was founded and constructed on quite different interests. This other interest can be seen in the fact that Zen masters typically ridicule speculation about whatever is "beyond time" because *we* certainly aren't. The focus is resolutely on the "here and now" that is fundamentally composed of finite temporal-spatial structures. Huang Po's Zen instructs us concerning how we might live within time rather than how we might get out of it.

The final issue of mind requiring our attention is also the most difficult. We must read Huang Po – and our own minds – in search of an answer to the question of the role of thinking in "Zen mind." What place, if any, within the mind of Huang Po, or any Zen practitioner, is occupied by reflective thinking? At first glance, this question presents no difficulty. The answer, stated repeatedly in Zen literature, is that "conceptual thought" plays no role, or at least "should" not. In the process of translating and analyzing Huang Po, this was John Blofeld's conclusion. For the most part, he thought that the intention of Buddhism is to "arrest the karma-forming processes of conceptual thought."[53] "Prajna," he wrote, "is that intuitive knowledge of Reality which lies far above the level of conceptual thought; indeed it is interrupted and blocked out by conceptual thought."[54] On this view, thinking serves only to generate "mental sediment"[55] which obscures and prevents an

---

[53] Blofeld, The *Wheel of Life*, p. 131.   [54] Blofeld, The *Wheel of Life*, p. 133.
[55] Blofeld, The *Wheel of Life*, p. 133.

immediate perception of reality. Because "Intuitive Knowledge" lies "infinitely beyond the highest point ever reached by the human intellect,"[56] the essential element of Huang Po's Zen practice must be "throwing off the burden of concepts."[57]

Moreover, a dichotomy between "conceptual thinking" and "direct awareness" is an important element in the Huang Po texts. Holding a doctrinal position (*chien*) at all is represented as an "obstruction."[58] Nevertheless, it would be difficult not to notice that Huang Po's substantial critique of "conceptual thinking" is itself an impressive act of "conceptual thinking." It constitutes a specific "view" about a specific matter of thought. This is inevitable. Any claim that reflection obscures, prevents, or cannot match "experience" is itself already the result of reflection on experience. Even the act of distinguishing between "experience" and "thought" is an act of thought, an abstraction from experience. Thus it is impossible to assert that "One Mind" cannot be an object of thought without, in that very assertion, making it just such an object.[59] Realizing this, we might improve clarity on this point if we retranslate Huang Po's statement that "the moment in which you realize the nature of mind can be said to be beyond conceptualization"[60] as follows: "The moment in which you realize the nature of mind *can be conceived* 'as' beyond conceptualization," not to mention *as* "the nature of mind," *as* "sudden breakthrough," and *as* other predicates that the texts encourage us to "conceive." "Beyond conceptualization" is precisely the form of its conceptualization.

Although the critique of thought is one ample area of thought in Huang Po, it is certainly not the only one. Thinking has other roles to play as we see in the example above. One extremely important role for thought is the construction of "ideals," frameworks of thought in relation to which experience of ideals is shaped. Concepts of "mind," "emptiness," "practice," "Buddha," and many more, shape both practice and realization in Zen. Although Huang Po claims that "If you

---

[56] Blofeld, *Huang Po*, p. 17.

[57] Blofeld, *Huang Po*, p. 51. Elsewhere Blofeld reflects on his own practice of thinking: "I spent some time reasoning discursively about the meaning of life and the place of each individual in the universe according to the understanding I had developed during the last twenty years, particularly my understanding of Buddhist doctrine – but this exercise, though fascinating, is quite unprofitable, as the Lord Buddha was fond of pointing out . . . to ponder such questions is not especially conducive to Enlightenment" (*The Wheel of Life*, p. 250). In spite of this negative judgment about "doctrinal thinking," however, Blofeld's many books consist primarily in such thinking.   [58] T. 48, p. 384c; Blofeld, *Huang Po*, p. 71.

[59] On this question, I am indebted to the thought of Robert Scharlemann. See, for example, *The Reason of Following*, p. 128.   [60] T. 48, p. 384b; See Blofeld, *Huang Po*, p. 70.

conceive of a Buddha you will be obstructed by that Buddha,"[61] the truth of the opposite point is so obvious as hardly to need stating. That is, if you *don't* "conceive of a Buddha," you not only won't be able to understand what Huang Po has said, you will also be "obstructed by" all the human failures that "Buddhism" was constructed to overcome. For a Buddhist, these conceptions are not optional; they are "essential" to "the way" insofar as they present it to mind. Huang Po's admonition above against "conceiving of a Buddha," is intended for those who already have that conception well in mind, so far "in mind," in fact, that it has displaced much else that once occupied that mental space. Huang Po's instructions concern what to do with that concept. The function of Zen concepts, once "in mind," is to restructure experience; not to leave it "as it is," but rather to reform it along new lines.

It is important to realize that the "referents" of Zen concepts, that to which they refer, differ from most in that they come into being (in the mind) only through conception and not additionally through being perceived as objects in the world. While they can be experienced in relation to objects in the world, they are nonetheless of a different order than the objective. Concepts of this "order," such as "One Mind," "emptiness," "Buddha nature," lacking perceivable referents, have their origins in the imagination. They require the person thinking them to begin by imagining, not some special object or entity, but the ordinary world around them now seen in some special light. These conceptions show the ordinary world "differently," and thus open up modes of experience other than those with which we are already familiar. This difference in the appearance of the ordinary is at first fictional and abstract, a provisional projection of an imagined possibility. But as the concept is "used" or "practiced," it becomes more "natural," not a projection onto the world so much as the actual appearance of the world itself. This, I believe, is what Blofeld had in mind when he wrote:

My months in the Zen monastery were not wasted. I believe I may claim to have made some progress in converting from theoretical knowledge to partial realization two supremely important truths . . . When a Zen Master declared that "Nirvana is here and now," or that "the Present is the only reality," I think I really did understand the truth at which those teachings point.[62]

"[T]heoretical knowledge," Blofeld suggests, needs conversion to "realization," and, I would add, it needs this conversion in order to be

---

[61] T. 48, p. 384c; See Blofeld, *Huang Po*, p. 71.　　[62] Blofeld, *The Wheel of Life*, p. 170.

actualized as successful "knowledge." Just like playing the piano, swinging a tennis racket, and sitting in *zazen*, the practice of theoretical thinking comes to fruition when it becomes second nature, when its abstract and awkward character has been converted into intuitive instinct. So long as "One Mind" or "emptiness" remains in the mind as a definition or a set of rules for thinking, it will be experienced apart from the world rather than within it. When the practice of these definitions has matured, "One Mind" or "emptiness" will be experienced on or in the world rather than (or in addition to) as a concept in the mind.

Blofeld writes that, through his months of Zen practice, he came to understand the truth of the saying "Nirvana is here and now." What this simple conceptual phrase demands is that the "here and now" (and nirvana) be reconceived, and that this conception be practiced in contemplation until the "experience" of the "here and now" has been transformed in its light. Practicing this concept, Blofeld underwent estrangement from the ordinary "here and now" that he had experienced prior to Zen. Through the practice of thinking the idea that "Nirvana is here and now," of looking through the concept at what is now here, the "here and now" takes on a different character. The "present moment" and "this place" become ever-present signs of "nirvana." Following the movement of the concept in the act of thinking it, experience is restructured. Although it requires considerable reflection to see it, this is no less true of the concepts "here and now" or "things as they are" than it is of "otherworldly" religious thoughts. Religious concepts function to show the world in some new light. Their relation to "practice" is not one of opposition, but rather of essential correlation. Concepts provide what it is that we practice; apart from these concepts, there is nothing to practice.

In Huang Po's system of conceptual practice, "One Mind" occupies a primary position. Particular moments of experience fill in the content of the concept, but no experience can exhaust it. No matter what we might experience personally, the "One Mind" exceeds that as the concept that encompasses all experience.[63] In addition to its conceptual status, however, the "One Mind" names the experience that defines the point of Huang Po's practice. As experience, "One Mind" can never be grasped in a concept. "One Mind" names, for Huang Po, that which is

---

[63] In this section, I work from a Kantian distinction between a concept that cannot be exhausted by any intuition, and an intuition that cannot be exhausted by any concept. I inherit this scheme from Robert Scharlemann, "The One of the Many, and the Many of the One," in *Inscriptions and Reflections*.

systematically and in principle "inconceivable." This is so because in the act of thinking the concept "One Mind," we violate it by breaking the unity that we seek to conceive. "I," the subject self, think "One Mind" as the object of my thought, and, in the process, disrupt its oneness and immediacy. This, for Huang Po, is the one destination to which thinking can never fully arrive, yet, at the same time, the only destination worth seeking. Nevertheless, this limit to thinking is itself limited precisely because it is a limit that we think. We can articulate, as we have above, and understand that thinking is systematically excluded from "One Mind," and we can think why or how this is so. Put succinctly, "We can understand the inconceivability of the one which we conceive *as* the one."[64]

In addition to its role in generating Zen experience in the first place, Zen thinking brings prereflective, pretheoretical experience[65] into the light of reflection and articulation. Thinking does this retrospectively, looking back over what has emerged in experience, evaluating it, criticizing it, reshaping and refining it. Why is this important? Without rigorous conceptual practices to accompany other modes of practice, Huang Po would not have known whether the "Zen mind" that was transmitted to him, and that he was passing on to others, was anything worth inheriting. He would have no way to evaluate it, or even to know what it was. Lacking reflective capability and a critical mind, Huang Po would not have been able to take responsibility for, or give any account of, the ideals that he was so vociferously advocating. In the absence of critical thought, only dogmatism remains – assertions grounded in desire but lacking justification.

That no Zen master was ever completely without the capacity to give justification to Zen shows the inevitability of "thinking" as a component of "Zen mind." On the other hand, given a literal reading of Zen "no-mind" (*wu-hsin*) and "no-thought" (*wu-nien*), relatively "unreflective" Zen is a real possibility, one that has also been actualized on historical occasion throughout the tradition. There is indeed a "fundamentalist" urge

---

[64] Scharlemann, "The One of the Many," in *Inscriptions and Reflections*, p. 221.

[65] Because it goes so heavily against the grain of "Zen thinking," let me clarify here once again that although this experience is neither "reflective" nor "theoretical," it is not on that account either "preconceptual" or "prelinguistic." Embedded within all experience are the concepts and the linguistic structures that make that experience possible as experience. In "immediate experience," however, they stand in the background and are not explicit or thematic to the experience. No exercise in thinking need be performed for the linguistic, cultural shaping of the world to have effect. Without the language of Zen, we could not experience "things as they are," *as* they are for Zen.

written into the basic tenets of the Zen tradition that has emerged full-force from time to time. "Fundamentalism," in this case, can be defined loosely as the tendency to select a limited set of basic doctrines – "sudden enlightenment," "no dependence of language and text," "everyday mind is the Way," and so on – that are literally and narrowly interpreted, and taken to be a timeless essence of the tradition. To the extent that "no-thought" is included in this list and interpreted literally, the abilities of Zen Buddhists to understand their practice and their achievement will be limited.

One problem that the tradition has not faced is a pronounced tendency not to recognize Zen doctrine *as* doctrine. Perhaps due to the influence of the "no dependence" slogan, Zen Buddhists have tended to assume that traditional pronouncements about "the Way" are something other than doctrine, and therefore not susceptible to critical thought. As long as ideas are naively thought to "flow directly from experience" (or, in other traditions, directly from God), they will be held dogmatically. Although unreflective Zen is certainly possible, it is not desirable, and constitutes a self-imposed limitation that has, on occasion, weakened the tradition. In much of the tradition, of course, this has not occurred. Creative minds, deeply immersed in both "One Mind" and "everyday mind," have transmitted a tradition to us that is in some senses unparalleled in its reflective and conceptual capacities. The sophistication of both the Zen literary tradition and Zen practice demonstrate those capacities.

A dialectical relationship between the practice of thought and Zen experience is essential to the tradition. Thought pushes experience further, opens up new dimensions for it, and refines what comes to experience. Experience pushes thought further, opens up new dimensions for thinking, and sets limits to its excursions. The brilliance of Zen thinking is its tentative and provisional character, the "non-abiding," non-grasping" mind. Knowing, through thought, that all thought is "empty," Zen masters have explored worlds of reflection unavailable to other traditions. Trained to experience the "void" of finitude, they face it without fear, playfully "thinking" what lies beneath "common sense."

Although essential to Zen, "conceptual thinking" is only one of its practices, and only a fragment of "One Mind." Thinking is to the whole of "Mind" as the tip is to the iceberg. Yet the "tip" that protrudes into the light is the element of mind that communicates to the unconscious totality both what it is and how it ought to practice its identity. Huang

Po's capacity to say what "Zen" is, in riveting and persuasive style, set him up as the master of reflective understanding among the many Zen minds in the monastery. From his mind they learned both how they were to conceive of themselves and how to practice that identity. To what did these monks attribute Huang Po's superior capacity? To the awakening of his mind – enlightenment!

CHAPTER 10

ENLIGHTENMENT: the awakening of mind

> Do not say that Huang Po's enlightenment is incomplete. How can someone like Joko tell what level Huang Po has reached or what his words mean? Huang Po is an ancient Buddha and he sacrificed his life for the transmission of the *dharma*.
>
> Dogen[1]

> What is enlightenment?
>
> Immanuel Kant[2]

Following the literary custom adopted in the nineteenth century, John Blofeld drew upon the European word "enlightenment" to translate the highest goal of Zen Buddhism. In actual fact, however, among the most widely employed symbols for the goal of Zen used in the Huang Po literature, none could be translated literally by our word "enlightenment."[3] Why, then, did Blofeld opt for *this* word rather than simply translating the symbols that were to be found in the texts? One reason would clearly be that the precedent for this rendering had already been firmly established. Earlier translators, including D. T. Suzuki, had interpreted both Buddhism and its particular "Zen" form *as* traditions focused on the quest for "enlightenment." This answer, however, simply forestalls our question: why had they chosen the word "enlightenment" as the most general rendering of an array of terms for the goal of spiritual practice in Buddhism? No doubt they would have responded to our question with the simple claim that "accuracy" was the primary criterion of selection,

---

[1] Dogen, *Shobogenzo*, p. 143.
[2] Immanuel Kant, *Foundations of the Metaphysics of Morals, and What is Enlightenment?* (New York: Liberal Arts Press, 1959).
[3] The list of symbols for the goal of Zen is extensive, and changes over time. One of these, used in the Huang Po texts, but only seldomly, could be rendered into English literally as "enlightenment." This symbol is *ming*, etymologically composed of the graphs for the sun and moon, which clearly has carried the meaning of "to enlighten" – "to shed light upon, to clarify, and hence, to become aware of."

not necessarily "literalness" of translation but overall correspondence to the authentic meanings being transmitted. "Correspondence," however, is two-dimensional. It entails an understanding of two vocabularies, two contexts of meaning, and two evolving traditions – one for the tradition out of which a meaning will be taken and one for the tradition into which it will be placed. What matters, therefore, is not just what Buddhist "enlightenment" means, but also the meaning of European "enlightenment" in relation to which the Buddhist version will be understood. Having received this translation, what Buddhist enlightenment would mean to westerners has been dependent upon what "enlightenment" had already come to mean in their own linguistic and historical context.[4]

What had this word come to mean in the west at the time when it was chosen to include within its variety of connotations what Buddhists seek as their goal? The European Enlightenment was the epoch of rationalism, the historical era in which it was thought that the clear light of human reason, scientifically purified, would dispel the darkness of superstition, finally making it possible to verify the truth that in the past could only be taken on authority. For Immanuel Kant, the foremost prophet of "the Enlightenment," the emancipatory aim of enlightenment would be to make possible an "exodus from the condition of self-imposed immaturity," wherein both immature thinking, and its consequent need for authority, are overcome. One rhetorical figure drawn from European rationalism that came to be particularly affixed to the western conception of Buddhist enlightenment was the idea of an unconditioned and unprejudiced perception of "things as they are." Although very distant from its Cartesian roots, this phrase has come to define Zen enlightenment. On this point we can see an interesting connection between the monastic origins of both traditions of "enlightenment." These origins in Europe can perhaps be seen most clearly in the Cartesian *Meditations*. For Descartes, contemplative, meditative purification precedes the capacity to see clearly and without prejudice. "Things as they are" only appear as they are to one whose mind has been cleared of unauthorized assumptions and emotional excess. In both east and west, such clarification has religious and monastic roots, and is traceable in interesting ways to a variety of religious practices and conceptions.

Although the rationalists of the European *Aufklärung* had valorized the

---

[4] In China this same process had already taken place when words were sought in the Chinese cultural sphere to communicate what translators understood "nirvana" and other analogous terms to mean in the very distant Indian cultural context.

Chinese Confucians for constructing a non-theistic system of ethics, and, to a lesser extent, the "original" Indian Buddhists for their hard-headed analysis of mind, it is not the rationalist tradition that accounts for our interest in Zen. Instead, Zen "enlightenment" would draw most of its images from the European tradition of thought that had opposed Enlightenment rationalism – romanticism. This tradition, by virtue of its modern opposition to the emerging shape of modernity, would reverse many of the preferences expressed in the Enlightenment. Whereas Enlightenment thinkers typically assumed the progressive triumph of *logos* over *mythos*, romantics would criticize the shallowness of rationality and seek wisdom in ancient myth. Whereas Enlightenment thinkers dismissed the traditional past as immature in contrast to its modern replacement, romantics typically sought ways to find in the past a source of depth otherwise unavailable in the economy of modern cal-culative thinking. It was this set of images that drew John Blofeld and other romantic thinkers to the mysterious and ancient "orient." Nevertheless, given the power and prestige of Enlightenment thinking even in the midst of modern romanticism, the word "enlightenment" more than any other would come to symbolize what Buddhists like Huang Po could offer.[5]

What did Huang Po's "enlightenment" mean to John Blofeld? Reflections on this topic can be found voluminously throughout Blofeld's long career as an interpreter of Asian religious traditions. Huang Po's enlightenment was simply one very powerful version of a generalized religious state that Blofeld sought through numerous other figures as well. Enlightenment, whether from Huang Po or elsewhere, is what Blofeld sought to understand and to appropriate into his own life through his practice as a Buddhist. How did he conceive and represent it?

The initial characteristic of "enlightenment" for Blofeld is its connec-tion to "reality." Enlightenment is "the experience of standing face to face with Reality."[6] It is one form of experience set in contrast to all others, the form in which what was previously taken to be real is reduced to a subordinate status through its juxtaposition to the sudden and self-evident appearance of "Ultimate Reality."[7] "Reality will flash upon us,"

---

[5] Paul Ricoeur takes these "two fundamental philosophical attitudes" – rationalism and romanti-cism – as definitive of the scope of modernity. Although they opposed the Enlightenment in explicit doctrine, romantics would be unable to escape the terms of the discussion defined by its opposition. Thus, even in their opposition to the spirit of modernity, romantics would remain within the sphere of Enlightenment vocabulary, as well as within the range of issues posed by scientific rationalism (*Hermeneutics and the Human Sciences*, p. 66).

[6] Blofeld, *The Wheel of Life*, p. 180.   [7] Blofeld, *Beyond the Gods*, p. 20.

Blofeld asserts in the future tense, "the whole universe of phenomena will be seen as it really is."[8] The capacity to see the universe as it really is, although innate as a capacity to human beings, results from an extensive practice of cultivation. Only purified minds will see reality. Drawing upon images that had been controversial throughout the history of Zen, Blofeld figures the mind *as* a "mirror" and cultivation *as* an act of "polishing." "[O]ur minds will become like polished mirrors," he wrote, "reflecting every detail of the passing show and yet remaining unstained, perfectly unaltered by reflections of things, whether beautiful or hideous."[9]

The separation between the Ultimate Reality of Huang Po and the apparent reality in which we live is constructed in Blofeld's doctrine of enlightenment through the metaphor of the "veil." Although right there before us, reality is veiled from our view. Having figured the structure of the human situation in terms of the veil, the human task comes to be understood *as* "striving to pierce the veils of sensory perception and conceptual thought in order to arrive at an intuitive perception of reality."[10] Those few, like Huang Po, who have "pierced the veil" sense a further "duty" "to carry back the secret from beyond the veil."[11] Although the image of "carrying back" implies a substantial separation between realms, Blofeld is quick to qualify the otherworldly implications of this doctrine. While enlightenment appears distant to us now, when it is suddenly manifest, what is shown is the truth of this world.

In spite of these qualifications, however, the otherworldly implications of the doctrine continue to assert themselves. The experience of enlightenment, Blofeld claims, entails an "unqualified liberation from the human state."[12] Enlightenment is "an Ultimate Perfection lying beyond the realm of ever-changing forms,"[13] and "a final escape from the bondage of life's Wheel."[14] That enlightenment requires such an "escape beyond" can be seen in the predicates Blofeld places upon it. Reality, he says, "is spaceless and timeless."[15] "[T]he state of mind of an Illumined man is independent of time-relationships"[16] and "does not discriminate at all."[17] That reality thus constructed is literally unthinkable and unimaginable is clear to Blofeld. In fact, it is an article of faith. Although we cannot currently imagine it, the great masters like Huang

[8] Blofeld, *The Zen Teaching of Hui Hai*, p. 31.　　[9] Blofeld, *The Zen Teaching of Hui Hai*, p. 22.
[10] Blofeld, *The Zen Teaching of Hui Hai*, p. 11.　　[11] Blofeld, *The Wheel of Life*, p. 17.
[12] Blofeld, *Beyond the Gods*, p. 17.　　[13] Blofeld, *The Zen Teaching of Hui Hai*, p. 27.
[14] Blofeld, *The Wheel of Life*, p. 62.　　[15] Blofeld, *Huang Po*, p. 16.
[16] Blofeld, *The Zen Teaching of Hui Hai*, p. 131.　　[17] Blofeld, *The Zen Teaching of Hui Hai*, p. 140.

Po are read in such a way as to provide assurance that the unimaginable will in fact be revealed.

The footnotes supporting the foregoing description of Blofeld's understanding of enlightenment reveal that some of this doctrine has been gleaned from works that are not explicitly on Huang Po or even on Zen. Zen doctrine, at this highest level at least, is not distinguished from Blofeld's reading of the doctrines of other traditions. This "merging" of traditions is intentional on Blofeld's part, and our account here simply follows his lead. On this dimension of his thinking, Blofeld had identified with an influential English tradition of thought known as the "Perennial Philosophy." Blofeld concurred with this tradition in maintaining that hidden within the various historical traditions, can be found one ahistorical, "perennial," mode of thinking that is unified no matter where or when it is found because it derives, not from culture or from thought, but from direct, mystical contact with "Ultimate Reality." Thus Blofeld would place Huang Po in a cross-cultural context and claim: "The experience of standing face to face with Reality never changes. Mystics of every age and every continent, Plotinus, the Buddha, Lao-tse, Eckhart, Blake, countless Hindu sages and the adepts of Sufi wisdom, though separated by immense distances of time and space, are remarkable for their unanimity."[18] The assumption that "there can be only one form of Supreme Enlightenment"[19] enabled Blofeld to interpret Zen texts like the *Huang Po* through categories supplied by other traditions – Buddhism, Hinduism, and, above all, romanticism. But it would also blind him to the particularity and specificity of Huang Po's Zen. The assumption of underlying unity is a powerful interpretive tool. No matter how different Huang Po's words might be from a Hindu's, for example, they could be understood *as* describing precisely the same experience.[20]

it is only that, while groping for words in which to clothe the experience, he is apt to choose terms most readily understandable to those around him. Thus the Catholic mystic speaks in terms of Catholic theology, the Sufi in terms of Allah, and so on.[21]

Underwriting Blofeld's claim here is the instrumentalist doctrine of language that we have considered earlier. According to this view, language "clothes" reality in a particular cultural style, but bears no essential relation to that reality. Therefore Blofeld's understanding is that, even

---

[18] Blofeld, *The Wheel of Life*, p. 180.   [19] Blofeld, *The Wheel of Life*, p. 51.
[20] Blofeld, *The Wheel of Life*, p. 254.   [21] Blofeld, *The Wheel of Life*, p. 180.

though Huang Po is thought to have seen reality as it is – unclothed – he communicates the meaning of this vision to others through a media- tion in the cultural "clothing" most understandable to them.[22] In Blofeld's view, enlightenment is unaffected by the linguistic form of its subsequent communication. Nor would enlightenment have a history, or a form particular to the tradition of Huang Po's Zen. Although it is true that Blofeld's "Perennial Philosophy" has provided a forum for a modern, western transmission of Zen, what the Huang Po texts might say is unconsciously censored in advance by the liberal doctrines of its host.

Beyond differences in language, Blofeld would also maintain that, although different traditions might follow different practices or methods, this would not affect the underlying unity of their goals. Nirvana, there- fore, is thought to be just what it is on its own, regardless of what might be done in different traditions to attain it. Consequently, on this view, Theravadins and Mahayanists "differ only as to method and never as to the Goal."[23] Moreover, the unanimity that Blofeld finds among the "mystics" is taken as evidence for the truth of their vision. Citing Aldous Huxley, Blofeld claims that the unanimity of the mystics "makes it impossible to suppose that they were the victims of their own delusions, for how could a thousand men unknown to each other dream the same dream? There *must* be a reality underlying their vision; their unanimity is marred only by their understandable attempts to describe the inde- scribable in words their respective co-religionists could understand."[24] On this point, Blofeld will not resort to critical doubt: "I do not for one moment doubt that Huang Po was expressing in his own way the same experience of Eternal Truth which Gautama Buddha and others, Buddhist and non-Buddhist, have expressed in theirs . . . Could one suppose otherwise, one would have to accept several forms of absolute truth!"[25] Although the cultural importance of the kind of openness and tolerance expressed in Blofeld's "Perennial Philosophy" should not be forgotten, it is difficult at this historical moment not to be aware of the dogmatic limits that it had placed upon critical thinking. Moreover, if we are to read Huang Po with an eye toward the possibility of learning something new, we must initiate the act of reading without having already subsumed the texts under the "perennial" that we already know.

[22] The Zen master is thought "to clothe invisible Reality in the garments of the religion then and there prevailing" (Blofeld, *The Zen Teaching of Hui Hai*, p. 18).

[23] Blofeld, *The Wheel of Life*, p. 25.　　[24] Blofeld, *The Wheel of Life*, p. 205.

[25] Blofeld, *Huang Po*, p. 9.

Thus, although we have explicated the primary points of Blofeld's interpretation of Huang Po's doctrine of enlightenment, it is not at all clear what aspects of this interpretation derive from a reading of Huang Po's texts and what derives from elsewhere, since Blofeld's overarching theory explicitly denies the difference.

Blofeld is certainly correct that a sense of unity and wholeness are fundamental to the doctrine of enlightenment in the Huang Po texts. The central concept of "One Mind" unifies the text in the same way that, in Buddhist practice, it unifies experience. But this unity is an abstract, high-level unity and stands as the centerpiece of the text and system only insofar as it is supported by various other dimensions of wholeness, some so rudimentary as to be ignored by the texts as presuppositions for what is said. To clarify this, and to show the importance of concepts of wholeness in Huang Po's Zen, it may be helpful to outline the major structures of wholeness both implicit and explicit in the texts.

An initial role for the idea of unity might be that the decision to enter the monastery and pursue Zen practice is, ideally, a decision to seek a unified meaning for the self, a wholeness for one's life. Although it is true that there is an important sense in which Huang Po's Zen should be understood as attentiveness to the present moment in its vivid particularity, there is another more basic sense in which this same Zen seeks to recall the self out of its absorption in the present so that broader perspectives could develop without the distraction of the current moment. "Leaving home," the monastic call, seeks at its most basic level a withdrawal from the activity and plentitude of the world so that, through contemplative exercise, a deeper, more unified sense of that same world might emerge to guide daily comportment and experience. Huang Po's text laments that "the people of the world do not awaken . . . they are blinded by their own sight, hearing, feeling and knowing."[26] The rich plentitude of the world can be blinding. Meditation in all its forms pursues authentic being in relation to the whole of things. It aims to release the self from its inattentive entanglements in the world; it demands a temporary withdrawal from active preoccupation with everyday affairs. The goal of this contemplative disengagement is to provide a cultural space for the development of an enlarged sense of awareness, an attentiveness to broader dimensions of the whole. For the individual practitioner, the initial task is simply to see each moment of one's life as an expression of the whole of life and its meaning.

---

[26] T. 48, p. 380b; Blofeld, *Huang Po*, p. 36.

A second dimension of the cultivation of wholeness sought through the structures of Zen monastic practice, but presupposed rather than discussed in the Huang Po texts, is a textured awareness of the larger social totality of the monastery. Upon entering the monastery, the practitioner begins a process of socialization into a particular way of conceiving and practicing the self's relation both to other selves and to the whole of the community. One's own interests are at first subordinated to, and, later, to some extent, identified with, the interests of the Zen monastic community as a whole. The practitioner relearns in a new and more thoroughly theorized way what was already in most cases learned in his or her earlier upbringing – that the part is subordinate to the whole, the self to the community.

A third dimension of cultivated wholeness, this one more explicit in the texts, extends the communal sense of unity beyond the whole that can be directly experienced in the monastery. This is the historical unity of the lineage, developed in chapter 6. The rhetoric of the Huang Po texts draws extensively upon images that connect current practice to the practice of "patriarchs and buddhas" even though these mythical, genealogical themes rarely become the central focus of discussion. Recitation of lineage and rituals of historical transmission, although not as highly developed in Huang Po's historical era as they are in Zen today, were clearly significant preparatory dimensions of conception and practice. Just as authentic Zen practice required, first, release from the narrowness of current activity, and, second, release from immature focus on one's own self, we find that it requires, third, release from exclusive identification with one's own historical time so that it becomes possible to contextualize one's own era in relation to the larger history of enlightenment. In each case, cultivating a sense of the whole functions to place each individual part in greater and more coherent perspective, and thus to transform one's experience of what is present and at hand.

Fourth, however, the self, the community, and the lineage can be set in a larger context, a greater totality than the human. Although still not the principle theme of the Huang Po texts, this sense of cultivated wholeness does come to frequent articulation. As we have seen, the concept of "emptiness" articulates, and makes available for experience, an awareness of larger relational complexes within which the human can be situated. According to this concept, all sentient beings and all beings of any kind, "co-arise"; each originates conditioned by others and in turn conditions their very possibility. Aside from "air, earth, fire, and water," there is no Zen practice. Although everyone already "knows" this in some sense, cultivating this sensibility beyond that initial knowledge gives rise to "wisdom and compassion," a deep understanding of the nature of all things and a corresponding sense of gratitude and responsibility. One dimension of enlightenment is clearly the capacity to experience oneself in relation to being as a whole.[27]

Although the whole of things can be thought in principle, and awareness can be enlarged, finite practitioners can never experience this totality directly. The finitude of enlightenment means that even the Zen master must be here right now, and not in all places at all times. Therefore, fifth and finally, more important as a dimension of cultivation than the whole as totality is the whole as the ground of all things. Although the teaching of Huang Po presupposes the previous four dimensions, this one is the focus of his explicit *dharma* discourse, and the primary content of enlightenment as it is defined there. Generalized terms in Huang Po's vocabulary suggesting something like the "ground" of all things include *pen*, "root"; *yuan*, "source"; and *li*, "principle." Specialized words, each arising out of the context of Buddhist and Chinese myth and philosophy include *k'ung*, "emptiness"; *hsin*, "mind"; *fo*, "Buddha"; and *fo-hsing*, "Buddha nature," among others. Although each of these arise in different contexts and are conceived differently, their identity is proclaimed in the Huang Po texts and in other Buddhist literature. Each names that which is experienced in enlightenment.

A significant proportion of Huang Po's *dharma* talk is concerned with correcting the *conception* of "that which is experienced in enlightenment." This is the conception of "mind" or "Buddha" still conceived dualistically as something to which the practitioner must come to be related. Turning away from ordinary things in the world, the "source" is sought as something extraordinary but still some-thing, one being among the many, even if more mysterious, more powerful, and so on. Taking one rhetorical pose after another, the Huang Po texts assert that the "source" is not anything at all, but rather that within which all things are encountered. The ground is encountered, not in a separate relation, but in the midst of all other relations. Thus the practitioner is not to establish an independent relation to the ground in addition to, and distinct from, all other relations. Instead, practice is to cultivate the understanding and the awareness that every relation to things in the world is simultaneously a relation to the ground of all things which has no "existence" independent of the "worldly things" through which it is manifest.

---

[27] For a contemporary version of this dimension of wholeness, see Hunt-Badiner, *Dharma Gaia*.

This ungraspability of "mind," "Buddha," or "emptiness" is a constant theme of Huang Po's sermons:

You may say that it is near, yet if you follow it from world to world you will never catch it in your hands. Then you may describe it as far away and, lo, you will see it just before your eyes. Follow it and, behold, it escapes you; run from it and it follows you close. You can neither possess it nor have done with it.[28]

Because it is only experienced within other experiences, a subtle form of awareness is cultivated to make possible a manifestation of this "source," one which doesn't turn away from things completely, but at the same time is not compelled by things and thus obstructed. As the mind shifts in succession from one situation and object of awareness to another, the enlightened mind stays attuned to the "one mind" at the "root" of all things. Conceived in terms of the concept of emptiness, we are led to understand that all forms – all appearances – make their appearance in and through "emptiness." Yet conversely, "emptiness" appears only in and through appearances.[29] Whether the Huang Po texts make this point in theoretical language or in concrete images, it is clear that the overall point is to introduce the content of these thoughts into daily living and experience. The concepts and images provide a depth to the surface of awareness that is to be integrated into ordinary experience.

This understanding of the matter leads Huang Po, like other Buddhists, into paradoxical situations. Although they have gathered in the Zen monastery to seek the Buddha, Huang Po announces playfully, yet with great seriousness, that the Buddha cannot be sought. Furthermore, such seeking is unnecessary; the Buddha is always already there in anything ever encountered. If you left the world in search of nirvana, how would you ever find it?[30] This line of religious thinking, as it developed in Chinese Buddhism, led to the idea of "intrinsic enlightenment." The Huang Po texts introduce this idea in various ways, including:

Even if you go through all the stages of a bodhisattva's progress towards Buddhahood, one by one; when at last, in a single flash, you attain to full

---

[28] T. 48, p. 387b; Blofeld, *Huang Po*, p. 107.

[29] A corollary point is that emptiness itself is an empty form, which is to say that everything said of all other forms applies to emptiness as well. When the concept or experience of emptiness is the focal point of one's attention, at that moment, its own ground is hidden from view. The ground escapes one's grasp even in the form of high-level concepts and breakthrough experiences.

[30] The *Lin-chi lu* proclaims: "You who come here from every quarter all have the idea of seeking Buddha, seeking Dharma, seeking emancipation, seeking to get out of the three realms. Foolish fellows! When you've left the three realms where would you go?" (Sasaki, *The Recorded Sayings of Lin-chi*, p. 26. T. 47, p. 500c).

realization, you will only be realizing the Buddha nature which has been with you all the time; and by all the foregoing stages you will have added to it nothing at all.[31]

Your true nature is something never lost to you even in moments of delusion, nor is it gained at the moment of Enlightenment.[32]

Enlightenment, on this account, is a re-establishment of contact with that to which we already belong, and apart from which we could not exist. Nevertheless, it is a conscious "re-establishment." The beginning of Zen practice initiates a process of meditative opening through which the practitioner makes contact with, and begins to retrieve, the depth into which all human beings are born. Aware of this dimension in the experience of enlightenment, the practitioner realizes what was given to awareness all along. Although the task is to be the one we already are, that attunement is indeed a task, a challenge, something which must be developed and brought into conscious realization.

The form that this "conscious realization" takes, however, is not the "closure" of conceptual determination; there is nothing objective that can be grasped or represented to consciousness. This claim in the Huang Po texts is clear: the activity of placing "mind" or "emptiness" before the mind simultaneously excludes the possibility of awareness of mind. As the open space within which all knowing takes place, mind is not anything that can itself be known. Because there is no standpoint that is external to that which is experienced in enlightenment, no position from which "mind," "emptiness," or "Buddha" could be grasped, Huang Po adopts two distinct postures in addressing the question of enlightenment. The first is irony. The inquiry into the content of enlightenment is ironic in that there is "nothing" there to be experienced. It is the experience of absence and finitude. The figure of irony deflates the expectations and the posture of grasping taken by practitioners. Huang Po's favorite line is the Buddha's own disclaimer that in enlightenment he attained nothing.[33] And as Lin-chi would claim, Huang Po's enlightenment is "nothing special."[34] The ironic power of these passages, however, works to open the practitioner to the more subtle, nonobjective sphere within which awareness of mind or emptiness occurs as an event of disclosure or breakthrough.

The other posture taken by Huang Po in addressing enlightenment

---

[31] T. 48, p. 380a; Blofeld, *Huang Po*, p. 35.   [32] T. 48, p. 387a; Blofeld, *Huang Po*, p. 93.
[33] For example, T. 48, p. 387a; Blofeld, *Huang Po*, p. 35.   [34] T. 47, p. 504c.

follows the pattern established in irony. Lacking a way to assert general propositions about enlightenment, the texts work rhetorically toward the possibility of evoking its manifestation directly. They show how the open space of mind is unavailable for thematic articulation and yet so near that nothing is more fundamental to the self. Experiencing enlightenment is like "tasting taste," or "touching touch." Both taste and touch are so near that, paradoxically, nothing could be more remote from conscious awareness. Taking "mind" and "Buddha" as explicit themes of discourse, however, and bringing their "distant proximity" to mind, sets up the possibility that advanced practitioners might enter this extraordinary open dimension and experience the event of its disclosure.

Perhaps the most distinctive feature of the kind of Zen taught by Huang Po – the "Hung-chou" style – is its sustained interest in converting the Mahayana realization that "nirvana is samsara" into a mode of practical enlightenment. The sayings from Ma-tsu that generated this line of Zen – "everyday mind is the Way" (*p'ing-ch'ang hsin shih tao*), and "this very mind is the Buddha" (*chi hsin chi fo*) – functioned to break the notion of nirvana as a timeless sphere apart from the human context of time and situation.[35] This objectification of enlightenment was a tendency inherent in both monasticism and philosophical Buddhism – the more you talk about nirvana the more it appears to be both something and something beyond this world.[36] Huang Po's version of the doctrinal reversal of this tendency takes several forms. For example: "Wherever your foot may fall, you are still within the sanctuary of enlightenment, though it is nothing perceptible. I assure you that one who comprehends the truth of 'nothing to be attained' is already seated in the sanctuary where he will attain enlightenment."[37] For Huang Po, the solution would be found both in the return to the ordinary, and in a deconstruction of the distinction between the ordinary and enlightenment. "If you would only rid yourselves of the concepts of ordinary and enlightened, you would find that there is no other Buddha than the Buddha in your mind."[38]

Tsung-mi, a contemporary of Huang Po, saw danger for Chinese Buddhism in this development of Hung-chou thought. Although he

---

[35] The primary doctrinal form that this realization had taken in China was the idea of intrinsic or innate awakening. On the effect of this idea on the dualism of "ordinary" and "enlightened," see LaFleur, *The Karma of Words*, p. 21.

[36] As Bernard Faure shows in discussing this doctrinal development, even the Hung-chou insight that nothing is attained in enlightenment is susceptible to "hypostasization." See *The Rhetoric of Immediacy*, p. 27.   [37] Blofeld, *Huang Po*, p. 128.   [38] T. 48, p. 383a; Blofeld, *Huang Po*, p. 58.

could sympathize with the critique of Buddhist otherworldliness that had generated the Hung-chou emphasis on ordinary life, he worried that turning to the opposite form of spirituality would entail too easy a surrender to the way human beings already happen to be.[39] The point of Buddhism was not an exaltation of the way things already are; it was instead their transformation. Although the monastic aspiration to purity was indeed susceptible to denial of life, and to the projection of a goal beyond life, the Hung-chou remedy for this tendency seemed too extreme to Tsung-mi.[40]

For western Zen readers it is important to notice that this is another position upon which the transmission of Zen to the west has been able to make contact with the romantic tradition. Like many of us, Blofeld's early English education would have been steeped in the writings of romantic authors for whom the spiritual significance of the ordinary was a primary theme. The "transfiguration of the ordinary" and its elevation into the "sublime" would motivate several generations of writers and artists in Europe in their opposition both to Enlightenment rationalism and to established Christian institutions.[41] And as Tsung-mi could see in its Zen form, this ideological emphasis carries with it inherent dangers that would no doubt emerge in certain contexts. On the basis of this precedent in romantic literature, we find emerging already in the first generation of American advocates of "Zen," a strong emphasis on the elevation of the "ordinary." "Beat Zen" would, in some contexts at least, appear to require the denunciation of all qualitative distinctions. Although implicitly advocating a particular form of human excellence, this form could be reduced to simple acceptance of what is – the idea that whatever is going on, and whatever we do in response to it, is just fine. Moreover, an emphasis on the *rejection* of an otherworldly quest for purity in "Beat" romanticism would tend toward a form of sensualism in which reflection would be repressed in order that the "immediacy" of impulse could be accommodated. Lacking sufficient internal or communal restraint, this acquiescence to "the present moment" would, in some circumstances, eventuate in distinctly unenlightened forms of life.

Although references to "wild monks" do appear in traditional Zen literature, it appears that the force of the monastic tradition in Buddhism would keep many of the excesses inherent in Hung-chou doctrine in

---

[39] See Broughton, *Kuei-feng Tsung-mi*, p. 152.   [40] See Yanagida, "The *Li-tai fa-pao chi*," p. 35.
[41] On this development in Europe, see Taylor, *Sources of the Self*.

check.[42] Opportunities for extreme interpretation of these doctrines, at least by modern standards, were few. Furthermore, we can see clearly that Huang Po's qualifications on the return to the ordinary are of central importance, one of them so significant that Blofeld would present it in capital letters: "DO NOT PERMIT THE EVENTS OF YOUR DAILY LIVES TO BIND YOU, BUT NEVER WITHDRAW YOURSELVES FROM THEM. Only by acting thus can you earn the title of 'A Liberated One.'"[43] Enlightenment entails that one be fully in the world, but never quite of it, never forced along blindly by one attraction after another. Enlightenment includes "freedom" as one of its primary characteristics. Freedom, as we have seen, is not release from the destiny of finding oneself in a situation of constraint. Constraints are always in place, and this placement structures the human situation. Instead, freedom is conceived as an awakening to the particular contours of the given situation, a heightening of the awareness of one's own basic situatedness. Although this awakening requires the practice of defamiliarization in initial stages, such that the ordinary ceases to appear so ordinary, the purpose of this intentional estrangement from the world is an authentic recovery of lived experience. The practitioner of Zen returns to where he or she always was, but now in the spirit of awakened contact.[44]

That this "return" occurs as an event of disclosure, a "sudden" breakthrough that reorients experience in a single moment, is perhaps the best-known facet of Zen. Huang Po was a forceful advocate of the teaching of "sudden awakening." His historical position placed him at the height of persuasiveness of this way of understanding enlightenment. How should we understand the import of this emphasis? If enlightenment is construed as an ongoing state of being, characteristic of the lives of Zen masters, then it makes no sense to say that enlightenment *is* sudden awakening, since that would restrict the time of enlightenment to a single moment. The Huang Po texts would seem to prefer to say that enlightenment first occurs in a sudden breakthrough, or that enlightenment is initiated in one moment of experience. Given the innate

---

[42] It is important to notice also that the monastic structures of Buddhist life would prevent Hung-chou Zen from returning to "everyday life" in most of its dimensions. Monasteries continued to separate men and women, to prohibit sexual activity, to keep themselves immune from the difficulties of childbirth, nurturance, education, and, to some extent, even the economic exigencies of family life. The monastic "ordinary" was not exactly everyone's "ordinary."

[43] Blofeld, *Huang Po*, p. 131.

[44] Faure is right that "in a sense, Mazu's Chan marked a return to gradualism, since it no longer advocated seeing one's true nature im-mediately, but mediately, through its function" (*Rhetoric of Immediacy*, p. 51). But if the only possibility for "seeing one's true nature" is mediation through some "rhetoric of immediacy," then there are no alternatives to "gradualism."

temporality of human experience, however, all life, whether enlightened or unenlightened, is "gradual," that is, susceptible to change over time. How would this be true of enlightened mind? Unless we conceive of this state of mind as permanent, not subject to change and not amenable to deepening or transformation of any kind, even enlightenment would be understood as gradual, that is, as process. Although no reflection on this question appears in the early Huang Po literature, we can glean an answer to the question from later *koan* practice into which these texts were drawn. The sequence of *koans* and the ongoing character of practice beyond initial "sudden awakenings" both imply that enlightenment entails the unfolding of mind over time. Although Buddhist mythology can imagine an end to this process – the state of Buddhahood wherein non-finite powers have been attained – Zen texts don't always concur. Instead, the openness and bottomlessness of reality sometimes lead Zen reflection toward the conclusion that enlightenment is not something definite at all, but rather the ongoing opening of awareness and the continual perfecting of responsiveness without end. Although Huang Po's sermons don't include reflection on the subsequent unfolding of enlightenment, neither do they imagine an infinite state beyond ordinary life in the world. Huang Po's earliest literature has already demythologized the state of enlightenment. To be enlightened is still to be human, and, therefore, always to be on the way, always immersed in particular circumstances in response to which finite decisions will need to be made.

If we assume this understanding, then what can we make of the suddenness of awakening? The figure of suddenness appears in two forms in these texts. The first invokes the agency of the practitioner. It takes the discursive form: "If you would suddenly let go of your concepts, then you would awaken." Here "sudden awakening" is a leap that "ought" to be made, an act of agency. Secondly, however, sudden breakthrough is presented as that which befalls the practitioner, less something done than something to which one might fall prey. In the first place, this discourse shows the practitioner the goal toward which one must gradually practice, the ability in faith to let go of the forms of subjectivity that secure our present state of being. The second form would appear to describe the experience of awakening subsequent to the act of letting go. In this case, having released the subjectivity of agency or control, awakening is experienced as that which comes upon the practitioner beyond his or her own doing. These dimensions of sudden awakening both require further specification.

The "leap" is an important image in the Huang Po texts, as it is elsewhere in Zen literature. Huang Po's image of awakening is a decisive "leap off a hundred foot pole." How is this act of suddenness related to gradual practice? Like everyone else, Zen initiates cannot simply set aside their current self-understanding in order to be someone else – suddenly. Self-understanding can, however, be gradually called into question, but only through the postulation of some new form of understanding (even if the new understanding is simply that all understanding must be released). The new understanding, accumulated in both doctrinal and non-doctrinal meditation, gradually dislodges the old. The difference between them, ideally, is that the new one embodies "emptiness"; it contains structures signifying openness and lack of closure, and it illustrates this openness in its own tentativeness about itself and all other doctrinal positions. Emptiness proclaims its own emptiness, and, in so doing, points beyond itself. The process of questioning and self-questioning is inherently gradual; old structures of experience slowly dissolve, first intellectually and then down to the level of practice and daily comportment. This process is implied in the character of the Huang Po texts. The texts say, implicitly, "think these thoughts, and, having done that, think these other thoughts." This is a gradual, disciplined process, as all reflection is. For example, Huang Po chastises the thought of gradual achievement. Instead, he instructs us not to regard ourselves as the cause of sudden transformation because such regard only closes off the posture that will enable breakthrough – openness to what is beyond the self. Nevertheless, this thought does function gradually to condition the possibility of sudden breakthrough.[45]

The final act of agency is pictured as a leap. The leap abandons the secure and familiar dimensions of ordinary subjectivity. In this act, the practitioner releases him or herself into "emptiness," the groundless ground that the texts call the "great mystery." Because what ground there is is groundless, this leap into the abyss is described as frightening, the abandonment of the known self and its secure ground. It is frightening because what lies ahead is unknown, a mystery beyond the practitioner's control and determination. Only the well-cultivated practitioner can and will make this leap; it clearly requires the gradual accumulation of faith. Yet this act appears as a requirement. One version of it, in the *Mumonkan koan* collection, number five, is Hsiang-yen's parable of the Zen practitioner hanging

---

[45] See Gregory, *Sudden and Gradual*, for a variety of Buddhist interpretations of the meaning of sudden breakthrough and gradual accumulation.

by his teeth from a branch high up on a tree. The question posed to him as he hangs there – why had Bodhidharma come from the west? – can only be answered in the act of letting go. Until he can let go, he hangs there in agony and anxiety. When the agony and anxiety are finally released, so is the self – sudden breakthrough.

Why is sudden awakening envisioned as release into the void; why not into the graceful arms of the Buddha or into the Pure Land or onto the solid ground of greater security? The image here fits the conception, and, no doubt, the experience. As Huang Po pictures it, the Buddha obtained "nothing" in enlightenment – no knowledge, no secure ground, no assurances, no certainties. In enlightenment, the Buddha did not escape the contingencies and exposures that are inherent to life in the flux. He was not enlightened in the sense of being infused with the light of complete knowledge. Instead, the Huang Po texts pictured enlightenment as a shattering of subjectivity, a de-centering of the self in its exposure to the groundlessness of all beings. The illusion of human mastery is dispelled and the contingency of freedom acknowledged. Therefore, the Huang Po texts have Bodhidharma pose the challenge of "enlightenment" as follows: "When we recognize the nature of mind, all we can say is that it is unthinkable. In understanding, nothing is attained; when we obtain it, we cannot say we 'know.' When I teach you this matter, can you withstand it?"[46] Enlightenment, in this image, is a human comportment in view of the abandonment of all solid grounds, including the search for such grounds. Release into the experience is simultaneous with release of all claims to possess, to grasp, and to know. It follows the concept "emptiness" into its denial of all claims to truth and absoluteness, including its own claim to know something ultimately truthful about all claims.

Even though the practice of seated meditation is rarely a theme in the Huang Po texts, it is clear that we cannot imagine their meaning without reflecting on the conjunction of the text's doctrinal assertions and med-itative exercise. After realizing, once again, that the thinking practice prescribed in the texts *is* meditation, we must also imagine the role of non-conceptual meditation in this context. Although the practices differ, both, it seems, serve the same function. The emptying capacity of the doctrine parallels and supports the emptying capacity of mental exer-cises aimed at stilling the mind. The thoughts prescribed by Huang Po can only be thought in the context of a disciplined and quiet mind; the

[46] T. 48, p. 383ab;

discipline of quieting the mind can only be performed in the context of thoughts which present and articulate "reasons" for such quieting. Both seek to de-center the ego and to clear the mind, creating in it an opening within which the manifestation of images within the mind, or forms within emptiness, can occur without grasping and securing. This expansive openness is described as difficult and anxiety-provoking. Opening to larger spheres beyond the self discloses the self's groundlessness and mortality – its own emptiness. In this sense, enlightenment is not simply a matter of personal fulfillment, a psychological self-improvement. Instead, abandoning the security of self-understanding, it entails exposure to transpersonal contexts beyond the self.

One image of enlightenment in Huang Po and in other Zen texts from this period was that of a "mind like wood or stone." This image was so much in contrast to Blofeld's understanding of what "enlightenment" was, cross-culturally, that he continued to use these metaphors as images of "unenlightenment," in spite of their obvious use to the contrary in both *Huang Po* and *Hui Hai*. Therefore, while translating the images in the text one way, in his introductions to these translations he continued to write: "Yet this does not mean that we should make our minds blank, for then we should be no better than blocks of wood or lumps of stone; moreover, if we remained in this state, we should not be able to deal with the circumstances of daily life."[47] We can surely sympathize with Blofeld's reluctance to accept a "mind like wood or stone" as an authentic image of awakening. After all, wood and stone are relatively unresponsive, unattuned, and unaware. In what sense are they *like* the mind? In alternative senses, obviously. All metaphors are limited in their analogical capacity. To be a metaphor requires both identity and difference. In the numerous passages where mind is to be understood in terms of the images of wood and stone, some dimension of their identity is explicated. Enlightened mind is like wood or stone in that "they do not discriminate"; in that "they do not seek for anything"; in that "they accept what is as it is and open themselves to be moved by reality." In other respects, clearly, wood and stone are not like the enlightened mind. The sense in which they are, however, is important in Huang Po. This sense corresponds to the negative dimension of practice, the conception of the way as abandonment, letting go, non-grasping and non-seeking. Huang Po instructs his hearers to practice the thought that "in reality, there is nothing to be

[47] Blofeld, *Huang Po*, p. 20; or see Blofeld, *The Zen Teaching of Hui Hai*, p. 132.

grasped."[48] Therefore, let go of the search for security, for stable and permanent ground. Place yourself in the open, exposed to the world. Do not grasp for anything because, no matter what image of the goal guides your seeking, it will prove to be inadequate. "Above all, have no longing to become a future Buddha; your sole concern should be, as thought succeeds thought, to avoid clinging to any of them."[49] No doubt, initially, the state of non-seeking must be sought. The Huang Po texts are certainly aware of the fundamental role of effort and discipline. Yet, in the end, effort is to circle back in upon itself, emptying its own activity, until non-effort is indeed effortless. Therefore, Huang Po says: "This is not something which you can accomplish without effort, but when you reach the point of clinging to nothing whatever, you will be acting as the Buddhas act. This will indeed be acting in accordance with the saying: Develop a mind which rests on nothing whatever."[50] This same kind of self-negation in the state of enlightenment appears to apply to Buddhist thought or to doctrine. Although the ideas of Buddhism must be thought, at the highest level the content of this thought is the relinquishment of thought, its emptiness: "Relinquishment of everything is the Dharma, and he who understands this is a Buddha, but the relinquishment of all delusions leaves no Dharma on which to lay hold."[51] Holding to the teachings that teach release was essential to the practice in Huang Po monastery. Consistent releasement, however, requires that, in the end, these teachings also be released. This is the image of Buddhas, the image of enlightenment in Huang Po. The process of Zen practice is thought to lead, not to definitive knowledge or grounding in certainty, but rather to an openness better characterized by "letting go." Therefore, the literature of Huang Po does not propose a conception of the "true self," nor does it conclude in an account of "the way things really are." Instead, it suggests practices of thought and images of masters who let go of thought even while thinking. Although the text is therefore unsystematic and sometimes inconsistent, what it offers instead is a mode of textuality and form of practice that are inventive, ironic, open, and free.

"Letting go" is Huang Po's worldly and practical analogue to the formal Buddhist concept of "no-self." For Huang Po, letting go is "losing oneself in enlightenment." Correlatively, the kind of truth experienced

---

[48] Blofeld, *Huang Po*, p. 111.   [49] Blofeld, *Huang Po*, p. 106.
[50] T. 48, p. 383b; Blofeld, *Huang Po*, p. 62.   [51] T. 48, p. 381a; Blofeld, *Huang Po*, p. 40.

in enlightenment is ungraspably not a possession of the experiencing subject. Instead, individual subjectivity is lifted up out of itself and transformed, not just on its own initiative but in the event of sudden disclosure. This event incorporates the self into a higher subjectivity that, while including subjectivity, transforms it by opening it to what is other than the self. Given this image, the creativity and inventiveness of the Zen master is not his or her own ingenuity. It is rather an openness of the self beyond itself in listening and attunement.

To be enlightened, then, is to be a willing and open respondent, to have achieved an open reciprocity with the world through certain dimensions of self-negation. Huang Po pictures the enlightened patriarchs in real-life situations effacing themselves so that the true contour of the situation comes to disclosure in them. They encounter the world, not through acts of will and mind primarily, but through relinquishment. Opening their own minds and will, the larger context of the situation comes to manifestation through them.[52] Two Buddhist examples might prove helpful in our attempt to imagine this kind of selflessness. Our first is the character of Zen conversation, often translated as "encounter dialogue," which is chronicled in a great deal of Zen literature. These narratives of dialogical encounter between two Zen practitioners display release of self in practice. Conversations, like games, move back and forth, neither participant controlling or preplanning the movement of words and images. Each, to the extent of their awakening, opens him- or herself to the encounter as a purified respondent, responding freely and without preplanned intention to what has just been said by the other. Neither the conversation nor its resultant disclosure are the subjective accomplishment of either interlocutor. Nor is it, in another sense, their joint construction. Opening themselves to the unexpected, both await disclosure, the moment in the conversation when open minds find themselves in an event of insight that is not their own product. The *Lin-chi lu* is especially interesting as a record of encounter dialogue[53] in that it pictures Lin-chi attuned, more than anything else, to moments of failure in dialogue. These are moments when Lin-chi catches his interlocutor in

---

[52] To my mind the best model for this overarching form of mental practice is Gadamer's analogy of the game. In playing a game, we are lifted up out of ourselves and put into play. Our actions are not determinations of our own wills and minds primarily; they are determined both by the understanding and rules of the game and by the particular movements of the game. Our actions are responses to the moves of others and to the point of the game. See *Truth and Method*, pp. 91–108.

[53] Many of these dialogues include Huang Po as interlocutor even though they were written several centuries after his life.

hesitation, planning or thinking out the next response even before the appearance of that to which response is to be made. These are called moments of "faltering" when the exchange fails because one speaker has withdrawn into the self and out of the open space of dialogue.

Our second example is the Mahayana Buddhist teaching that enlightenment necessarily includes compassion. Compassion entails a sensitive awareness of a context larger than the self. Being selfless is being attuned to others. Open to others, the enlightened person is pictured as moved by others, responding to their plight as if it were his own. Compassion is not imagined as a duty for those who have succeeded. Nor is it considered, strictly speaking, an act of will. It is rather the opening of oneself to the possibility of being moved by others, an experienced identity between the self and the social world beyond the self. In this context, moving and being moved are indistinguishable. The Huang Po texts excel in teaching this reciprocity of human life in the world. They maintain that enlightenment is "neither subjective nor objective."[54] Neither activity nor passivity encompasses the simultaneity of grasping and being grasped. Beyond the duality of self and other, active and passive, the enlightened mind encompasses both poles. Active, the mind is resolute; it strives to open itself and to regard the other's welfare as its own. Passive, the mind openly awaits the disclosure of truth: silent composure, no grasping. In Zen and Buddhist thought, this opening is not simply a psychological attitude. It is more importantly an occurrence situated reciprocally within multiple relations to the world. On the basis of this reciprocity, enlightenment is described, from one "Mahayana" perspective, as enacted by forces beyond the individual self. Although the self must strive to open itself, and must adopt certain postures in that effort, it cannot on its own accomplish the event of "awakening." But it can be opened. There is indeed an art of existing being recommended by Huang Po in the texts. It entails taking certain postures, thinking certain thoughts, and comporting oneself in certain ways. All of these entailments, however, stand in service of living life as a temporal process, a movement of multidimensional occurrences that are not fully of our own doing. The texts teach both the practices of opening and the event of being opened.

The active component of enlightenment includes a wide variety of exercises, following Huang Po's principles, practices, and precepts. Enlightenment goes beyond that activity, however, to the kind of

---

[54] T. 48, p. 380b; Blofeld, *Huang Po*, p. 38.

spontaneous responsiveness we have described. The archetypical Zen life is described as fully spontaneous. Although spontaneity is constructed, both by oneself and by the tradition upon oneself,[55] the Zen ideal of excellence is that Buddhist cultivation proceed until the construction process has disappeared from view. This relationship between practice and spontaneity is analogous to that between doctrine and realization or thought and feeling. After one gives rise to the other, its presence in the other has been thoroughly transformed. Thus, Huang Po insists that "if one does not actually realize the truth of Zen from one's own experience, but simply learns it verbally and collects words, and claims to understand Zen, how can one solve the riddle of life and death?"[56] Realizing the truth of Zen takes time, practice, and effort. First one has to "learn it verbally" and "collect [some] words." Then, over time, this learning and these words must be internalized, until they are embodied and thus made spontaneous. Spontaneously feeling the truth of Zen occurs not in opposition to thinking this truth, but rather, in part, as a result of this practice of thought. "Feeling is not contrary to thought. It is thought made ours."[57]

The images and conception of enlightenment we have now described were, to some extent at least, unique to the Zen tradition in the era following Huang Po's time. What enlightenment had meant to earlier Chinese Buddhist monks was considerably different. Earlier images of enlightenment included a greater emphasis on a philosophical articulation of Buddhist thought. Earlier enlightened figures were often writers rather than orators like Huang Po. Few earlier images of the ideal feature excellence in the kind of "encounter dialogue" that comes to be stressed in Zen texts from Huang Po's time on. Comparing saintly images of the ideal in the Zen "recorded sayings" and "transmission" texts with the ideal as projected in the earlier "illustrious

---

[55] Bernard Faure is insightful in showing the ritualization of spontaneity in Zen, the "framing of ultimate truth by conventional truth." He wonders whether spontaneity or immediacy was "affirmed at the very historical moment when it is about to disappear, when mediations come to play an increasing role" (*Rhetoric of Immediacy*, p. 314). Faure's point is important and can be extended by being reversed. The "disappearance" of spontaneity is really its appearance, the moment when spontaneity is noticed and brought into thought and practice *as* spontaneity, as something desirable and worth cultivating. The mythical spontaneity that existed *in illo tempore*, before anyone knew it *as* spontaneity, was of a fundamentally different kind than that conceived and practiced after the "fall" into awareness of spontaneity. The entire Zen tradition, just because it is a tradition, postdates the kind of unconscious spontaneity that had by then become a theme – something to be valued, practiced, and theorized.

[56] T. 51, p. 266; Chang, *Original Teachings*, p. 105.

[57] Ricoeur, "The Metaphorical Process as Cognition, Imagination, and Feeling."

monks" (*kao-seng*) literature yields strikingly different ways of imagining what the goal of Buddhism might be. The meaning of enlightenment had changed.

Moreover, Huang Po's image and conception of enlightenment have not continued to be fully persuasive, either in China or elsewhere. Criticisms of that image have, at various times and in various ways, come to be widely known and accepted. Following the height of Zen in China, for example, Neo-Confucians rose to ideological power in China; their image of human excellence came to prevail. Although these practitioners of *Tao-hsueh* had borrowed a great deal from the Zen of Huang Po, they were also very critical. Neither Huang Po nor other Zen masters ever had much to say about ethical and moral issues, about political issues, about artistic and other cultural practices. They seemed to be of little help when it came to economic and social organization; they had no suggestions concerning "right livelihood" for laypeople, and little advice to give concerning education, family life, and so on. Although Zen stories clearly had morals to tell, none of them seem to educate readers about issues of conscience. Neo-Confucians were harsh in their critique of these absences in the ideals and modes of excellence that Zen had to offer. Reformulating the image of human excellence, they added what seemed missing to them and subtracted what seemed irrelevant or unworthy of further valorization. This process has continued. Neo-Confucian images of excellence continued to evolve over centuries and, in the nineteenth and twentieth centuries, were upstaged altogether by modern images, first from scientific rationalism, and then from others, especially Marx. Marxist/Maoist conceptions of the human ideal, even though adopted only recently, are currently under heavy pressure, already yielding to the formation of new ideals. An analogous process constitutes the history of western cultures, and continues today.

This history of human idealization is visible to us today in ways that it never has been to any culture in the past. We have available for our contemplation an unprecedented range of possible human ideals. Each representation of the ideal, precisely because it is an idealization as seen from a certain historical location, claims timeless truth for its image of excellence. When a newly emerging ideal is radically new, that is, when the change is as dramatic as a paradigm shift rather than a revision that stands more clearly within a traditional lineage, claims to finality and certainty tend to be heightened. Yet, in each case, historically conscious spectators can see that each claim to timeless truth is itself time-bound, a function of a specific set of historical convergences. An assumption about the timelessness of enlightenment as it is conceived in the texts can also be seen in Huang Po. The authors of these texts, and perhaps Huang Po himself, would not have been able to imagine that "true enlightenment" could possibly be much different than they had represented it. As we have seen, the kind of historical understanding at work in these texts assumed a "transmission" of mind from one enlightened master to another without substantial change. What that meant, in effect, was that the Buddha, from Huang Po's angle of vision, appeared to be a Zen master possessing all the powers and virtues of medieval Chinese life. In spite of the "emptiness" of all forms, enlightenment was conceived as a timeless essence, and thus no "impermanence" was predicated of it.

We have found one intriguing exception to this pattern, however. Although enlightenment was represented in one context as a permanent essence passed on from one master to another, in another context Huang Po was expected to "go beyond" his teacher in the form that his enlightenment would take. The teaching of "going beyond" shows the extent to which the tradition at that particular point was open to the possibility that enlightenment itself might be "impermanent." Clearly, the question had been posed: if all things are empty, what does the application of this concept to enlightenment mean? This is perhaps the most difficult question, more perplexing even than the "emptiness of emptiness." The conceptual elements to begin to answer this question are clearly there in the texts of Huang Po. Enlightenment is empty, and that implies that no thought or experience of enlightenment is final and absolute. What elements might encourage this answer? To a great extent, enlightenment in Huang Po has been defined as openness. Openness comes to be the virtue that it is in Huang Po because, among other reasons, impermanence was basic to the Buddhist world view. All things change; closure unwisely resists the change that is always under way. Openness to change is therefore wisdom itself. That even "openness" could take different forms and continually undergo change is no doubt difficult to see from any point of view. Clearly, however, some version of this principle has been seen, not only in Huang Po and his authors, but elsewhere in the Buddhist tradition as well. How does it occur that enlightenment will always entail some form of "going beyond?"

One impetus to change can be noticed in any sufficiently well-developed tradition of practice. Our understanding of the goal of practice changes as we progress toward it. Our understanding of excellence, in any dimension of human culture, is altered by our striving to attain it. We make progress not only in our proximity to the goal, but in our conception of it as well.[58] If a cultural practice is successful, it will lead to a series of reformulations of its own "reason for being."[59] Huang Po's Zen is part of just such a reformulation. As the tradition evolves, each image of the goal ends up serving as a means to some future goal. Although the present form of enlightenment always takes the form of the unsurpassable, its ultimacy is sooner or later undermined by transformations in other dimensions of the context or point of view from which its unsurpassability seemed obvious. Even new ways of speaking about the goal, new means of practicing it, and new ways of expressing it, will eventually lead to the necessity of "going beyond" what was previously sought.

While the Enlightenment rationalism that is still very much our heritage assumes progress or "going beyond" primarily in the form of greater rigor and consistency in current thinking and practice, romanticism attunes us to the possibility that insight might open entire dimensions of thought, practice, and experience not now available to us. Romanticism is the dimension of our selves and culture most open to thoroughgoing transformation in light of some form of otherness. Moreover, these two dimensions of heritage are, and always have been, so thoroughly intertwined that openness to radically new dimensions of human life is also an imperative placed upon us by critical reason. Critical reason, which now recognizes more thoroughly than it ever has the finitude and historicity of all culture, comes to the realization that a conception and practice of "ongoing enlightenment" is superior to "static" conceptions of enlightenment. "Ongoing enlightenment" in this sense is a process without end. Since all forms of excellence give way to new and revised forms, ongoing attentiveness to the process of deepening current conceptions of excellence is perhaps legitimately the most enduring and important dimension of "enlightenment."

In the current world cultural situation, it is clear that the most promising resource for insights that might reshape our ideals is cross-cultural and cross-historical reflection. Just as modernity in Europe derived in part from Europe's encounter with Islamic culture and, through it, Europe's first full-scale appropriation of a legacy from Greece and

---

[58] "The very process of trying to obtain what one values may change what it is that one values" (MacIntyre, *Whose Justice*, p. 41).

[59] "It is one of the marks of the flourishing of such a developing system of thought and practice that from time to time its telos is reformulated" (MacIntyre, *Three Rival Versions*, p. 149).

Rome, similarly China and other Buddhist cultures have reshaped their thinking and practice through creative encounter with the west. Openness to previously underdeveloped forms of enlightenment – science, political structures, and so on – although no doubt forced upon Asia by the exigencies of historical pressure, have brought far-reaching transformation to traditional Asian ideals. Chinese enlightenment in the tradition of Huang Po and others has been broadened and expanded by encounter with images of enlightenment provided by Darwin, Mill, and Marx. Since, in view of Kant's definition of enlightenment, the "immaturity" from which we would be liberated turns out to take a surprising range of historical forms, so must enlightenment. The process of such revolutionary reflection continues in China today.

Can those of us in English-language cultures be similarly transformed by our encounter with Asia? We not only can, we already have, although perhaps not to the extent and depth of the East Asian transformation. Although romanticism has shown us ways in which it might be possible to learn from Asian culture, both the range of possibilities and the scope of this learning are so far limited – immature. Nevertheless, it is already the case that "enlightenment" in English has incorporated connotations and nuances from Asia. When the word "enlightenment" is said, Huang Po, via Blofeld and now others, is there, however distant in the background. This inevitable inclusion, which we can still choose either to cultivate or to ignore, expands and deepens the repertoire of possibilities for meaning and practice already inherent in the traditions of western culture. If "enlightenment" is to symbolize excellence of human being, the best form of life currently imaginable, however defined, then the question posed by Kant and Dogen at the beginning of this chapter – what is enlightenment? – is ours as well. We have no choice but to answer the question by filling in its content for use in our lives. Although we may or may not do this in principle, that is, in thought, we will all do it in practice by living one way rather than another, for better or worse. If we do it thoughtfully and with integrity, then our meditations on Zen will simply be part of this questioning process wherein we too ask ourselves – what is the form of enlightenment most worthy of our striving? Moreover, by criteria acceptable to both Huang Po and Kant, the individuals and the cultures that are most authentically open to the possibility of learning something new and valuable from others, and who most creatively and rigorously engage in the process of "application" to their lives, will also be the individuals and cultures that will come to define for us our own future images of enlightenment.

CONCLUSION. *Zen in theory and practice*

When we discover that we have in this world no earth or rock to stand or walk upon but only shifting sea and sky and wind, the mature response is not to lament the loss of fixity but to learn to sail.

James Boyd White[1]

During Huang Po's time, he left all the monks who followed him and became involved in the general work at Ta-an Monastery, where his continuous practice consisted of sweeping out all the rooms. He swept the Buddha hall and the Dharma hall. But it was not continuous practice done for the sake of sweeping out the mind, nor was it continuous practice performed in order to cleanse the light of the Buddha. It was continuous practice done for the sake of continuous practice.

Dogen[2]

Zen Buddhism has been practiced in East Asia for well over a millennium. During this lengthy historical period, the Zen tradition incorporated into itself many of the spheres of culture – or cultural practices – that were dominant in its time. Theoretical thinking, or philosophy, was one of these, and the Huang Po texts are fine examples of its Zen form in the early Sung period. Nevertheless, Zen Buddhism is not primarily a philosophical movement. Indeed, criticism of theoretical reflection from the perspective of Zen meditation practice is ever present in Zen literature. Even when Zen Buddhists do philosophize, as Huang Po certainly did, practice, not theory, is the emphatic focus of reflection. Therefore, it seems important that we conclude these meditations by asking, first, how should we understand the relation between meditation and philosophy in Zen Buddhism, and, second, how should we understand the relation between our own theoretical reflections on Zen and the practice of Zen?

---

[1] White, *When Words Lose their Meaning*, p. 278.　　[2] Francis Cook, trans., *How to Raise an Ox*, p. 198.

207

Once again, we can take our initial lead on this issue from John Blofeld. Following the discussion of "Zen doctrine" in his introduction to the translation of Huang Po, John Blofeld addresses the topic of "Zen practice." The practice he had in mind, and the one that he knew would need to be discussed, was meditation. The word "Zen" means "meditation" and this practice, variously conceived, has always been important to the tradition.[3] The issue of Zen meditation posed a serious problem for Blofeld's understanding of his own book, however, because, as he admitted, Huang Po seemed to have very little to say about this topic. Uncertain about what to make of this absence in the Zen master, Blofeld wrote that "Huang Po seems to have assumed that his audience knew something about this practice – as most keen Buddhists do, of course."[4] This was, of course, a sound assumption on Blofeld's part: practitioners in a ninth-century Chinese Buddhist monastery would have known something about this practice, so much in fact that, whether a Zen text discusses it or not, we can be confident that this practice could be found not too far in the background of the discussion. Nevertheless, the question must be significant: if the origins and early centuries of the Zen tradition were heavily focused on seated meditation, why do we find in Huang Po and in the avant-garde Zen tradition of his time a relative disinterest in meditation? Why do we find the practice of meditation being so frequently criticized in the Zen monastic discourse of that period?

Answers to these historical questions can be found in a number of places. Let us take just one, however, as an impetus to our own reflections on the issue of theory and practice. It is clear from many sources that, in addition to their practice of silent meditation, Chinese Zen monks of this period pursued a theoretical practice aimed at rethinking the entire domain of meditation. One theory being practiced to this end claimed that there is nothing for meditative effort to achieve since all human beings already possess the "Buddha nature" that has been their birthright all along. Therefore, Ma-tsu, the lineage founder, would speak as if to absolve monks of the necessity of "constant sitting" because "everyday mind is the Way," not the extraordinary mind of prolonged disciplinary sitting. Following Ma-tsu's theory, Huang Po would instruct his followers that "since you are fundamentally complete in every respect, you should not try to supplement that perfection by such meaningless practices."[5] This theory was taken to be worthy of considerable

---

[3] Foulk is right, however, to insist that there is no single element of the Zen tradition that can legitimately b e conceived as the essence of the tradition throughout its history ("The 'Ch'an School").   [4] Blofeld, *Huang Po*, p. 19.   [5] T. 48, p. 379c; Blofeld, *Huang Po*, p. 30.

meditation; dedicated monks would "practice it day and night," both when they were in seated meditation and when they were not.

In the time that Huang Po's text was being composed, it appears that the relations between thought, practice, and all other activities were being radically reconceived. One form that this reconceptualization seems to have taken is a critique of the idea that meditation practice is a special activity located outside the domain of ordinary life. Meditation was thought to be more effectively practiced when it was not considered a separate and sacred dimension of life, but rather as the conscious awareness present in all human activity. If the point of meditation was to elevate the level of awareness in daily life, transforming all moments and all activities in enlightening ways, then raising meditation above and separating it from daily life would be counterproductive. Instead, meditation was to be universalized; that is, all acts, no matter how ordinary, were to be performed as though they too were meditative practices. Rather than limiting meditation to a certain number of hours in the meditation hall, monks were encouraged to live all moments of life meditatively, no matter what the external form of the activity currently under way. When properly theorized, meditative practice was to encompass everything: daily monastic labor, ordinary conversation, eating, bathing, breathing, and so on. When monks pondered the common Zen phrase, "In chopping wood and carrying water, therein lies the marvelous Way," they were simply practicing the most transformative Zen theory of their time, a theory aimed at making all of life one continuous act of meditation.

One of the many forms that meditation could take was theoretical or philosophical reflection. Thus, "theory" could be refigured in the mind as "practice." Although in some ways this may seem an odd conclusion, it would not have surprised anyone in the Buddhist tradition. On the contrary, from very early on, meditation was divided into two basic forms. One form (*samatha*) is non-discursive silence – stopping thought activity and pacifying the mind – and the other (*vipassana*) is philosophical meditation, a conceptual meditative practice. Zen meditation can be found abundantly in both kinds. When *zazen* takes a non-discursive form, the intention of its practice is to calm the mind of pointless and frenetic activity. In this case it seeks to clear away the meaningless chatter that obstructs mindful presence in the world; it opens the senses to experience the world in ways that are otherwise obscured. This is a non-discursive, non-conceptual practice, even though, upon reflection, theories can be found in the background: theories about the relationship between silence and enlightenment, theories about what the mind is and how it can be transformed, theories about what reality is and how it can be experienced, not to mention practical theories about how to do it. In the actual practice, however, theory stands in the background, framing the practice by making it self-evident to practitioners why and how it might be performed.

When, on the other hand, *zazen* takes a linguistic and thoughtful form (*vipassana*), the mind is to be enlightened through a sustained transformation in thinking. In this case mental images provide the lens through which new dimensions of reality are opened to view. John Blofeld alludes to this in his discussion of Zen practice when he includes in a list of practices "unremitting effort to see all things in light of the truths we are learning."[6] "Truths," in the form of thoughts and images, shed a light on "all things" that transforms the way they are experienced. How things appear differs in accordance with alterations in the mental "light" that is shed on them. Light reflected through the doctrine of emptiness, for example, shows the world one way, while the doctrines of compassion, sudden enlightenment, and mind-to-mind transmission will display it in other ways. The point here is that, by traditional Zen standards, dwelling in Zen light by thinking its doctrines *is* Zen meditative practice.

This point, however, is frequently misunderstood. Both scholars and practitioners, east and west, tend to misrepresent the role of thought in meditation by holding to an untenable dichotomy between thought and meditation. Taking this point of departure, they might assume the obverse of Blofeld's claim that "if we practice Zen it must surely be because we accept its cardinal doctrines" because one cherished doctrine in this tradition is that Zen is a religion without doctrines.[7] But this doctrine about Zen can neither account for itself nor the presence in Zen of precise forms of thought that support its sophisticated practice. Zen theory is a form of Zen practice that sustains other practices by showing how, why, and to what end they might be worth performing. It is not an optional addition to Zen practice. Although practitioners may proceed with practice on the belief that doctrine is dispensable, the net result is not non-doctrinal practice. Instead it is practice guided by doctrine that is naive and poorly developed, because it has not undergone thoughtful appraisal. Zen scholars have tended to accept this view of Zen without the critical evaluation that has been applied so carefully to other dimensions of Zen.

---

[6] Blofeld, *The Zen Teaching of Hui Hai*, p. 40.
[7] We should note that in later years Blofeld too began to teach that not only Zen but Buddhism itself did not depend upon doctrinal truths.

There are important limits, however, to this way of setting Zen theory over other forms of practice. Perhaps most important is the realization that all thinking or theory, whether religious or not, is already shaped by practice. The word "practice" here means, simply, "what we regularly do," the patterns of activity that we share with others and that form our socially constructed world. Human practices, or patterns of activity, establish the background or context within which thought takes place. Everyone's perception of the world and their sense of what is possible within it are pre-formed by these practical forms of life. They construct the basis or context for thinking. Although all human beings share this common ground, differences are significant. Our patterns of thought will come to be shaped quite differently depending on whether we spend many hours each day with others in *zazen* or farming or doing social work or analyzing the stock market. Each practice in each of these social worlds directs and shapes the mind with its own distinct language, set of concerns, hopes, and fears.

Therefore, from this angle of vision, we can see the role that practice plays in shaping theory, and thus, their reciprocal character. Intertwined, theory and practice continually shape each other. The way you live your life and the way you understand it are mutually determining. In Buddhist terms, they "co-arise," neither one able to sustain itself in the absence of the other. "Practice" is the actualization and embodiment of theory, which, in implementing theory, continually hones, revises, and reorients the world view that gives rise to it. Reflective thinking seeks to make practice explicit, self-conscious, and subject to criticism and revision. It helps everyone continue asking: practice of what, why, and toward what end? These theoretical questions show the essential reciprocal relation between practice and theory in Zen and elsewhere.

In the Zen tradition, the purpose of saying that everything is religious practice is to bring daily life to awareness, to point out the patterns of daily activity to the one living them. This is a very productive theory. Anyone who practices it will be less likely to ignore any aspect of their life; cultivating the practice, they gradually perform each activity with greater and greater awareness. The danger of the theory that "everything is practice," however, is that it may obscure the opposite point: that in the midst of the many practices people perform, a few are worth elevating because they have an important bearing on the quality of all others. Both meditation and philosophy might be placed in this group. "Everything is practice" should not be taken to mean that it doesn't matter, therefore, which ones are chosen or how they are placed in relation to each other. It does matter. Not all practices are equal in their qualitative powers. What the theory is meant to highlight is the state of mind in which all activities are performed. This should not, however, be confused with the question of which among the many activities are most worth choosing to do. When they do get confused, the danger is that, in attempting to elevate ordinary life, spiritual life is debased or lost. Although one goal in the Zen tradition is to eliminate the distinction between "ordinary" and "spiritual," this elimination is only effective when the ordinary has been elevated to the level of the spiritual, and not vice versa. That the distinction is "empty" in Buddhist terms does not mean that it is without important function. Lacking some distinction like this, no transformative awakening would ever be sought, nor attained.

To test these meditations, an experiment in thought is productive. Reversing the idea that theory is actually practice, consider whether, in contrast, philosophy and meditation might both be regarded as theory. Framed in this way, both theoretical reflection and meditation could be considered "theory" insofar as both require a temporary step back out of ordinary life; they are exceptional practices requiring the suspension of ordinary practice. They are both temporary, artificial, experimental removals from worldly activities for the intended purpose of reconfiguring one's overall orientation to daily life. Philosophical thought and silent meditation are the same in this fundamental respect. While all practical tasks are performed on the world, so to speak, these two practices suspend work on the world, requiring instead a self-conscious step back to work on the "spirit" of the performer him- or herself. It is in this sense that they are spiritual activities, in clear distinction from most other dimensions of daily activity or practice.

This gives us two seemingly contradictory alternatives. Is philosophical reflection really a form of practice, like all activities, or is it better to regard reflection and meditation as two forms of theoretical removal from ordinary life? In this case, we can have it both ways, since both bring into view some dimension of the matter inaccessible to the other perspective. In fact, it is counterproductive to think of either as the final word on the matter. "Skill-in-means" – the Buddhist virtue of flexibility in conception – is the ability to move in principle between points of view, each informing the other so that greater and greater comprehension results. Stopping short of this comprehension to finalize a doctrinal position is a self-imposed limitation that is unnecessary and misleading. While philosophical meditation is clearly a practice, like non-discursive meditation, it is a practice that removes one from the practical sphere of everyday life so that greater perspective on life might be gained. The step back into theoretical practice is made in order that other practices might be transformed and elevated.

Stepping back out of the rush of everyday life to reflect or meditate is also, in effect, stepping back out of the self; it sets up an opportunity to consider being (theory), or to strive to be (practice), something other than what you have been so far. That is clearly the overarching point of Buddhist practice: to transcend yourself, to go beyond yourself, to become someone wiser, more insightful, more compassionate, more flexibly attuned to the world than the self you have been. In Zen Buddhism, this transformative process is deeply ensconced in institutional structures and is maintained over time in the form of relatively stable traditions. This, of course, does not match the image of Zen we find in much western literature where a significant degree of tension exists between "institutional structures" and the spirit of Zen. The iconoclastic dimensions of Zen are interpreted frequently to encourage the search for enlightened self-transcendence on one's own, individually, thus avoiding the alienating features of hardened institutions and overbearing traditions. This form of individualism, however, is rarely found in East Asia, in the Zen tradition or elsewhere. Even where it is found, it has been made possible by the traditions and institutions that encourage individuals to consider such a quest. Lacking institutions and traditions altogether, Buddhists don't inherit the "thought of enlightenment" at all, in any of its forms; they would not receive the bequest of models, ideals, images, and symbols, all of which give rise to the quest, sustain it and, on occasion, bring it to fruition. In every culture, institutional traditions place images of excellence before individuals and lay out for consideration the alternative forms of practice at their disposal. As has been the case in most traditions of self-cultivation, "transcendence" occurred in Zen through processes of idealization, the projection and internalization of ideal images of human cultivation handed down from one generation to another in the form of traditions by the institutions responsible for them. Zen monks studied the masters before them, in person and in literary image, and then adapted their own comportment to those models. Through these texts and these ideals, monks studied who they could be and what kinds of practice might be entailed in attaining those identities. The initial posture required in this practice of self-cultivation would have been one of self-effacement before images of excellence – the enlightened masters of Zen. Imitation of these ideals was neither unenlightening nor impossible since monks understood these images of excellence to be instances or models of their own true nature – the Buddha nature inherent within them.

Placing emphasis on the institutional "givenness" of these cultural ideals as they are experienced by practitioners, and upon the imitative reappropriation of these ideals, should not be taken to imply, however, that the self's role in Zen practice was simply passive, or that the tradition was so conservative that it was not open to change. Accordingly, we should notice that classical Zen texts project not just one image of excellence but thousands of them – an enormous pantheon of historical and historically constructed saints. The repertoire of possible ways to be a self was immense, showing that previous efforts to construct an enlightened identity each demanded some degree of differentiation. Emptied of previous selves, monks were initiated into processes of constructing identities by synthesizing and reshaping the variety of patterns bequeathed to them through the tradition. "Established convention" and "distinctive identity" were not held to be in opposition since the established models *were* distinct identities, and since one's own act of self-construction would inevitably push in some new direction.

Indeed, as we have seen, one of the most intriguing images in the texts is the example of Zen masters rejecting convention and refusing to follow custom and pattern. This custom was itself a focal point of imitation, a pattern of Zen practice. Although the quest for enlightened life begins when the practitioner is moved by admiration to imitate the image of previous masters, the practice of imitation is not itself enlightened behavior. It does begin the quest, however, by teaching the practitioner how to recognize his or her own deficiency in relation to the model and how to begin the process of self-modification.

Through this process, each participant defines a distinct relationship to traditional resources, and, in doing so, the tradition is transformed. Newly revised images of the ideal emerge as new generations adapt the tradition to new circumstances. It is here, perhaps, that we find the greatest theoretical strength of the Buddhist tradition. In the wake of the doctrines of no-self, impermanence, dependent origination, and emptiness, human beings could easily be understood in flexible and non-essentialist terms, as capable of differentiated possibilities. Indeed, the greatest of the traditional Zen masters were understood to be innovators, who, like Huang Po, put substantial pressure on the traditions they were inheriting. Like others before and after him, Huang Po was expected to "go beyond" the figures of excellence that he had idealized and imitated.

Lacking a fixed essence, what possibility for human cultural transformation could be ruled out in advance?

The tension between traditional models of excellence (the results of prior activities of "going beyond") and the current act of going beyond those models through critical innovation is potent in its creative force. Positive idealization gives substance and concrete shape to the tradition; critical appropriation builds the tradition by pushing it beyond its old forms into further refinement or reformulation. Zen practice requires correlating these positive and negative functions so that they sustain each other over time.

Each practitioner had to do this on his or her own. Doing it, however, required "awakening." Only when stirred out of complacency do practitioners ask crucial questions. In the Zen tradition, one of the critical functions of the awakened masters like Huang Po was to expose the sleepy routines of everyday life, to show the ways in which even Zen discourse tended to objectify and substantialize the self, such that "the self" became a topic about which one could hold forth, all the while forgetting *who* it was that was holding forth. To counteract this tendency in discourse, Zen masters sought to force the self as "I" into manifestation, to bring the self out of its place of hiding within the language and customs of the tradition. When Hui-hai Ta-chu, the "great pearl," came to the master Ma-tsu to study Zen, Ma-tsu shocked him with the question, "why are you here searching when you already possess the treasure you're looking for?" "What treasure?" In response to which Ma-tsu replied: "The one who is right now questioning me."[8] This was Ma-tsu's favorite line and the text has him present it to all of his students at precisely the right moment: the moment when, through prior cultivation, the "I" is prepared to emerge into self-awareness. This is about *you*, not "the self" in general, or some other self! Who are *you*, and what are *you* doing? When, on another occasion, Ma-tsu was asked, "What is the meaning of Bodhidharma coming from the West?" he bent the inquiry back upon the asker: "What is the meaning of your asking at precisely this moment?"

As a question posed to modern, western interpreters of Zen, Ma-tsu's question could hardly be improved upon. What is the meaning of "our" asking at precisely this moment in our own history? Why are we interested, and what is the point of the modern western engagement with Buddhism? Asking these questions brings our own act of reading and

[8] Pas, *The Recorded Sayings of Ma-tsu*, p. 94.

thinking into view. Who are we, the ones who engage in these meditations across cultural and historical lines? These questions are crucial for the reflective reader of Zen Buddhism today. They are also similar to questions that Zen texts like *Huang Po* sought to evoke in meditative readers of earlier times. The connection between these questions across historical eras is the focus on self-awareness. Thus we realize that when we are studying Zen, what we are also inevitably studying is . . . ourselves, regardless of when we are studying or why. And that, clearly, is the point of Huang Po's Zen. Realizing this, and imagining the gleam in Huang Po's eye, is all that it takes to bring these meditations to fruition.

Bibliography

Almond, Philip C. *The British Discovery of Buddhism*. Cambridge University Press, 1988.

Altieri, Charles. *Canons and Consequences: Reflections on the Ethical Force of Imaginative Ideals*. Evanston: Northwestern University Press, 1990.

Ames, Van Meter. *Zen and American Thought*. Honolulu: University of Hawaii Press, 1962.

Arnold, Sir Edwin. *The Light of Asia*. New York: Crowell and Co., 1884.

Austin, J. L. *How to Do Things with Words*. Cambridge, MA: Harvard University Press, 1962.

Barthes, Roland. *The Empire of Signs*. Trans. Richard Howard. New York: Hill and Wang, 1982.

Bergmann, Frithjof. *On Being Free*. Notre Dame: Notre Dame University Press, 1977.

Berling, Judith A. "Bringing the Buddha Down to Earth: Notes on the Emergence of *Yü-lu* as a Buddhist Genre." *History of Religions* 21.7 (1987): 57–88.

Bernstein, Richard J. *Beyond Objectivism and Relativism: Science, Hermeneutics, and Praxis*. Philadelphia: University of Pennsylvania Press, 1983.

Bielefeldt, Carl. *Dogen's Manuals of Zen Meditation*. Berkeley: University of California Press, 1988.

Blofeld, John. *Beyond the Gods: Taoist and Buddhist Mysticism*. New York: Dutton & Co., 1974.

The Tantric Mysticism of Tibet. New York: Causeway Books, 1974.

The Wheel of Life. Berkeley: Shambhala Publishers, 1959, 1972.

The Zen Teaching of Hui Hai on Sudden Illumination. New York: Rider and Co., 1962.

The Zen Teaching of Huang Po on the Transmission of Mind. New York: Grove Press, 1959.

Bloom, Harold. *The Anxiety of Influence: A Theory of Poetry*. New York: Oxford University Press, 1973.

Bodiford, William. *Soto Zen in Medieval Japan*. Honolulu: University of Hawaii Press, 1993.

Bols, Peter K. *This Culture of Ours: Intellectual Transitions in T'ang and Sung China*. Stanford University Press, 1992.

217

Broughton, Jeffrey. *Kuei-feng Tsung-mi: The Convergence of Ch'an and the Teachings.* Ann Arbor: University Microfilms, 1975.

Bruns, Gerald. "Canon and Power in the Hebrew Scriptures." In *Canons.* Edited by Robert von Hallberg. University of Chicago Press, 1983. 65–83.

Inventions: Writing, Textuality, and Understanding in Literary History. New Haven: Yale University Press, 1982.

Buswell, Robert E., Jr. *Chinese Buddhist Apocrypha.* Honolulu: University of Hawaii Press, 1989.

The Formation of Ch'an Ideology in China and Korea: The Vajrasamadhi-Sutra, a Buddhist Apocryphon. Princeton University Press, 1989.

"The 'Short-cut' Approach to *K'an-hua* Meditation: The Evolution of a Practical Subitism in Chinese Ch'an Buddhism." In *Sudden and Gradual Approaches to Enlightenment in Chinese Thought.* Edited by Peter N. Gregory. Honolulu: University of Hawaii Press, 1987. 321–377.

Buswell, Robert E., Jr. and Robert M. Gimello, eds. *Paths to Liberation: The Marga and Its Transformations in Buddhist Thought.* Honolulu: University of Hawaii Press, 1991.

Cavell, Stanley. *In Quest of the Ordinary: Lines of Skepticism and Romanticism.* University of Chicago Press, 1988.

Chang, Chung-yüan. *Original Teachings of Ch'an Buddhism.* New York: Vintage, 1969.

Chappell, David W., ed. *Buddhist and Taoist Practice in Medieval Chinese Society.* Honolulu: University of Hawaii Press, 1987.

Cleary, Thomas, trans. *Sayings and Doings of Pai-chang.* Los Angeles: Center Publications, 1978.

Cleary, Thomas, and J.C. Cleary, trans. *The Blue Cliff Record,* 3 vols. Boulder: Shambhala Publications, 1977.

Collcutt, Martin. *Five Mountains: The Rinzai Zen Monastic Institution in Medieval Japan.* Cambridge, MA: Harvard University Press, 1981.

Cook, Francis H. *The Record of Transmitting the Light: Zen Master Keizan's Denkoroku.* Los Angeles: Center Publications, 1991.

Cook, Francis H. trans. *How to Raise an Ox.* Los Angeles: Center Publications, 1978.

Crossan, John Dominic. *Cliffs of Fall: Paradox and Polyvalence in the Parables of Jesus.* New York: Seabury Press, 1980.

Davidson, Donald. *Inquiries into Truth and Interpretation.* Oxford University Press, 1984.

Dawson, Raymond. *The Chinese Chameleon: An Analysis of European Conceptions of Chinese Civilization.* Oxford University Press, 1967.

De Man, Paul. *Allegories of Reading: Figural Language in Rousseau, Nietzsche, Rilke, and Proust.* New Haven: Yale University Press, 1979.

Blindness and Insight: Essays in the Rhetoric of Contemporary Criticism. New Haven: Yale University Press, 1983.

Derrida, Jacques. "The Law of Genre." Trans. Samuel Weber, *Glyph: Textual Studies.* 7 (1980): 202–232.

The Margins of Philosophy. Trans. Alan Bass. University of Chicago Press, 1982.

Of Grammatology. Trans. Gayatri C. Spivak. Baltimore: Johns Hopkins University Press, 1974.

"White Mythology: Metaphor in the Text of Philosophy." *New Literary History* 6 (1974): 5–74.

Dogen Zenji. *Shobogenzo.* Vol. II. Trans. Kosen Nishiyama. Tokyo: Nakayama Shobo, 1975.

Dumoulin, Heinrich. *Zen Buddhism: A History.* 2 vols. Trans. James W. Heisig and Paul Knitter. New York: Macmillan, 1988–1990.

Ebrey, Patricia B., and Peter N. Gregory, eds. *Religion and Society in T'ang and Sung China.* Honolulu: University of Hawaii Press, 1993.

Eco, Umberto. *Semiotics and the Philosophy of Language.* London: Macmillan Press, 1984.

Faure, Bernard. *Chan Insights and Oversights: An Epistemological Critique of the Chan Tradition.* Princeton University Press, 1993.

The Rhetoric of Immediacy: A Cultural Critique of Ch'an/Zen Buddhism. Princeton University Press, 1991.

Fish, Stanley. *Doing What Comes Naturally.* Durham: Duke University Press, 1989.

Foucault, Michel. *Language, Counter-memory, Practice: Selected Essays and Interviews.* Ithaca: Cornell University Press, 1977.

The Order of Things: An Archaeology of the Human Sciences. New York: Vintage/Random House, 1973.

"What is Enlightenment?" In *The Foucault Reader.* Edited by Paul Rabinow. New York: Pantheon, 1984. 32–50.

Foulk, Theodore Griffith. "The Ch'an School and Its Place in the Buddhist Monastic Tradition." Ph.D. dissertation. University of Michigan, 1987.

Gadamer, Hans-Georg. *Philosophical Hermeneutics.* Trans. and ed. David E. Linge. Berkeley and Los Angeles: University of California Press, 1976.

Reason in the Age of Science. Trans. Frederick G. Lawrence. Cambridge, MA: MIT Press, 1981.

Truth and Method. Revised translation by Joel Weinsheimer and Donald G. Marshall. New York: Seabury Press, 1989.

Gardner, Daniel K. "Modes of Thinking and Modes of Discourse in the Sung: Some Thoughts on the *Yü-lu* ('Recorded Conversations') Texts." *Journal of Asian Studies* 50.3 (1991): 574–603.

Geertz, Clifford. *Local Knowledge: Further Essays in Interpretive Anthropology.* New York: Basic Books, 1983.

Gimello, Robert M. "Mysticism and Meditation." In *Mysticism and Philosophical Analysis.* Edited by Steven Katz. New York: Oxford University Press, 1978. 170–179.

Gómez, Luis O. "D. T. Suzuki's Contribution to Modern Buddhist Scholarship." In *A Zen Life: D. T. Suzuki Remembered.* Edited by Abe Masao. New York: Weatherhill, 1986. 90–94.

Gregory, Peter N. "Tsung-mi and the Single Word 'Awareness.'" *Philosophy East and West* 35.3 (1985): 248–269.

Tsung-mi and the Sinification of Buddhism. Princeton University Press, 1991.

Sudden and Gradual: Approaches to Enlightenment in Chinese Thought. Honolulu: University of Hawaii Press, 1987.

ed. *Traditions of Meditation in Chinese Buddhism.* Honolulu: University of Hawaii Press, 1986.

Guojun, Lui. *The Story of Chinese Books.* Beijing: Foreign Language Press, 1985.

Habermas, Jürgen. *The Philosophical Discourse of Modernity.* Cambridge, MA: Harvard University Press, 1987.

Hansen, Valerie. *Changing Gods in Medieval China, 1127–1276.* Princeton University Press, 1990.

Hanson, Chad. *Language and Logic in Ancient China.* Ann Arbor: University of Michigan Press, 1983.

Hartman, Geoffrey. *The Fate of Reading and Other Essays.* University of Chicago Press, 1975.

Heidegger, Martin. *Being and Time.* Trans. John Macquarrie and Edward Robinson. New York: Harper and Row, 1962.

On the Way to Language. Trans. Peter D. Hertz. New York: Harper and Row, 1971.

Heine, Steven. "Does the Koan Have Buddha-Nature? The Zen Koan as Religious Symbol." *Journal of the American Academy of Religion* 58.3 (1990): 357–387.

Dogen and the Koan Tradition: A Tale of Two Shobogenzo Texts. Albany: State University of New York Press, 1994.

Existential and Ontological Dimensions of Time in Heidegger and Dogen. Albany: State University of New York Press, 1985.

"From Rice Cultivation to Mind Contemplation: The Meaning of Impermanence in Japanese Religion." *History of Religions* 30.4 (1991): 374–403.

Heise, Steven, and Charles Wei-Hsun Fu. *Japan in Traditional and Postmodern Perspectives.* Albany: State University of New York Press, 1995.

Hoover, Thomas. *The Zen Experience.* New York: New American Library, 1980.

Hoy, David. *The Critical Circle: Literature and History in Contemporary Hermeneutics.* Berkeley and Los Angeles: University of California Press, 1978.

Hunt-Badiner, Allan, ed. *Dharma Gaia: A Harvest of Essays on Buddhism and Ecology.* Berkeley: Paralax Press, 1990.

Iriya Yoshitaka. "Chinese Poetry and Zen." *Eastern Buddhist* 6.1 (1973): 54–67.

Denshin Hoyo Zen no Goroku Vol VIII. Tokyo: Chikuma Shobo, 1969.

Jan, Yün-hua. "Buddhist Historiography in Sung China." *Zeitschrift der Deutschen Morgenhändlischen Gesellschaft* 114 (1964): 360–381.

"Tsung-mi: His Analysis of Ch'an Buddhism." *T'oung Pao* 58.1 (1972): 1–50.

Jean-Luc, Nancy. *The Experience of Freedom.* Stanford University Press, 1993.

Jorgenson, John. "The Imperial Lineage of Ch'an Buddhism: The Role of Confucian Ritual and Ancestor Worship in Ch'an's Search for Legitimation in the Mid-T'ang Dynasty." *Papers on Far Eastern History* 35 (1987): 89–133.

Kasulis, Thomas P. *Zen Action / Zen Person.* Honolulu: University of Hawaii Press, 1981.

Kim, Hee-jin. "The Reason of Words and Letters: Dogen and Koan Language." In *Dogen Studies.* Edited by William LaFleur. Honolulu: University of Hawaii Press, 1985. 54–82.

Klein, Anne C. *Meeting of the Great Bliss Queen: Buddhists, Feminists and the Art of the Self.* Boston: Wisdom Publications.

Klemm, David E. *Hermeneutical Inquiry,* 2 vols. Atlanta: Scholars Press, 1986.

The Hermeneutical Theory of Paul Ricoeur. Lewisburg: Bucknell University Press, 1983.

Kraft, Kenneth. *Eloquent Zen: Daito and Early Japanese Zen.* Honolulu: University of Hawaii Press, 1992.

Kraft, Kenneth, ed. *Zen: Tradition and Transition.* New York: Grove Press, 1988.

Kuhn, Thomas. *The Structure of Scientific Revolutions.* 2nd edn. University of Chicago Press, 1970.

LaCapra, Dominick. *Rethinking Intellectual History: Texts, Contexts, Language.* Ithaca: Cornell University Press, 1983.

LaFleur, William R. *The Karma of Words: Buddhism and the Literary Arts in Medieval Japan.* Berkeley: University of California Press, 1983.

ed. *Dogen Studies.* Honolulu: University of Hawaii Press, 1985.

Lai, Whalen, and Lewis R. Lancaster, eds. *Early Ch'an in China and Tibet.* Berkeley: Asian Humanities Press, 1983.

Levering, Miriam. "Ch'an Enlightenment for Laymen: Ta hui and the New Religious Culture of the Sung." Ph.D. dissertation. Harvard University, 1978.

"Ta-hui and Lay Buddhists: Ch'an Sermons on Death." In *Buddhist and Taoist Practice in Medieval Chinese Society.* Edited by David W. Chappell. Honolulu: University of Hawaii Press, 1987. 181–209.

Liu, James J. Y. *Chinese Theories of Literature.* University of Chicago Press, 1975.

Lopez, Donald S., Jr., ed. *Buddhist Hermeneutics.* Honolulu: University of Hawaii Press, 1988.

MacIntyre, Alasdair. *After Virtue.* Notre Dame: University of Notre Dame Press, 1981.

"Relativism, Power, and Philosophy." In *After Philosophy.* Edited by Bohman, Baynes, and McCarthy. Cambridge, MA: MIT Press, 1987.

Three Rival Versions of Moral Enquiry: Encyclopaedia, Genealogy, and Tradition. University of Notre Dame Press, 1990.

Whose Justice? Whose Rationality? University of Notre Dame Press, 1988.

Maraldo, John. "Hermeneutics and Historicity in the Study of Buddhism."
    Eastern Buddhist 19.1 (1986): 17–43.
"Is There Historical Consciousness Within Ch'an?" *Japanese Journal of
    Religious Studies* 12.2–3 (1986): 141–172.
McGann, Jerome J. *The Romantic Ideology*. University of Chicago Press, 1983.
McRae, John R. "Encounter Dialogue and the Transformation of the Spiritual
    Path in Chinese Ch'an." In *Paths to Liberation: The Marga and Its
    Transformations in Buddhist Thought*. Edited by Robert N. Buswell, Jr., and
    Robert M. Gimello. Honolulu: University of Hawaii Press, 1991.
    The Northern School and the Formation of Early Ch'an Buddhism. Honolulu:
    University of Hawaii Press, 1986.
Michelfelder, Diane P., and Richard Palmer, eds. *Dialogue and Deconstruction: The
    Gadamer–Derrida Encounter*. Albany: State University of New York Press,
    1989.
Miura, Isshu, and Ruth Fuller Sasaki. *Zen Dust: The History of the Koan and
    Koan Study in Rinzai (Lin-chi) Zen*. New York: Harcourt, Brace, and World,
    1966.
Napper, Elizabeth. *Dependent-Arising and Emptiness: A Tibetan Buddhist Interpretation
    of Madhyamika Philosophy*. Boston: Wisdom Publications.
Nattier, Jan. *Once Upon a Future Time: Studies in a Buddhist Prophecy of Decline*.
    Berkeley: Asian Humanities Press, 1991.
Nietzsche, Friedrich. *The Use and Abuse of History*. Trans. Adrian Collins.
    Indianapolis: Bobbs-Merril Company, 1957.
Noakes, Susan. *Timely Reading: Between Exegesis and Interpretation*. Ithaca: Cornell
    University Press, 1988.
O'Leary, Joseph S. *Questioning Back: The Overcoming of Metaphysics in Christian
    Tradition*. Minneapolis: Winston Press, 1985.
Ogata, Shohaku. *The Transmission of the Lamp*. New Hampshire: Longwood
    Academic Press, 1990.
Pas, Julian F., trans. *The Recorded Sayings of Ma-tsu*. Lewiston, ME: Edwin Mellen,
    1987.
Pollack, David. *The Fracture of Meaning: Japan's Synthesis of China from the Eighth
    through the Eighteenth Centuries*. Princeton University Press, 1986.
Powell, William F., trans. *The Record of Tung-shan*. Honolulu: University of
    Hawaii Press, 1986.
Prip-Moller, J. *Chinese Buddhist Monasteries: Their Plan and its Function as Setting for
    Buddhist Monastic Life*. Hong Kong University Press, [1937] 1982.
Ricoeur, Paul. *Hermeneutics and the Human Sciences*. Trans. and ed. John B.
    Thompson. Cambridge University Press, 1981.
    Interpretation Theory: Discourse and the Surplus of Meaning. Fort Worth: Texas
    Christian University Press, 1976.
    "The Metaphorical Process as Cognition, Imagination, and Feeling." *Critical
    Theory* 5.1 (1978): 143–159.
    The Symbolism of Evil. Boston: Beacon Press, 1967.
    Time and Narrative. 3 vols. University of Chicago Press, 1984.

Rorty, Richard. *Contingency, Irony, and Solidarity*. Cambridge University Press, 1989.

Philosophy and the Mirror of Nature. Princeton University Press, 1979.

Said, Edward. *Orientalism*. New York: Vintage Books, 1979.

Sasaki, Ruth Fuller, trans. *The Recorded Sayings of Ch'an Master Lin-chi Hui-chao of Chen Prefecture*. Kyoto: Institute of Zen Studies, 1975.

Sasaki, Ruth Fuller, Yoshitaka Iriya, and Dana R. Fraser, trans. *A Man of Zen: The Recorded Sayings of Layman P'ang*. Kyoto: Institute for Zen Studies, 1971.

Scharlemann, Robert P. *Inscriptions and Reflections: Essays in Philosophical Theology*. Charlottesville: University of Virginia Press, 1989.

The Reason of Following: Christology and the Ecstatic I. University of Chicago Press, 1991.

Sekida, Katsuki. *Two Zen Classics: Mumonkan and Hekiganroku*. Edited by A. V. Grimstone. New York and Tokyo: Weatherhill, 1977.

Sharf, Robert H. "The Idolization of Enlightenment: On the Mummification of Ch'an Masters in Medieval China." *History of Religions* 32.1 (1992): 1–31.

Smith, Barbara Herrnstein. *Contingencies of Value: Alternative Perspectives for Critical Theory*. Cambridge, MA: Harvard University Press, 1988.

Stout, Jeffrey. *Ethics After Babel: The Language of Morals and Their Discontents*. Boston: Beacon Press, 1988.

Suzuki, D. T. *Essays in Zen Buddhism (Second Series)*. London: Rider, 1970.

Zen Doctrine of No Mind. New York: Weiser, 1973.

Taylor, Charles. *Sources of the Self: The Making of the Modern Identity*. Cambridge, MA: Harvard University Press, 1989.

Taylor, Mark C. *Deconstructing Theology*. New York: Crossroad Publishing Co., 1982.

Teiser, Stephen F. *The Ghost Festival in Medieval China*. Princeton University Press, 1988.

Thurman, Robert A., trans. *The Holy Teaching of Vimalakirti: A Mahayana Scripture*. University Park: Pennsylvania State University Press, 1976.

Ui, Hakuju. *Zenshushi Kenkyu*, 3 vols. Tokyo: Iwanami shoten, [1935–1943] 1966.

Van Hallbert, Robert, ed. *Canons*. University of Chicago Press, 1983.

Vickers, Brian. *In Defense of Rhetoric*. Oxford University Press, 1989.

Wachterhauser, Brice, ed. *Hermeneutics and Modern Philosophy*. Albany: State University of New York Press, 1986.

Warnke, Georgia. *Gadamer: Hermeneutics, Tradition and Reason*. Stanford University Press, 1987.

Watts, Alan. *In My Own Way*. New York: Random House, 1972.

Weinsheimer, Joel. *Gadamer's Hermeneutics: A Reading of "Truth and Method."* New Haven: Yale University Press, 1985.

Imitation. London: Routledge and Kegan Paul, 1984.

Philosophical Hermeneutics and Literary Theory. New Haven: Yale University Press, 1991.

Weinstein, Stanley. *Buddhism under the T'ang*. Cambridge University Press, 1987.

Welbon, Richard. *The Buddhist Nirvana and its Western Interpreters*. University of Chicago Press, 1968.

White, Hayden. *Tropics of Discourse: Essays in Cultural Criticism*. Baltimore: Johns Hopkins University Press, 1978.

White, James Boyd. *When Words Lose Their Meaning: Constitutions and Reconstitutions of Language, Character, and Community*. University of Chicago Press, 1984.

Yampolsky, Philip B., trans. *The Platform Sutra of the Sixth Patriarch*. New York: Columbia University Press, 1967.

Yanagida Seizan. "Goroku no rekishi: Zen bunken no seiritsu shiteki kenkyu." *Toho gakuho* 57 (1985): 211–663.

———. "The *Li-tai fa-pao chi* and the Ch'an Doctrine of Sudden Awakening." Trans. Carl Bielefeldt. In *Early Ch'an in China and Tibet*. Edited by Walen Lai and Lewis R. Lancaster. Berkeley Asian Humanities Press, 1983.

———. "The Life of Lin-chi I-hsüan." *Eastern Buddhist* 5.2 (1972): 70–94.

———. "The 'Recorded Sayings' Texts of Chinese Ch'an Buddhism." Trans. John R. McRae. In *Early Ch'an in China and Tibet*. Edited by Whalen Lai and Lewis R. Lancaster. Berkeley: Asian Humanities Press, 1983. 185–205.

———. "Shinzoku toshi no keifu." *Zengaku kenkyu* 59 (1978): 1–39.

———. *Shoki Zenshu Shisho no Kenkyu*. Kyoto: Hozokan, 1967.

Yanagida Seizan and Umehara Takeshi. *Mu no Tankyu*. Vol. VII. Tokyo: Kadokawa, 1969.

Yu, Lu K'uan. *Ch'an and Zen Teachings*. Second series. Berkeley: Shambhala Publications, 1970.

Zengagku Daijiten. Tokyo: Taishukan, 1978.

Index